Trust Me, You Will Survive

Trust Me, You Will Survive

Dominik Stoltman

The Pentland Press Limited
Edinburgh • Cambridge • Durham

© Dominik Stoltman 1994

First published in 1994 by
The Pentland Press Ltd.
1 Hutton Close
South Church
Bishop Auckland
Durham

All rights reserved.
Unauthorised duplication
contravenes existing laws.

ISBN 1 85821 129 8

Typeset by CBS, Felixstowe, Suffolk
Printed and bound by Antony Rowe Ltd., Chippenham

In Memory of my
mother, Leokadia, whose
deep faith has sustained
me all my life.

FOREWORD
by Neal Ascherson

When Alfred Jarry wrote *Ubu Roi*, his fantasy about tyranny, he set it 'in Poland, that is to say: nowhere'. And at that time, before the first world war, there was indeed no Poland on the atlas. The three Partitions at the end of the eighteenth century had abolished the Polish state and distributed its territory and people between the empires of Russia, Prussia (later Germany) and Austria.

And, when it has 'existed' in the atlas sense, Poland has taken many different shapes and sizes, extending at one moment to a vast ramshackle Commonwealth filling the space between Baltic and Black Sea, or vanishing altogether for over a century, or appearing briefly as a semi-independent satellite of France in the Grand Duchy of Warsaw. Finally, after 1945, Poland was moved bodily several hundred miles to the west, without the consent of the Poles, to the place in Europe which it now occupies.

Poland, in short, has paid the full price down the centuries for the ambitions and ideologies of other powers. And yet Poland, even when it could not be found on a map, has always existed. It has existed as a nation and a culture. But it has also existed as a series of reproaches, even satires, against the grand ideas of other countries. In Poland, the human reality of those grand ideas is relentlessly exposed. 'Stability' can mean foreign occupation; 'democracy' can mean a one-party dictatorship: 'victory' in a world war can actually mean defeat, the loss of national independence and the seizure of Polish territory by others. Even 'patriotism', the most passionate of Polish feelings, is not some pure and incandescent emotion but a way of confronting terrifying dilemmas.

This is why Dominik Stoltman's memoir is such an important book.

It is a priceless contribution to the history of our own times, not just to Polish history, precisely because it is not a tale of simple heroism. It is a lesson in dilemmas. It is a course in how ordinary people can find their winding path through the moral maze of an inhuman system - the Nazi occupation - and make compromises which do not dishonour or diminish them, but reinforce their humanity. *Trust Me, You Will Survive* is about the complicated condition we call decency.

After 1939, Poland suffered what can be called the Fourth Partition. Once again, after just over twenty years of independence, Poland was wiped from the map. In the east, Polish territories were annexed by the Soviet Union. Central Poland was reduced to the so-called 'General-Government', a German colonial territory or 'native reserve' under martial law in which some of the worst atrocities in the history of Europe were committed. Poland's northern and western lands - where the Stoltman family ran a shop in the village of Powalki - suffered a more complicated fate. These lands were annexed to the German Reich. The design for their Polish inhabitants, the majority, was that they should either be 'Germanised' or eventually deported, and in the fullness of time their farms and houses would be handed over to ethnic Germans, either from within the 'old' Reich or from the ancient German colonial settlements in the Balkans and Russia. The Jewish inhabitants were to be exterminated. The German minority in those territories was suddenly promoted, after the German invasion in 1939, to the status of a ruling caste which in practice held powers of life and death over its Polish neighbours.

The Stoltman family, submerged in this nightmare from the first days of the war, clung to two principles: to survive physically and as a family, and to remain loyal to Poland. The fourth Partition, in all its complexity, offered different ways of fulfilling those principles. It depended largely where you lived. In the east, under Soviet rule, most of the Poles were deported into slavery: the options there were nil, and the struggle was simply to stay alive. In the General-Government, there was the limited choice of whether to live as a slave, keeping a family alive by black-marketeering, or to join the Resistance and risk the massacre of one's family in reprisal. In the regions annexed to the Reich, there were more

– and more dangerous – choices. There it was often possible to apply for German status. This could and occasionally did mean genuinely changing sides; throwing in one's lot with the Nazi occupiers as a collaborator. But it could also mean a dangerous double life: using the slight privileges of 'Class Three' German identity in order not only to hold the family above the starvation line but – much more importantly – to cover illegal activity which ranged from supporting Polish partisan and underground units to hiding numerous family members and friends who were being sought by the Gestapo.

Through this moral maze, Dominik and his family kept their integrity and found their way. He escaped a firing-squad, worked as a forced labourer on German-owned farms (one next to the Stutthof concentration camp), absconded several times to flee home, and managed to postpone call-up into the German army by horrible feats of self-wounding and self-poisoning (drinking vinegar and eating cigarette-butts was only one of his methods). The family kept going, with several of its members in hiding, by bribing Nazi officials and local ethnic Germans with food. This meant the illegal buying, slaughtering and butchering of pigs, at which Dominik became an expert.

All this time, the family was overshadowed by the danger posed by German neighbours – or by 'Polish' neighbours who had decided to opt for German citizenship. They too had to be neutralized by all kinds of illegal favours. This book shows how the Nazi occupation transformed rural Poland into a fantastically resourceful underworld of dealing and trading, an agile, lawless but vital way of life which was never quite abandoned and which served as a sound preparation for the challenges of capitalism in our own day.

In the end, Dominik could no longer dodge the call-up and was drafted into the Wehrmacht. He used the German uniform to cover a visit to his brother, a priest hiding from the Gestapo, and to gain all sorts of access: in reality, he had already been sworn in as a member of a resistance unit near Powalki. After many adventures, Dominik Stoltman ended the war in Belgium as an American prisoner-of-war. From there he joined the Polish armies in the West and was finally demobilised in Scotland. Back in Poland, the Germans around Powalki fled as the

Russians approached, and the Stoltman family – less one son who had died rescuing children from an anti-tank missile – set about adapting to the bleak new reality of Communist Poland.

The virtue of this book is its simple humanity. It has, at times, something of Jaroslav Hasek's *Good Soldier Schweik*: the obstinate practicality and kindness of the Stoltmans which shows up all the posturing madness of Ubu and his lieutenants for the absurdity it is. Dominik saw terrible things done during the occupation. And yet he also met – and was able to recognise – Germans who were no more than good, kind men and women caught up in the vast machinery of injustice, who saved his life and his faith in other human beings more than once. The Stoltmans did not hate other people just because they were Germans. In this they were unlike many Poles who experienced the hell of the General-Government, for whom even the sound of the German language would induce physical nausea for many years. The Stoltmans hated Poland's enemies, in a general way, but it was cruelty, treachery, selfishness in another human being which made him or her an enemy, not national origin. Dominik Stoltman's mother, the real heroine of this book, never ceased to pray for her persecutors and to seek to understand them. In the end, her son came to share her sense of the brotherhood of man. And that is the message of this book.

Neal Ascherson

PREFACE

For two decades we had enjoyed our s̶e̶c̶o̶n̶d̶ ̶f̶reedom since Poland had been torn apart, divided and occupied by Austria, Russia and Germany. During 1939 Poland and its people were once again faced with an uncertain future.

The threat of a German invasion was constantly on our minds and discussed often. Who could guess what the outcome would be? All we could do during those anxious times was offer daily prayers for peace. Sometimes it felt like we were living in the shadow of a smouldering volcano which we hoped would not erupt but knowing if it did, our lives would be shattered.

Fear grew as the invasion seemed more imminent. Parents refused to send their children away from home to be educated. Families living close to the border tried desperately to sell their properties or, failing that, left everything behind to look for a safer place to live – or so they hoped. Little did we know that such words as 'SAFETY' and 'SECURITY' would have no place in our lives in the days ahead; rather 'DESPAIR' and 'HOPE'.

For some amongst us, the threat of invasion held no fear or loss. They hoped and waited for Hitler's occupation. They were mainly well-to-do business people and landowners of German origin who, after Poland's independence from Germany, Austria and Russia in 1918, had taken Polish nationality, in order to keep their properties, and acquired wealth. They belonged to the ethnic minority who, on the very day of Hitler's invasion, turned so much against us. Even those members of the ethnic minority who had not gained riches were eager for German supremacy in Poland so they, too, could gain more in the way of wealth and power for themselves. They were all eager to acquire German nationality after the occupation and very quickly became Class 2 Germans known as the Volksdeutsche, forsaking their Polish upbringing.

Over the years, they had lived equally amongst us, having the same rights to education, work and possessions – there had been no deprivation. Thus we were not able to understand at all WHY these people, who were our friends, neighbours and workmates and who had been part of our daily and social lives began to treat us as enemies. As individuals they were even more dangerous than the invaders of our land and personal privacy.

I have tried to record accurately what the situation was like so that you, the reader, can judge for yourselves. The changing attitudes and actions of so many, but not all, of the ethnic minority living in our midst affected our lives greatly as we struggled to survive the overpowering forces.

'WHY? WHY is it happening?' we often asked ourselves but no sane answer was ever forthcoming.

CHAPTER 1

During the pre-war period, whilst people were selling their properties and moving away from the German border, my own family did the opposite. They sold their retail business and moved about seven miles closer to the border to a place called Powalki with a population of 800.

Lag, the place we left behind, was a village of about 2,000 inhabitants where my family had run a grocery and drapery business. By the time my parents had decided to move, there were nine grocery shops in Lag. As the number of grocery businesses increased, the income from our own decreased.

As my father was involved in the very expensive, all-year-round hobby of hunting, my mother's income as a midwife was often required to supplement it. The expenses for my brothers' and sisters' education had to be met and it was becoming harder to make ends meet. We relied even more on my mother's income as a midwife to keep us going. Eventually, my father's costly hunting trips had to stop. We all sympathized with him as his whole life had been taken up with his hobby. Shortly after that, our nanny, Francesca, who had been with us for many years, was reluctantly asked to leave to reduce the overheads even further.

The change in our financial position was not helped by mother's kind heart. She loved to look after the poor. After delivering a child to a poor couple, instead of making the usual two visits, she would make half a dozen, always taking some groceries with her at no extra cost to them. Often my father would say, 'That's the blessings for your generosity' and I remember our whispering to our mother not to answer back. However, sometimes she would reply that because of her 'hobby' the blessings would be more, not only for her but for the rest of us.

In summer, quite a few of the older men and women from the

poorhouse would come to our house for a meal. At these times Father would eat his meal alone as not all the people were grateful for what my mother was providing for them and it hurt and annoyed my father to see this. Many of the old folk would complain that the meals were too cold, too hot, there was not enough or too much salt, etc.

In winter, when the snow was lying deep, I would take their midday meal to the poorhouse for them. I remember one old man who was so grateful for all we did for him. After each meal, he would tell me of the huge estates he had, of how the hills were covered with gold and that after he died it would all belong to my family. Although his mind was wandering, he tried to reassure us that one day our efforts would be rewarded. I often thought about this old man who was so willing to part with his gold-covered hills for just a few meals. I sometimes found myself walking home as proud as a peacock, at times almost believing his promise!

There was one old Jewish lady, Mrs Kunz, and her daughter whom my mother loved to visit. She often talked about them and how much she admired their strong religious belief. My mother's charity work was very important to her.

The main reason my family had moved closer to the German border was because my mother's brothers and two sisters were involved in farming there. However, things did not turn out as we hoped. We found we were expected to help them work the land and receive nothing in return. As a result, the atmosphere was strained at times. Our lives were cloudy with very few silver linings.

Eventually our situation began to improve as we settled down to running the general store my father had set up. We continued to assist relatives with the farming when time permitted, and Mother successfully settled down in her continuing role as midwife.

My father would often reminisce about his hunting days. He would talk for many hours about his adventures, always producing a cigar and beer when talking to his friends about hunting. I would eagerly listen to his tales about stalking wild boar or stags. Although I was already 18 years old, I was not given a beer - an unspoken rule made by my father, as he felt that it would not look good in front of his guests.

Often, during conversation somebody would say 'There's not much talk about war.' For the older people, it became a form of greeting. 'Long may it continue, Lord,' would come the reply. 'For ever and ever, amen.'

CHAPTER 2

In the few years leading up to 1939 and the outbreak of war, the Polish army had been preparing for a possible invasion of our country and the soldiers were constantly on manoeuvres, which took place perhaps fifteen miles from the border.

During the summer of 1939, the army moved closer to the border and dug in only four or five miles from it. At this time they fully expected Hitler's army to attack. We talked to the soldiers most days. Some were so sure of victory should Poland be attacked whilst others, however, had no faith at all; neither of victory nor even of presenting reasonable opposition. To add to all the worries we already had, news reached us that Russia and Germany were intending to sign a non-aggression treaty, but it was difficult to believe that such a pact would be made between such sworn enemies. If this proved true though, we felt we were lost.

My brother, Victor, who was in his late thirties, was ordained as a Franciscan priest on 25 August 1939 and it was the biggest event for some years in the small village – the first Franciscan priest to be ordained in our parish. After the big event, we tried to persuade Victor to stay with us as we expected war to break out any day but nothing would stop him from going back to the Franciscan Order in Panewnik, near Katowice.

One day my twenty-year-old brother Bruno said, 'Once we are invaded by Hitler's army, the Polish forces won't be enough for Hitler's breakfast.' I remember being surprised at how angrily my father reacted to Bruno's comment. 'Have you no faith at all in your country?' he asked. I was quite taken aback as I had never heard my father being so patriotic. It was very rare for him to talk of politics and I remember being so proud of him and his beliefs. My own feelings were every bit as strong. I believed very much in victory if we were invaded.

Our family had all come home for Victor's ordination. When he returned to the Order my brother, Jan, who was 22, returned to the Polish Army; my sister, Lucy, went back to her convent at Pelplin, not far from the Baltic; and another sister, Gertrude, returned to nursing in a mental institution in Kozborowo.

We believed that war would soon be declared. Even at that time there were some people who tried to benefit from all the miseries facing us, especially those of the old people. Gypsies would come with fiddles and guitars and sing verses from the Bible's prophets. They would sing of the devastation of our land and at the same time sell their holy pictures. Nothing would stop the old ladies from spending their money on the pictures and then praying before them, crying.

We had just finished the harvest a few days before the invasion when my Uncle Frank, who was married to my mother's sister, asked me to visit him. I was rather surprised and wondered why, but off I went to his farm, which was only about 200 yards or so from where we lived. He wanted me to help him dig a hole so that he could bury meat, which he had salted, in barrels. For obvious reasons, this work had to be done during the night. I agreed to help, provided we killed a pig from his stock for my parents. Why leave the pigs for the Germans to eat if they invaded our country?

The following night when I returned we killed two small pigs, salted all the meat and then through the night, dug two deep holes. When that was complete, a stack of corn was forked on top of the hidden barrels packed with meat. It was the hardest work I had ever done in my life.

For two or three days before war was declared, the police ordered that civilians patrol the main road during the night. This was a compulsory order and it was left to the local councillors to arrange which men were to be chosen each night and delegate their duties. We worked in pairs and changed over every four hours. However, the way in which we were asked to arm ourselves had left a lot to be desired. What a beginning! There we were, defending our borders with spades and forks and similar farm tools. Two miles closer to the border, the Polish army was dug-in. There was no alternative but to obey orders.

During the night, lots of people were on the move, leaving their properties behind to get away from the German border. As patrolmen, we were required to check their papers, if they had any at all. I was under the impression that all the people intending to leave from the borders had already done so, but this was not the case. There had already been a constant stream of loaded wagons passing by with families sitting on top of their belongings. Our job on night patrol was to stop everyone. My partner was doing his duty as ordered and stopping everyone for identification.

I will never forget one incident. We were lying in an small plantation of fir trees watchIng the road, when we spotted a lady cycling towards us. My good companion, Bronek, insisted we had to stop her, although I did not think it necessary. He quickly jumped out of hiding and shouted for her to halt but she cycled even faster. Catching up with the terrified and now weeping female, we learned that the poor soul was trying to meet up with her parents who had travelled on ahead. The startled cyclist had not known who we were, and in her frightened state had chosen not to find out. That was to be our last duty on patrol.

My dad asked me and my brother to call on Uncle Andrew, who lived about twenty miles away, and get horses and a wagon to transport whatever valuables we had in the house to a place of safe keeping. It was only then I told my mother about the meat I had buried, in case anything should happen to me and I failed to return.

The day before we were attacked was nerve-racking. There was a ghostly atmosphere in our village, Powalki. No order had been given to evacuate, yet no one was to be seen on the streets. Everyone in the village was busy packing to go, and even the soldiers who were constantly patrolling the village had disappeared.

We tried to persuade my father that we should stay together but in the end he insisted we should go to Uncle Andrew's for the wagon. My brother Bruno and I set off, he on a lady's bike and myself on a gent's. After a few miles we encountered an incredible sight. The road was choked with fleeing families with their loads, on bikes, too large for a horse to carry. One person would pull the laden bike with a rope and another would balance the load. There were no proper roads, only sandy tracks. Some families had small hand-wagons but they, too, were grossly overloaded. I told Bruno that I didn't think we would ever reach our uncle's that night.

All of a sudden, there were screams and cries coming from all directions. Someone had spread word that the German army had been given an order to execute every able-bodied man captured. The whole stream of traffic came to a standstill. Wives with crying children screamed to their husbands to run to safety. Many families did stay together despite the panic. Various loads of belongings were strewn over the track leading to safety, causing even more chaos. As we couldn't make much progress on the road, we decided to take a short cut as we knew the area well. However, we stumbled upon a Polish routine patrol. After being questioned for five hours and suspected of spying, we were released.

By the afternoon of 1 September 1939, we had reached our uncle's farm in Osieczna. He could not believe that our family had not stayed together. He was even more surprised when we told him what had happened on the way. As there was nowhere for us to run to, Uncle Andrew told us to tell Father to stay where he was. The whole family listened with alarm to our experiences. My uncle left the room and came back with a small tray carrying vodka and beer for each of us. I felt that I had become an adult. This was the first 'real' drink I had been offered, which showed just how concerned Uncle Andrew was although he tried to hide it. We finished our drinks as we talked about what we should do.

Osieczna was in turmoil: the Polish army was retreating through the village, and it was hard to believe that it took my brother and me nearly twenty hours to reach it. As we sat with my uncle watching the army retreat, I couldn't help thinking of my brother's comment that our army would not be enough for Hitler's breakfast.

We decided to go back home. Suddenly, the door opened and a sergeant burst in. Shocked, I thought 'How dare you come in without knocking.' He tried to reassure us and told us not to worry. He also said that the Germans were not as bad as we were all thinking. I noticed my uncle, who had been in the German army himself during our occupation in the First World War, remained quiet in response to the sergeant's comment. Personally, I could have choked him, as it was obvious to me that he was pro-German. I thought it was an insult that he should be allowed to wear Polish army uniform and hold the rank of sergeant. I was an optimist and truly believed in my own mind that we would win. After the sergeant had left, my uncle said that we should stay with him as it would be too risky to try to return. We, however, decided to go back and look for our parents.

CHAPTER 3

As we left for home, we were perplexed by how peaceful the roads had become. The long track disappeared into the distance and there was not a single soul to be seen.

As we reached a small town called Czersk, about eighteen miles from our home, we were again surrounded by crowds of people. No one of authority was about to advise anyone what to do or where to go. All the civilians had been abandoned and left to the mercy of fate. The Polish army was on the run. The Germans were advancing and the Polish people were in the middle. After a while, German planes began to swoop over our heads adding to the panic. There were screams and cries from all around. Thankfully, for some unknown reason we were not fired upon. One plane did fire short bursts nearby, but no one was injured, and we knew that if it had been their intention to shoot us, it would have been impossible for any bullet to miss its destination.

I came across a family from our own village who told me that my mother had been asked to deliver a child and she had gone as asked. My father, with my two younger brothers and two sisters, Maria and Sophie, had gone into hiding, as we lived only about seven miles from the German border.

As I talked to the family, my brother approached and said that a border patrolman had taken his bike. Luckily, I still had my gent's bike and we were still mobile. We wondered what to do next: turn back and follow the crowds away from the border, or continue on to find out about Mother who was perhaps alone. We decided to head for home. My brother winked at me as if to say 'Look back.' I did so and there was another border patrol. As expected, he asked me for my bike. I replied, 'How dare you terrorize people, stealing instead of helping. I see you have disarmed yourself or have you lost your arms?' He had not expected my response and disappeared faster than he had appeared.

We continued on our journey home, planning what we would do once we got there. We cycled for miles along the now deserted road. It looked so peaceful with woodlands on one side and the fir plantation on the other. It was hard to believe that we had been invaded and our country was now at war.

As we neared the village of Rytel, a lone Polish army patrol approached from the plantation and asked where we were heading and where we lived. He was surprised when we told him that his unit (he belonged to the Cavalry) was on the retreat about eight miles further back. We asked how far away the German army was. To our utter amazement, he told us Polish forces were fighting on German territory. We really were going home, or so we thought; the information proved to be deliberately misleading.

Our joy and excitement lasted only a few minutes. As we came out from the wooded area into farmland we could see Rytel. Bruno whispered for me to look to the right. 'Oh God! We are lost, Bruno,' was all I could murmur. The ditches were full of German soldiers. They were so well camouflaged we almost stepped on top of them. Their faces were covered with mud and grass, and little branches were fixed around their helmets. Two jumped out to stop us and they began to ask questions. We just looked at them before replying in Polish that we were unable to understand. At that many more came out. After debating among themselves for a while we were given a signal to walk to a little hill. A soldier walked each side of us and another half a dozen followed behind. Bruno and I eyed each other knowing the end was coming – this was to be our firing squad.

On reaching the hill a short distance from the road we found ourselves facing woodlands. The two soldiers gave us a signal to stop. I noticed the other six were waiting about fifteen yards from us. In these few minutes, my mind worked like lightning. I realized now that the Polish patrol had used us as a decoy to find out when we were going to be stopped. Even then, my thoughts were mainly for my mother. I felt sure that she would be trying to find us when we failed to show up. We were so near to home.

I turned once more to Bruno then cast my eyes down, looking to the ground in front of me and wondered if I would hear the crack of the rifle before being hit. I cannot say that we were frightened; rather we were in shock. Things were happening so fast. I could hear the sound of a motor cycle stopping near us on the road, then a voice screamed out. As I lifted my head, I knew it had something to do with us. We were taken back down to the road to a German officer and a civilian who acted as his interpreter.

First of all, we were asked if we knew what was happening. 'Yes, we are in front of the firing squad,' was my reply.

'You are to answer all questions truthfully. Any suspicion that you are telling lies and you will be going back to where I saved you from. Understand?'

'Yes, Sir,' came my quick reply.

During interrogation I could see no advantage in telling lies, so I told the truth to save our lives. I had a feeling that the civilian interpreter must have been a local man because of the questions he asked us later on his own initiative. First, he asked where we lived and then asked me to draw a map on the sandy ground of the roads from the Chojnice town to our village and out of the village. The German officer checked the drawing and compared it to his map. Then he asked me to add all the field roads that I knew of to my drawing. I knew these very well and did as asked.

He also asked which house we lived in coming from the direction of Chojnice. We told him it was the first on the right, a grocer's shop. He queried why we were so far from home and how we had landed in their front line. I answered that my father had sent us to collect my uncle's wagon to pick up some belongings. He then asked for my uncle's address and occupation, and also if he was following. I explained he was not, as we had decided to abandon our plans after seeing the Polish army retreating through their village.

At this point, I noticed the interpreter became interested. He wanted to know how many Polish soldiers were on the retreat but I was only able to tell him that they had been coming in batches during most of the day.

When asked what units they were from, I informed him that they were mostly Cavalry with very few soldiers on foot. As regards any other soldiers, there had only been the lone patroller who had told us that the Polish army was fighting on German territory.

Continuing his questioning, he asked about our family and I told him what I knew. I observed the interpreter nodding in agreement when I was asked and confirmed my mother was a midwife. This proved my suspicions that he was a local collaborator and knew of us. I also had to tell them that the Polish patrol had been roughly half a mile away: two men armed with machine guns quickly headed off in that direction. With the same speed, they returned. Then to our relief the now smiling officer, through his interpreter, told us that there was nothing to worry about and we could go home.

Having my brother on my bike with me made it difficult to cycle. The advancing German army took up the full width of the road with horse-drawn guns, covered wagons most likely with ammunition, and huge kitchen boilers. The soldiers were older and seemed to be rather friendly often calling out 'Heil, Hitler.' This made it rather difficult for me to cycle with my brother on the handlebars and constantly lift my hand to reply 'Heil, Hitler.'

As we were familiar with the terrain, we branched off into the wooded area. About a mile further on at Mlynki was Uncle Johan's farm. As we headed for the farm we observed quite a lot of cavalry horses walking about with their heads down and reins trailing on the ground as if looking for their masters. Wounded horses stood motionless and I couldn't help wondering what they had gone through to suffer like that.

At the farm we were surprised to see all the cattle and pigs inside the sheds. We let them all out before going into the house. His two dogs were inside and gave us a tremendous welcome. There was a bowl of water on the floor and a large loaf of bread of which we took a little. There was no sign at all of Uncle Johan - where could he be? We started off again to cover the last four miles of the journey home.

As we approached our neighbouring village, it was packed with German soldiers. We were stopped by a group of five who could hardly stand up as they were so drunk. By sign language, we knew they were asking for vodka and cigarettes but after turning our pockets inside out and showing that we could not help them they signalled us to carry on.

Our own village was also packed with German soldiers. As we approached our house, we could see some officers and soldiers inside. Our home had obviously been commandeered by the enemy. We decided to go in as there was nothing else we could do. There was a civilian who did the translating for the army personnel who were desperate for cigarettes. After telling them that we had sold out before leaving, they wanted to know where we normally kept cigarettes. On showing them, they swept the shelves with a piece of paper and from the loose tobacco gathered managed to roll two cigarettes. There was no sign of any member of our family.

Through the interpreter, they said that we could have a look through the house. It was spotless; typical army style. Eventually, we were told by the civilian to go to a certain farm in the village where we would be issued with identity cards. As we approached the farm square, it looked like general headquarters with three long tables covered with maps being studied by about twenty officers.

Again, civilians approached us and took us inside the farm building for more interrogation. Asking how we managed to get through the front line, we repeated our story. We were then told to go to our own town, Chojnice, four miles away to be registered.

We set off again like two lost sheep, never meeting one Pole we could talk to for comfort. To make our situation more difficult, Bruno had suffered since childhood from a nervous disorder and when excited he could not talk. If he was asked anything he would open his mouth but could not speak and I always had to take over.

On arrival in the town where we were to register, we found the main street packed with civilians watching columns of German troops marching to the front line. I voiced my fears to Bruno that we should stay there and not bother with registration but go instead to stay with our cousin but Bruno insisted we registered.

When we landed at the registry office, we were met by German police. More questions were asked and we had to empty our pockets. Being Catholics, my mother insisted we each carried a rosary. On seeing the contents of our pockets, I sensed one of the policemen felt a little sorry for us.

As it happened, our registration turned into a long trek to imprisonment - so near home and yet so far away. We were put into a prison cell. After half an hour, we whispered to each other that whatever we talked about, nothing was to be said about Germans. Every time there was a sound of footsteps, we thought we were getting some food but no such luck. It was fortunate we had pinched some bread from the dogs at my uncle's farm. We realized we were not going to receive any registration cards. All we could do was wait and see what their plans were for us.

CHAPTER 4

Some registration cards! Early the next morning, along with other prisoners, we were taken about ten miles away to a town in Germany called Schlochau. The lorry stopped in a market square. It must have been to show us off to the German public – a sort of propaganda exercise – the first Polish prisoners. As we were standing there, an old man using crutches and barely able to walk came close. With a threatening and hate-filled look in his eyes he lifted his stick and tried to strike out at us. Also observing us in the crowds was a group of younger people and I noticed the confusion and sadness in their eyes. The girls were quite emotional and some were crying. After that exhibition, we were taken out to a big farm. There were about 50 prisoners and our accommodation was a cattle byre with no blankets but plenty of straw.

By the second day, we still had not received any food. Eventually, in the evening, we got a thick slice of almost black army bread. At least there was a tap in the byre and we had any amount of water. A short distance from the byre about twenty Polish soldiers were being held separately. A few yards to the left of them senior German officers were studying maps spread on tables. We were not allowed to talk to the Polish soldiers and we were desperate for some news, although by now none of us had much hope after seeing the German might the Polish army was facing.

Two German soldiers arrived with another prisoner, a Polish captain in his early forties. I was surprised to see that one of the German officers got up and they saluted each other. He was allowed a few minutes with his soldiers. We felt a surge of hope. Despite being a prisoner, the captain stood proudly, anger showing in his face as he exchanged a few encouraging words with the soldiers who stood to attention. The Germans then took him to a house, just across the square from us. One of his guards carried a towel and eating utensils. I was very pleased to see the Polish captain getting a little VIP treatment.

By eight o'clock the metal gate of the byre was locked for the night. A German guard came inside trying to sort out the sleeping arrangements. What a mixture of ages we were, from 18 like myself to 60 years of age. One of the oldest men had a bad open wound just above his foot and walked with the help of a stick. To complete the mixture of prisoners, there was one beautiful gypsy girl of about twenty years of age. She kept very much to herself and was constantly on the verge of tears. We slept in one long row. The gypsy girl was put at the very far end away from the metal gate. Next to her a boy with a very unusual face, squint-eyed, was deliberately placed followed by all the older men and finally anyone else still needing a sleeping place.

As we lay there, my mind wandered over the blunders we had made. We should have stopped at my uncle's farm where we had deprived the poor dogs of some bread. On the other hand, we could have hidden on our way to the town to be registered. There were huge, young plantations on both sides of the road leading to town.

We were warned almost daily that any attempt to escape or disobey orders would result in the death penalty. I thought about my brother, Jan, and how he was getting on in the Polish cavalry with only a sword and a rifle against the might of the German tanks and planes.

The German regime was not very tolerant towards the Catholics and I wondered also about my brother, Victor, who had just been ordained and what was happening to him. He could have stayed at home but had chosen to return to the Franciscan Order. I thought, too, about my mother who would be rather sad and lost, and felt sad for her. I knew that after being missing for a fortnight she would knock on the doors of every police and army office until she found out our whereabouts. As I lay there in the straw throughout the night, I thought about all the members of my family. Hopefully, with everything that confronted them they would survive.

As for the war, we were all losing hope. We did not see much chance of winning the battle. As I dwelt on these matters, a guard burst in with his torch blazing and turned to where the gypsy girl was lying. We all sat up to see what was happening and were astonished to find her lying there stark naked staring up at the guard who was screaming at her to cover herself up. There was no response from her as she lay motionless, staring into his eyes. With his bayonet fixed to his rifle, he started tearing at her breasts. The poor gypsy girl lay still and silent, her breasts now covered in blood. We sat petrified, unsure of what was going to happen next. Eventually, he turned and ordered us to cover her up. There was now some reaction and movement from a few boys who quickly covered her with so much straw that she had almost disappeared under it. The guard did not say a word to the innocent-faced boy next to her who had obviously taken advantage of the female lying so close to him. With his unattractive looks it was easy to see though why the temptation had been too much for him to resist. We did not sleep much for the remainder of the night wondering what was in store for us. We could hear the gypsy girl trying to get out from under the straw to get some air.

In the morning, we each got our rations of bread and a two-litre aluminium container for coffee. Some thought that perhaps we were going to get something warm to eat. At the thought of a hot meal, our tummies were turning somersaults with joy! But our luck was not in: we were given coffee that we called brown water. As for our ration of bread, every one of us chewed his share very slowly, almost frightened to swallow it, in order to make it last. Our gypsy girl did not get up for her bread and coffee. One of the older men, who could speak good German, explained to the guard that she wasn't feeling well and eventually her rations were taken over to her by another prisoner. Tearfully, she looked up at him with gratitude, as if to say 'Somebody cares'. He asked her how she came to be here separated from her people. Again, she just shrugged her shoulders but didn't utter a word. Her bread and coffee lay untouched.

Another guard came in and opened one of the metal gates so that we could get out to exercise. Somebody commented that they seemed to be concerned for us and that it might not be so bad after all.

Two of the men in our group simply refused to speak to us in Polish. Instead they seized every opportunity they got to speak to the guard in

German in an attempt to try and prove that they were not Polish even though they lived in Poland. Eventually, they succeeded. They were issued with some papers, cigarettes and a small truck took them away. They were members of the German ethnic minority who later terrorized our people as we were to find out to our cost.

The peace was broken by terrifying screams and cries as the gypsy girl clung to the metal gate like a caged wild animal. Two of our boys ran to her and tried to quieten her but she was so hysterical she took no notice. German guards came and forcibly pulled her off the gate then twisted her arms behind her back before taking her outside. Seeing her, we all felt so downhearted. We knew of the freedom the gypsies had before the war, travelling with their caravans throughout the country. There she now stood sobbing so hard her body was shaking, her head hung down with her long hair covering her face. She was taken away from us in a lorry. She obviously missed her precious freedom so much.

A truck arrived in the afternoon and we were ordered to get on board. After a two-hour drive, the truck stopped at a huge camp with long, wooden army huts. A lot of Polish civilians were already there, including women and young girls. We were issued with two blankets each and marched into one of the barracks. After our meal which, as usual, was bread and coffee, we all sat around against the wall with our legs pulled up close to our chins and the blankets over our shoulders. There were no mattresses. We were not cold but our bones were very sore.

Next morning after our rations, our names and ages were checked against a list. Those over 50 years were separated from the rest, given some extra bread and told they were going home. I thought my brother might have been included as he was so gaunt he already looked like a concentration camp victim, and it would have been much easier for me not to have to worry about him. Also, if he was released my parents would know what had happened to me. Yet we were pleased to see the older people being sent home. As for the rest of us? Everybody was speculating – would it be labour camps, factory work or prison camps until the end of the war?

That same afternoon, our names were called out again and checked off the list. This was to be the morning routine. We were marched about half a mile into a fenced area where they told us that they were going to get rid of our Polish lice. Some of the guards were so nice, we thought they felt sorry for us. Then there was the other extreme, the ones who would kick you or hit you with the rifle butt at the first opportunity.

During next morning call, I tried to get Bruno into the middle line to save him from any abuse. We were told to strip and put all our belongings in one bundle and then carry them to huge steam boilers. As we were waiting, a group of women was marched in. Modesty was not respected. After they had stripped and put all their clothing into bundles, a guard came to us and asked us to take their bundles to the boilers. The heat in the boilers meant anything made of leather just crumpled. From then on belts were out, and trousers had to be held up by one hand.

The next time we stood to attention, our trousers just fell to the ground. The face of a German officer standing in front of us turned red with rage, thinking we had done it deliberately. But when the command 'at ease' came, everyone's hand went automatically for his trousers. When our spokesman explained to the officer, he was rather amused and, smiling, told the sergeant to issue us with string.

After our clothes had been disinfected, we were taken on another two-hour journey, this time to German barracks at Grossborn. These consisted of huge army buildings three storeys high. Here, again, there was any amount of water to drink and to wash with. As the barracks were fenced off with a high, solid-metal fence, we were allowed to move around, although there were signs warning 'ANYONE WITHIN THREE METRES OF THE FENCE WILL BE SHOT'. We all mentally extended this limit to ten metres to avoid any accidents. A loudspeaker told us to return to our rooms. It also announced, 'We have the pleasure to give you the news that Warsaw has capitulated. We are proud of the bravery of our soldiers and those who sacrificed their lives for our beloved Führer and our fatherland...' We didn't believe a word. To us, it was Goebels speaking. At the same time, we knew we were not going to win. All of us taken prisoner had the chance to see the strength of the German army advancing – the tanks against man with horse and sword.

Following the speech, we got our first warm meal in seven days. I remember it was thick rice with plenty of meat. In fact, it was so thick that my spoon could stand in it. Bruno couldn't finish his and I was only too pleased to help him. I had never enjoyed a meal so much in my life. Some of us jokingly commented that we hoped Warsaw would fall again the next day. Our bread rations, however, became smaller as we were now getting a midday meal of thick vegetable soup.

We started searching for people from our own district to exchange news. I realized that most of them had been captured after leaving their hiding places at night to feed the farm animals. Now it became clear why all the animals, including the dogs, had been inside when we had landed at our uncle's farm. Why hadn't we hidden on the farm? However, having been already in front of the firing squad and my brother insisting on obeying orders, here we were. We tried to console each other with the fact that the older people had been sent home. News was bound to reach our family and they would have a glimmer of hope that we were still alive.

During the five days we were at Grossborn, I noticed that every time we got our bread, some of the boys would try to swap half of their rations for just one cigarette. Some gave their gold rings to the German guards for tobacco or cigarettes.

One day, my good, law-abiding brother came with a banjo, apparently in exchange for a packet of cigarettes he had had all the time since leaving home. I could not believe that he could make such a deal and was annoyed that he had not given them to me. Eventually, though, the banjo turned out to be a treasure. One day, as our names were being checked as usual, we were told that after breakfast we would be issued with extra rations for a long trip. There was a lot of speculation. Some said we must be going home, but others remarked that there would be no need for extras if we were indeed going home.

We were loaded onto army trucks and within twenty minutes we were at the railway station and packed so tightly into cattle wagons that we were all forced to sit. Anyone sitting against the walls could relax a little, but those in the middle complained and quarrelled over the lack of room all through the long night. Each time the train stopped, we desperately tried to find out where we were, but the way the air vents were installed made it impossible to see. We could barely distinguish day from night.

Our first stop came after twenty hours. The door slid open and soldiers were positioned ten to twenty yards from each other in a field. We were ordered out to relieve ourselves, then received new rations and a drink of coffee. We realized that our journey was going to be a long one because the bread rations had been doubled. As we strolled about, I tried to stay close to the wagons so that when the order came to get in I could secure at least one place for Bruno against the wall.

It was mid-morning when we were ordered inside again and the doors locked as the train departed into the unknown. We had no clue of our whereabouts – our stops were in the middle of fields and woodland.

Moaning filled the wagon until someone suggested that we should all sit back to back and give each other support. That worked really well for the rest of the morning and all was quiet. The only sound then was the monotonous 'rat-tat-tat' from the wheels of the train. We stopped speculating as to where we were going. One thing was obvious, we were going in a southerly direction. The train stopped quite often; not that we were let out. We did notice that the rail traffic seemed to be very busy during the night. Each time the train stopped, we could hear each other's breathing as no one was talking in the hope that we could catch something from the guards' conversation about where we were heading.

Morning came and we stopped again and were allowed out for about half a hour. On the third day we had one stop near a small station. We could hear talking. One of the older men in our wagon thought he knew where we were. Before he had a chance to say anything else, somebody tried to be witty and said, 'I, too, know where we are – sitting in German cattle wagons in the middle of nowhere.' The man continued, 'I think I can tell you where. According to the dialect, it must be Bavaria.' He was later proved to be correct.

Later the same day about 10 o'clock, we pulled into a siding. The doors opened and we were told to get out for the toilet again, then back into the wagons. We could hear the German guards and the railway porters talking and eventually we were marched about half a mile to a convoy of about fifteen trucks. Thirty of us filled each truck, with two fairly friendly guards at the back. At long last, we knew where we were. A signpost read 'Nuremberg 8 Kilometres'.

Half an hour later we came upon long rows of huge tents and the convoy stopped. Two eight-feet-high fences surrounded the tents about seven feet apart, with coiled barbed wire inside and look-out towers every 100 yards. A spotlight would immediately fix on anyone who went near the perimeter fences. This was now going to be our home, but for how long?

CHAPTER 5

More soldiers awaited us here as we climbed out of the trucks and lined up four abreast. We were checked out from the list again and each issued with two blankets. In groups of 80, we headed for our tents. Again, we were given straw to spread on the ground. Between us Bruno and I put one blanket on top of the straw leaving three to cover ourselves with.

The next thing we did was to look for water - wonderful water - which, at home, we took for granted. As the whole area was brightly lit, we didn't bother trying to sleep, but started exploring. There was a long, troughlike basin with half a dozen taps for each line of tents. The toilets, on the other hand, looked rather frightening and dangerous. The toilet consisted of a pit about 10 yards long, 3 feet wide and 8 feet deep with a pipe about 4 feet in diameter passing through it. There was a pole, not very strong, to sit on, about 10 inches to the back and about a foot higher was another one to lean on. There was another pole in front of that for the person to hold on to. Every time a few men sat on the pole it started to bend, scaring all those perching on it.

At this camp, our first ration of bread and coffee, although not enough to live on, was too much to die on. With guards either side we had to walk about 300 yards to the kitchen outside the prison camp to collect our rations, then the camp rules were read to us.

We were told that rules and commands were to be obeyed and asked to choose our own leader; we were to be ready for inspection at 11 a.m. in front of our tents; any disobedience or stealing would be severely punished; we would be shot on sight if we attempted to escape. Our leader was to choose men required for work both around and outside the camp.

For the first few days, we visited the various tents hoping to find someone we knew to share our miseries with and to console each other. In between each block of six tents was a single six-foot-high fence. Across the fence from us there were four empty tents and Jews occupied the remaining two.

In spite of all the misery and uncertainty that was surrounding us, there were still some young men who always stood beside the fence and as soon as any of the Jews appeared at the water trough, they would swear and insult them, but the Jews just looked at them and didn't even bother to reply. I couldn't help recalling the two Jewish families we had once known. I tried to console myself that they were so old they were bound to have died by natural causes now as it had been almost five years since we had left that area.

My brother and I decided to report the boys to our tent leader. He picked half a dozen men, very tough ones, to put an end to it. They seemed only too eager to oblige and the following day, after our watery soup, we waited anxiously to see the performance. As we came out of our tent, there they were; the same abusive lot. The six men approached casually and then very quickly gave them their just desserts. As one of them picked himself up he asked, 'What was that for?' As he tried to tell him the reason, another one hit him again and said, 'That's for asking ignorant questions.' I think it was the first time since our capture that I really laughed from the bottom of my heart and so did the others. They then had to apologize for their behaviour to the Jews. The Jews stood in bewilderment at first, then with a little smile said, 'Thank you for sorting them out.'

Some of the troublemakers threatened to complain to the sergeant, thinking the Germans would approve of their actions and they were told they could do so but only if they were prepared to accept the consequences.

Sometimes the tents remained open until late into the evening and we could always hear the older Jews praying but, somehow, it seemed the good Lord did not hear their prayers or those of the other millions of people praying and screaming for help. At times, I wondered why, with all the millions of people praying to God, that no help was forthcoming.

On the fifth day there, we were marched to a much larger tent. A few doctors and male nurses were waiting to inject us against typhoid. The needle was so blunt you could hear it tearing the flesh. Quite a number of the boys were laid up with fever after the injection – especially my brother – but eventually they all recovered.

Next day, I volunteered for work because I knew I could get some cigarette ends if I was lucky enough to work in the German quarters. If the coast was clear, some of the soldiers would give you a full packet. Then again, some would throw a cigarette on the ground, stamp on it and look at you with hatred, almost saying with their eyes, 'I wish I could do this to you.' It was a great advantage to have some tobacco. Often at night, after bread rations were issued, I'd give half of my slice of bread to Bruno and I would enjoy a puff or two from my precious cigarette. It would knock me out and I'd fall asleep easily.

As the days progressed, our tent leader was getting on quite well with our guard. He managed to trade our banjo for four ounces of tobacco. I gave him one ounce and kept three for myself. From then on I was well off. For two cigarettes, I could get half a ration of bread or exchange a small one-inch-square piece of bread for a small 'bomb'. This was a little tobacco rolled in newspaper and put in a cigarette holder with enough for five or six good puffs. Being weak to start with, the boys smoking it went down like jelly and that's where the name 'bomb' came from.

One morning towards the end of September, the sergeant came with his two guards, all smiling, and called us out. Then through his interpreter he announced that Warsaw had fallen and that the Polish army had surrendered. That was the second time we had been told that Warsaw had surrendered. As had happened on the previous occasion, we had very thick soup for dinner. I landed very lucky. As the boiler they dished soup out of was almost empty, I could see some big bones lying at the bottom so I asked the cook for one. He looked at me and, to my surprise, pulled one out and with a nod said, 'Take it.' It must have been from a horse's leg – what grizzle was on it. What a feast Bruno and I had! After we'd enjoyed a good feed of the bone I gave the rest to our tent leader. It helped a lot as regards getting work. Our leader always put my name on the work list after that. That poor bone got the works at the end. It was smashed with stones and the marrow taken out.

Somehow, this time we did believe that Poland had surrendered and our war was over. At the same time, we consoled ourselves with the thought, 'Just wait until Britain starts, it won't be long until we will be free again.' Hopefully, the cook would get two bones in return for the one he had given to me, should he land in prison!

One day, a truck arrived carrying well-dressed Japanese civilians. They were put in one of the empty tents across the fence from us and we were rather surprised to see that every evening German families would visit them with food, chocolate and cigarettes. Two weeks later, they were taken back home again. The block of tents where the Jews were was getting more full as each day passed.

The days, but especially, the nights, were becoming rather cold. Some nights, we could hardly sleep for the cold. To add to all the misery we had to endure, we were covered in lice. On a warm day, we would strip and scrape them out from between the seams in our vests and shirts.

Towards the end of October, a table and chairs were set up in front of each tent. We were called out and our personal details checked - date of birth, place, occupation, parents' occupation. Everything was noted. Then an observing officer got up and announced that within the next two or three weeks we would be sent home as we came from West Prussia - the corridor. We were looked on as Germans and, therefore, we should consider ourselves privileged to join them in whatever duties would be put upon us and that it would be all for our fatherland and our beloved Führer. When he left, despite all the misery, the thought of going home did cheer us up. Comments were made about his speech - 'privileged to work for your fatherland' and 'our beloved Führer.' If he only knew what we were thinking about his fatherland and his beloved Führer.

Things were moving fast now. The next day the same officer with his sergeant were with us again as we lined up. The interpreter asked anyone serving a prison sentence from five to ten years to step forward. When four men stepped to the front, their names were taken before stepping back. Next it was the turn of those serving over 10 years to life sentences. Two men stepped forward. The officer at the table gave a sheet of paper to the sergeant who walked in front of the first line, now and again glancing at his paper, then ordered the whole line to move forward four yards. Again, he regarded each man then his paper. Suddenly, he stopped in front of one man and stared before hitting him repeatedly on the face and head. We thought he was going to finish him on the spot. Before departing, our tent orderly was told to have the seven men picked out and waiting at the gate at 10 o'clock the next day. For the rest of the day we all felt despair and sorrow for them. Anyone with tobacco, cigarettes rolled in newspaper or the little tobacco rolled 'bombs' gave them some. We seemed to rally around them and didn't want to know their crimes. They were each one of us and we belonged together.

Next morning most of us broke off a bit of our bread ration and gave it to them. Poor boys, they were quite emotional. But the one that was dealt the punishment was missing and this was reported. The six listed men were ordered into the guarded truck and the sergeant, raging with anger, warned us that should any of us be hiding the seventh man, we would be executed.

In the afternoon, a truck loaded with 30 soldiers arrived. There was a roll call of all 480 of us, then we had to stand to attention by the dividing fence closely guarded while an unsuccessful search was made of all the tents.

I had become alarmed during the roll call earlier as poor Bruno was unable to answer when his name was called. He could only look at me red-faced and nervous. I shouted 'here' for him. As they regarded me suspiciously, our tent orderly explained about Bruno's speech impediment. When Bruno, still blushing, was asked his name his mouth opened but he was unable to utter a word. The sergeant could not understand how someone like Bruno could be in this prison camp. I heaved a deep sigh of relief when the quizzing was over with. Had he been a ruthless Nazi, Bruno could very well have been dealt the same treatment as the now-missing man.

There was a lot of speculation amongst us concerning the man who had disappeared. It was impossible for him to get away. Surrounded by an eight-foot double fence, with coiled barbed wire inside, as soon as anyone went near it the spotlight was on them. We all believed that his escape route was a sewage pipe four feet in diameter. What a horrible way to go! To him it must have seemed the lesser of two terrifying decisions, preferring to die voluntarily by breathing in the gasses from the sewage pipe than face torture and eventual execution. We were rather surprised that the Polish Prison Authorities had not burned all their records before the German invasion. We consoled ourselves with the belief that, because they were taking all the previously jailed prisoners away, once free there wouldn't be any hardened criminals living in the community.

Conditions in the camp were seriously deteriorating. Food, as such, was issued as usual but the nights were so cold. We just could not sleep. Some would still try to joke saying we wouldn't starve without freezing. My tobacco ran out and that meant no extra bread, specially for my brother who only got up to march the 300 yards for food and crawl back under the blankets. He already looked like a ghost, with large bulging eyes and he said very little, only stared ahead. Even with the news of going home, he just shrugged his shoulders as if he couldn't have cared less what came next. I was very concerned for him. Should we be kept much longer, he would not survive.

One Saturday, late in the evening, we heard cries of agony coming from the Jewish tent. We learned later that somebody had stolen their bread rations. Our tent orderly asked some of us whom he could trust to watch for anyone who had more than their usual ration of bread but we observed without success. For some reason, the Jews were given their full day's ration of bread for the whole tent in a big willow basket. At midday they had to leave it unguarded to collect their soup like the rest of us. It was suggested to our tent leader that he should talk to the sergeant but he told us it may jeopardize our release for sympathizing with them. Yes, just for sympathizing with other human beings. I just wondered what was in store for us.

Sunday came and we received a surprise visit from our sergeant and his two guards. He called us out of the tent then produced a newspaper from his briefcase and called a name – Jan Novak. He was asked to step forward. The 16-year-old did so and he was shown the front page of the newspaper. The boy began crying and said that it was his father. Needless to say, he was taken from us. Next day, the sergeant returned and put up a big poster displaying the boy's father handcuffed to two soldiers. He had been accused of torturing a wounded German officer. What a fate – a boy of sixteen years most likely paying with his own life for his father's crime. He was a nice, lively boy from my home town, where his father operated buses to Danzig. He was always asking if we really believed that one day we would get home, hoping to get a reassuring answer. Yet because of his father's actions his dreams of home and freedom had disappeared forever. It made me realize how cruel fate can be at times.

We were now into our third month at Nuremberg and some of us were suffering from dysentery. The authorities would have to do something with us. If not, most of us wouldn't make it. The straw we were given to lie on turned into chaff. There was no difference now to lying on the bare ground.

Then one day the much-longed-for news came. The sergeant accompanied by his two guards announced that within the following two days or so we would be on our way home. What an atmosphere the news created, one of laughter and joy. Some went over to the sergeant and got a hold of him and started heaving him up. At the same time, others were calling out not to drop him in case the trip home would be cancelled. Now, somehow, through the night we didn't feel the cold or discomfort. There were a few in our company who looked very poorly and who continued staring into space, unaffected by the joyous news.

My brother, who was giving me so much cause for concern, became more lively. We couldn't stop talking. What were we going to eat on our first day home? Bruno and I were rather aware of one thing - everybody wouldn't be at home. We wouldn't even know where they were if they were still alive. Later, our suspicions proved to be right.

Next day, our dream became reality. We were again issued with the same amount of bread as in the camp which made some suspect that because we did not get any extra we weren't really going home yet.

Convoys of lorries arrived. What a welcome sight! The guards seemed much friendlier as we all climbed in. They didn't even sit with us at the back of the lorry but up front beside the driver. We arrived at a small station on the outskirts of Nuremberg. Surely it must be true we were going home now for there was straw in the cattle wagons. We were each given a paper carton of honey, which amounted to 250 gms, and an extra ration of bread. Even the ventilators this time were small open doors giving us some light during the day. Any sign of comfort worked like a barometer on us. Our hopes were building up. Before the train left, we got our containers filled with coffee. We were off!

Through the day, we managed to peep through the ventilators. We could see lots of fruit trees beside the road with some fruit still on them, despite the fact it was the middle of December. The sight of all that forbidden fruit made my mouth water. As darkness fell, we settled down for the night. This time there were quite a few less to each wagon so we could stretch our legs to some degree. Somehow, we managed to suffer each other more on our return journey.

What a wonderful flavour the honey had. I kept digging my finger in it. Once the trace of honey in my mouth disappeared, I would dig again until it was all gone.

The train stopped a number of times, sometimes up to three hours. We were allowed out for the first time at midnight, after almost twelve hours. Again, it was in the middle of nowhere. We felt uplifted as we knew we were near the Polish border. We were told that if we needed the toilet to get out and that the next stop would be our last. What a sight it must have been with almost half of us suffering from diarrhoea or the after-effects of sweet honey. Even the guards seemed amused.

There was a lot of excitement after boarding the train once more. Within six hours we would be in our home town. About 2 o'clock in the afternoon, after another few stops, we alighted at a place called Hamerstein, a small German town near the border. We lined up four abreast and marched about one kilometre guarded on either side. Our hearts dropped as we neared yet another camp gate with the same type of tents as in Nuremberg. Guards stood on either side of the gate. We were back to square one.

Once inside the camp, we were told that each prisoner was to join his tent leader. Again, we were issued with blankets, and the only consolation was plenty of fresh straw. All hope of freedom vanished. Civilians were standing all around the fence. After getting sleeping areas sorted out for the night, some of us went over to see what was going on. There were local people looking for relatives. Quite a few did find their own people and handed over food parcels. For some reason the guards seemed not to bother them. Those civilians who didn't find relatives divided their parcels but there were so many hands outstretched to them that we felt sorry for them as they hesitated about who to give to. There was one piece of good news, though. We were told by the civilians that it was a gathering point, a transit camp. After our addresses were sorted out, some were being sent home almost every week. Hopefully, it wouldn't be too long for our turn as Bruno was now in very poor shape.

Foodwise, the news we got from other prisoners already there was rather depressing. Daily a few people were carried out dead. Our bread portions got smaller, but then we did get a little blob of jam! At midday, our soup was so watery that the whole week's ration couldn't make up for one ration of the soup we got in Nuremberg.

Within a week of our arrival, many of us were again suffering from dysentery. The toilet pits were red with blood. Throughout the day, almost everyone just sat and stared into space.

Each morning a tractor with guards sitting on each side came with a delivery of potatoes and carrots. As our tent was the nearest to the gate entrance, some guards deliberately pushed carrots and potatoes off. If you were quick and lucky enough, you got some. You would take a little bite out of each with relish. It was always something extra, especially for Bruno.

The second week of our stay there, all 300 of our names were called out. We were marched back to the station and this time without any extra rations which we all understood to be a good sign. Should we be going home, within two hours we would be in our home town. The day everybody was talking and dreaming about constantly was perhaps here at last.

The train at last pulled in at our local station. Such excitement! We were all lined up four abreast and marched away through the town. People were running on the pavements on either side shouting and asking for names. I noticed Uncle Frank. I called over to him to tell my parents that we were back. As I had walked so often on these streets before the war, I felt almost every house was my home. What a marvellous feeling!

We were taken to a place two miles from the station which used to be an institution for the mentally handicapped, surrounded by a nine-foot-high wall. I did hope that we would get home from here. Home was another four miles away still. After being issued with our rations of bread and coffee, we tried to catch some sleep. This was the first time we had mattresses to lie on - what a luxury. Witty comments were made to the mattresses, apologising for the German lice we were going to leave behind! We were sure next morning our mother would be there waiting.

During the night, there was a lot of noise outside. Alongside the institution was a dairy. Milk was taken there from all the surrounding farms including the estate belonging to the institution which was worked by the patients. With all the excitement and the noise, we couldn't sleep much. Somebody mentioned a name, a Mr Kopf, who was a village councillor, and that every time new prisoners came he would come to the camp to see them. He took a lot of people out, always pretending he knew them. I knew him myself, a very friendly person. He had a farm and a smithy in our neighbouring village.

At daybreak, we all went outside and headed for the fence, shivering with the cold and hoping to meet somebody we knew. Many of the farmers were coming with their milk to the dairy. At 7 a.m. as the huge gate opened, there was my mother talking to the German guards, most likely explaining the reason for trying to enter. Then a German officer came and after more talking, she was eventually allowed in. As she neared the fence surrounding the institution building, a German guard stopped her and, quite abruptly, put his rifle across her breast and pushed her back. My mother begged him tearfully to be allowed to leave small parcels of food with us, but to no avail. As she turned away sadly to leave, I tried to control my emotions and called to my mother to go home and get in touch with Mr Kopf and this she eventually did. Bruno was so overwhelmed with emotion that he couldn't utter a word. As for me, I just looked at the guard. Most likely he could read my thoughts. I didn't give much thought to the food my mother had brought but, because of the treatment she had received, she would most likely have been crying the whole way home. If the good Lord had granted half of my wishes that morning, that guard would have dropped dead, the monster. I didn't dare think of what might be in front of us after that experience. We all felt the same watching my mother's treatment.

By 8 a.m. there were almost as many people outside the gate as there were inside, all waiting with food parcels but not being allowed in. As I watched the civilians walking about, I noticed there were none of the mentally handicapped amongst them. Whatever had happened to them?

At lunchtime, we got thick, milky soup with potatoes and barley. It was almost as good as the day Warsaw had surrendered the first time!

I thought the next morning would never come; the time passed so slowly. I was so excited at the thought of the family being together again. At long last, the big gates to freedom opened - if that was what one wanted to call it. It only followed with years of misery, persecution and executions as we were to find out.

As I anticipated, our dear mother was standing there right in front of the gates with Mr Kopf, the village councillor. As before, the civilians were not allowed inside. As the councillor, accompanied by two German officials, came towards the fence he took out a list and started calling out names. Those called were ordered to line up outside. Almost everyone seemed to know Mr Kopf. People called to Mr Kopf even after the list had ended and he just kept saying that he knew this one or that one. There was no end to it.

We marched out free to go. There were tears of happiness on all the faces. My mother whispered to me to say, 'Heil, Hitler.' I whispered back, 'Shit Heil, Hitler. Let us go home before they change their minds about releasing us.' My mother had organized transport with Uncle Frank who had come with the horse wagon. He didn't dare take the coach out in case of trouble. What a feast we had when my mother produced a flask of coffee, some nice sandwiches and fruit.

It was around 5 o'clock in the afternoon and we were home at long last. What a welcome! There was so much news to share. We heard from our parents of what was already sadly happening in our area. Visitors called during the evening and right into the early hours of the morning bringing fruit and cigarettes. Eventually, we did manage to get to bed. I couldn't believe a bed could be so comfortable after about eleven weeks lying in straw spread on the ground. The whole family lived for almost a week on all the presents brought to us on our return. We just hoped we would manage to stay together and survive whatever lay ahead.

Next day, we resumed our talking. There was no end to what we had to tell of how we had landed in the front line and our experiences of all the prison camps.

The family wondered about my brother, Jan, who was in the cavalry and whether he was still alive. Almost three months had passed since my other brother, Victor, had gone back to his Franciscan Order but there was still no word from him. Then there was my sister, Lucy, in the convent near the Baltic and also my sister, Gertrude, who had gone back to the hospital to nurse the mentally handicapped. Despite all, my mother was convinced that she would get all her chicks back. With yearning in her eyes she said, 'Before the war started, I prayed to God and asked, that if the war should break out, he would give my children back wherever they were and I know one day they will knock on the door and we will be together again.' Her beliefs, honesty, integrity and her generosity towards the underprivileged were hard to live up.

CHAPTER 6

The bell of the shop went. It was usually my father who went to serve because of the language problems, as often the police would come to the shop asking for addresses. In no time at all my father was back in the room. I could tell something was wrong as he said, 'Somebody wants to see you, Dominik.' I went through to the shop followed by my father. I could not believe my eyes as there stood my friend Alfons in SS uniform. Alfons's family, who now belonged to the ethnic minority, had one of the biggest farms in our area and now he was an SS party man. His first words to me were, 'You had better start learning a proper language. It is the end for your Polish yapping. We are free now from Polish persecution.' My father had to translate for me because Alfons had chosen to speak in German although his Polish was as good as mine. Then he asked, 'Who got you out of prison?' When I told him it was Mr Kopf, he said that he was getting too many out of prison and that something had to be done about it.

After Alfons had left and we were back in the room, my father's face was as red as a beetroot; he was so angry.

'Wait until the war is over and we are free again and I will talk to him,' he said.

'You will do no such thing,' my mother replied. 'Instead, you will go on your knees and thank God that you have survived. Let it be an SS man or any other, if they come and ask for help, your duty as a Christian is to help and not to persecute.' That was my mother - again full of compassion and forgiveness. She didn't know what the meaning of hatred was.

I did not say anything and just listened, but inside me I bore more hatred even than my father towards the people who had lived amongst us with the same rights and who had now turned against us. Hundreds of thousands of innocent people would die because of their kind.

It was possibly due to my father that we had been saved so far. For some reason, he had been very much against any of us joining any political organization before the war. Perhaps that was one of the reasons we still had our shop which was a great advantage as food was already rationed. There were always bits and pieces left over.

The same went for cigarettes which were worked on a 'points' system. Five in our family were issued with cigarette cards, but only I smoked, so we managed to save quite a few packs. If any of the ethnic minorities came asking for cigarettes without coupons, he would be given 20 or 40 with a careful explanation that it was because five of us had cards and only one smoked and, therefore, there were always a few left over. This was just to let the person know that we were acting within the law.

It was of great advantage to us to have some of the Germans on our side. My mother had a way with them. They always left the shop smiling. The local ethnic minority knew it would be a good bit harder to get rid of us. Of course, if the Nazis had known how deeply and far we were involved already, we would have been shot, every one of us.

We were just a few weeks at home from the prison camp at Nuremberg when one morning before the shop opened a car pulled up outside with two German policemen and one SS who asked for my brother, Bruno. How desperate the bloodthirsty Volksdeutsche (ethnic minority members) were to get rid of us. Someone had accused Bruno of murdering a German. My mother took them to the guest room and called Bruno in. The date my brother was alleged to have murdered the German did not correspond as we had been in Nuremberg prison at that time. They tried to question him. Because of his speech impediment, he just opened his mouth, head shaking, but couldn't utter a word. One of the police officers commented as he looked at Bruno, 'That's one of these unfounded accusations again.' Any charges were dropped.

Accusations of that kind were nothing unusual. They were always made by either the ethnic minority or the SS against any of us they hadn't liked before the war. Any accused person the police came to see had a chance to prove his innocence. But if the accusations were made by our ethnic minority now dressed in SS uniform, you had very little chance indeed.

Sometimes you would be beaten there and then, in front of your family, before being taken away and shot. Some of the SS, when they came for you, behaved like real gentlemen so that you almost believed everything was going to be all right. However, they made up for it once they took you away, and the end result was always the same.

When they called for Bruno, we were sure they had made a mistake and it was me they were looking for. When the police came and took you away for interrogation, there was always a slim chance they would let you go. There was no doubt it was the end for anyone taken by the SS though. Usually, you were taken to a place on the outskirts of the town. We called it the 'Valley of Death'. There you had to dig your own grave before being shot in the back.

All the mentally handicapped from the mental institution landed there in the Valley of Death. They seemed braver than all the other people who just obeyed their executioner's orders. As soon as the first shots were fired and the handicapped noticed their friends falling over, they took off scattering in all directions. After hours of chasing through the bogs and searching in adjoining houses, they were all recaptured only to be faced with the same procedure all over again. Another great deed completed for the glory of the Third Reich. Many people living along the Valley abandoned their homes because of the screams and cries and the fear that one day the same fate may be dealt them because they knew too much about the executions.

It was coming up to Christmas now and a very sad one for all, especially those who had lost parents or children. We were still awaiting the arrival of my two brothers and two sisters. Foodwise, it was going to be very poor. As for Christmas cake, nobody even mentioned it. Some people didn't even have bread. The amount of flour allocated to each family was far from sufficient. While baking bread, people resorted to adding boiled grain and potatoes put through a mincer two or three times and then mixed with the flour. Sometimes, if the substitutes were overdone, instead of well-baked bread nicely risen, one ended up with a toffee-like slab which of course still had to be eaten. Almost everyone baked enough bread to last two or three weeks in order to save fuel, so when someone said that they were on three weeks' penance, we knew what they meant - toffee-like bread.

Living in a farming community had one advantage - we had sufficient potatoes and milk which was our main diet, obtained from my Uncle Frank's farm. Again, my mother's income contributed mainly to our survival. On any occasion she was asked to assist with the delivery of a child to a German family, she always asked for payment in money. However, if her services were required by a Polish family, especially by farmers, she would return instead with a few bags of potatoes or grain, mostly rye. Sometimes she would have a few hens. In no time at all, we had about 40 hens and, of course, the eggs were particularly welcome.

By good fortune we discovered German farmers who were selling butter or poultry at black-market prices believing that the Third Reich would last forever. They would rather deal with us than ask high prices of their own people.

One day, Bruno and I received a letter asking us to report to the forestry office about one and a half miles away. On our arrival, we were told that we were to thin out an area of woodland. The trees had to be cleared of branches, the bark peeled and the wood carried to the roadside. They were then marked in Roman numerals, cut in different lengths and stacked ready to be taken to the coal mines. We were paid by the cubic metre for all the work.

As Bruno was not fit for work, we were concerned about what to do. My mother, who was always trying to protect us, came to the rescue. She took Bruno to the doctor and managed to get a certificate stating that he was not fit for work. As far as I was concerned, the work put a stop to my visits to Uncle Frank's where I had been spending quite a lot of time helping on the farm. He was sometimes busy as a member of the political organization called Organization West. (The Organization had been set up some considerable time before the war and the members consisted of businessmen of Polish nationality who had felt a need to join together as a force against the many Germans in the area.)

We were always on the alert, and when any Germans, police or gestapo were in the village the news spread within minutes. Anyone expecting to be in any danger just moved out of the village for half a day or even longer. Many people from our area who had been in the same organization as Uncle Frank were already resting in the Valley of Death.

The Jews were the first to be exterminated, second were teachers and intellectuals – anyone they suspected of being capable of organizing others to put up opposition against them. So many ended up in the Valley of Death.

Before the war, that area had been a small estate belonging to the mental institution. Now when I visit Poland, I go there, sometimes for the whole afternoon, and just stand beside the monument that was erected in memory of all the people executed there. Travelling in a northerly direction towards the Baltic from my old home town, there are monuments or signs almost every few miles marking where mass executions took place, listing the names of those who lost their lives in that spot. As if exterminating many of our people was not enough, to make sure that all Polish history and traditions vanished forever, all history books were banned in schools. For this, we had to thank the ethnic minority living in Poland who had led such a good life but then showed so much hatred towards us.

Eventually, once the German army reserve moved into our town to stay, things improved quite a lot. We assumed they had been told by some of the civilians about the treatment that had been dished out. Polish girls who became the girlfriends of soldiers would probably have talked about events. Such was the outcome that where German soldiers were regular customers in a restaurant, the German ethnic minority or gestapo kept away.

Then one day the gestapo arrested our village councillor, Mr Kopf, who had managed to free so many Poles. He was accused of treason against the German Reich for freeing so many Poles from the camp by falsely saying that he knew them. When interrogated by the gestapo, his only defence was, 'I had a good life here before the war and it is the least I can do to help them to get home.' He was taken away by the gestapo – his own people – never to be heard of again.

Two days later, they came back for his wife and children who were also to disappear without trace. With Mr Kopf out of the way, the gestapo had more opportunity to get rid of anyone they disliked.

Many of the prisoners held in our town had now been released. Some of them had to walk five, sometimes ten, miles to reach their home but some unlucky ones were caught by drunken members of the ethnic minority or gestapo who took them to the wood and told them to run before they shot them. Any who were hit or wounded would be finished off and left lying where they fell. The rest of us had to bury them. The survivors spread the news of what was happening and once this became known, someone always waited outside the camp for the released men and warned them not to walk alone and never at night. That did help, as there were not many accidents after that, but we do not know what might have happened to them after their arrival home.

A few days before Christmas, a car pulled up in front of our house. Four German gestapo, all tall and rather good-looking, stepped out. My mother went out to speak to them. We were fearful as they entered the shop, thinking they had come for my brother, Bruno, who had already been accused of murdering a German. We were all questioned about the whereabouts of my brother, Victor, the Franciscan priest. After questioning everybody, they began a search of the house and outbuildings. It was an hour before they left. I was terrified for my father as I thought they would start beating him. We all cried with relief when they had gone.

Considering the distance they had come from the south of Poland (for whatever the reason) they must have been desperate to find Victor and exterminate him. Our neighbour went quickly to my Uncle Frank who went into hiding, thinking himself in jeopardy because of his involvement in a political organization before the war. We were lucky in our village as none of the ethnic minorities lived there. After the alarming experience of the gestapo search, we tried to console ourselves with the thought that Victor must still be alive.

Christmas turned out to be a happy day for us all. Whilst my sister, Maria, was feeding the hens she called out to us. We ran out and there was my brother, Jan, marching in military style with only his sword missing and his long cavalry coat flowing. What a welcome sight and what tears were shed. We didn't know what to start talking about first. Only three more to come and then we would all be together again. There was nothing more sure for my mother than that one day we would be all together. She was running about bringing bits and pieces for Jan and looking adoringly at him. My father joked that he had never received such adoring looks from her. 'You can't complain. Look at the results - all the children. You had better pray for the rest to come,' she replied.

The following day found us all attention listening to Jan's depressing stories. Often he would say, 'If only we had proper equipment to fight with.' He couldn't get over the bravery of the Jews - they were fearless. They were always the last to leave their positions when it came to retreat and also the first to volunteer. What a cruel and sad end they had to face.

While Jan and his unit were retreating through Bydyoszcz in Poland, not only were they faced with the might of the German army but they were also fired upon from the houses *en route*. Hand grenades were thrown at them by men belonging to the ethnic minority. After that treacherous experience, the Polish cavalry received orders that, no matter what the losses, they were to recapture the town, which they did. The men were then taken from the houses to the outskirts of the town and executed. On hearing this, the Germans spread propaganda throughout Germany and Poland that the Polish army had tortured and killed civilians in the town. As a result, there was a new wave of indiscriminate killings amongst our people. The Germans named that day 'Bloodbath in Bromberg' (Bydyoszcz). To commemorate that day in the following war years, the Germans took two men at random from some of the towns each autumn and shot them, depending on the fanaticism of the ethnic minority living in the various towns.

After hearing of my brother's war experiences, we made a promise to each other not to repeat them even to our relations. Had the gestapo known about Jan's involvement in Bydyoszcz they would have waited for him on his arrival from prison in Chojnice.

I now had a partner to work with me in the wood. The three foresters in our area were Polish. One of them, Eddie, was courting my sister, Sophie. We would have liked to have worked for him but the distance to walk was too far. The woodland area we were allocated to was about three quarters of a mile from our home. On the opposite side of the road in front of our house, there was a ditch which led directly to our workplace, and this helped us tremendously.

Before finishing work, we would lay aside any dead trees, cut in manageable lengths. As darkness fell, we each took a log on our shoulders and set off for home. What a struggle it proved to carry their weight. On a calm night, we could hear each other panting heavily. Whoever reached the road first would drop his log and go to the house. When the other person saw the light from the corridor he knew the coast was clear. Some nights during cold weather, we would make two or three trips. On occasions, while walking along the ditch for a second supply, we would notice somebody ahead - panic! We would listen for a second or two then, with all the speed we could produce, return back home to find out that it was only someone else in desperate need of firewood. Back we would then go for our second load.

My father was always offering to come and help us. Eventually, we did accept his offer but it was a struggle for him. When I noticed this, I tried so much harder to reach the road first so I could turn back for his log, which he willingly handed over. He did not come with us again. It was enough to see the relief on his face when Jan and I returned home after making two or three trips. He would be a bundle of nerves, afraid of what may happen should we be caught. However, there was no alternative method for cooking and heating the house. To my father, it was stealing. To me, it was helping myself to wood we were entitled to and which we could buy any amount of before our country was overpowered.

Our Polish forester knew what we were up to, and he would always be given a few extra packets of cigarettes when he came to the shop. Often during conversation he would say, 'There are a lot of dead trees around this year,' as if to say, just go and help yourself until things improve. All we had to watch out for was our German neighbours or the gestapo. If we were caught, we could be severely beaten in front of our family. Even the head forester, Mr Hengst, who came from Germany and was in charge of the three Polish foresters, would rather turn his head the other way than prosecute a person taking dead wood.

Mr Hengst was a very keen huntsman and organized big shooting parties for Germans. The hunts were for stags, wild boar or hares. All the forestry workers, including young men from the surrounding communities, would be ordered to drive the game to the waiting guns. Two or three of us would group together without saying anything, just giving an approving smile, knowing that lots of game would turn back through the gaps we had created. This worked tremendously well. Our thoughts were so much attuned, anyone would have thought the way we worked together had been planned. It was almost painful to hear a shot, knowing that yet another beast had been killed for their benefit. Before coming out of the plantation, we would spread out again to avoid suspicion. Had they suspected our tactics of depriving them of some of the game we could have been severely punished.

We would return home satisfied with the day's driving. My father would also be pleased, as he knew there would be much more game to shoot once we were free again. To us there was nothing surer than that the Third Reich would be defeated one day. It was the only luxury we had - our hope and belief that one day we would be free. That's the main thing that kept us going.

During the last week in January 1940, we received a welcome visit from the son of our nanny, Francesca. He had cycled about twenty miles to let us know that my sister, Gertrude, was living with them. What welcome news! For some reason, none of her letters had reached us. In case he might be stopped and questioned, he hadn't been given much more news. To the boy, it was just another visit his mother had from my sister. He was told to say on his return home that Gertrude's visit had been long enough and for her to come home. That would mean that the coast was clear. Next morning he cycled home with a small food parcel my mother had made up. It seemed we would be all getting together again and my mother's prayers would be answered. Only two more to come.

We knew Victor was alive somewhere, in hiding from the enemy. The only one about whom we didn't have any news was my sister, Lucy, who was in a convent near Pelplin on the Baltic. We did know the convent had been abandoned, but just what had happened to everyone was still a mystery.

Unfortunately, the news we heard in our shop was always depressing. The atmosphere in the village was like that following a funeral. Far too often there was someone being taken away from the surrounding community and beaten up. For some unknown reason, a curfew was imposed and no one was allowed to leave the house after seven o'clock. This was difficult, especially for the farmers who had to take in turnip and potatoes which were stored in pits in the fields, or hay from the stacks.

Often, after working long hours, the farm boys would be sent to our shop for some messages. A boy of twelve years was so badly beaten by the gestapo that he refused to go for any messages even during the day. To safeguard ourselves, we put up a notice: 'NO SERVICE AFTER SEVEN O'CLOCK'. As for our ethnic minority or our gestapo, it gave them new powers to terrorize us after 7 p.m. The curfew made it so much harder for Jan and me to go for firewood at night.

Almost every farm had its own plot of 20 to 30 acres of woodland, but we were not allowed to cut any live trees without permission. There was no alternative but to persuade my father to ask the German forester, Mr Hengst, for firewood the next time he came to the shop. It worked and a few days later he handed my father a note stating that we were entitled as forestry workers to purchase dead trees and branches. We then had to hand the note to our Polish forester who was only too pleased to oblige because of the cigarettes he had been getting without his allowance card. No more worrying nights trying to obtain firewood at least.

As the months passed, we seemed to be getting better organized. The whole community was like one big family, helping each other. In our village, life was a little easier as we didn't have any German residents. In our neighbouring village, however, there were quite a lot of Germans, so people felt they were continually being watched.

It was now February, 1940, and snowing heavily. In the woodland, we had to use a shovel to clear away the snow, which was up to three feet deep, before cutting each tree. It was decided to give work a miss for a few days. I spent most of my days on the farm with Uncle Frank. One day when I was at home playing chess, Gertrude arrived. As we were such a close family, instead of smiles, we were shedding tears of joy. Gertrude was surprised that she had not received any replies to her letters - thinking something had happened to us, she hadn't come home. The stories she related of what had happened to all the mentally handicapped people in the institution were so very depressing and appalling.

The first time the gestapo visited the institution, they came with a lorry and the severely handicapped were executed on the spot and their bodies removed. Some of the mentally disturbed knew very well what was happening. They would cling to the nurses and not let go. As a result, much pulling and beating took place before they could be taken away to a place not far away from the institution called Kosborowo where they were all executed – the total number being 1,692. After the remaining mentally handicapped had been herded on to the lorries, the nurses were told by their superior, 'Just go, please go, don't delay any more – just go away.' To the Germans, the mentally handicapped were not human. This was the same treatment as that given to the mentally handicapped in our home town. Not having heard from us, my sister had decided to go to our nanny, Francesca, to find out what the situation was.

Jan and I were very much aware of the fact that we were not working in the wood. Hopefully, nobody would bother us and the snow would disappear very soon. Then one day, Bruno came running in saying that there was a policeman walking along the road with an alsatian dog. We waited to see if he was calling on us. Yes, he came into the shop. Jan didn't wait to find out why he had come but grabbed hold of his boots and went out through the window to Uncle Frank's place. Through his experience of fighting the Germans, he was more alert in making decisions. By the time I had decided what to do, my father was already walking towards the living room followed by a tall policeman in his early forties with a huge alsatian in tow.

I sat while my father stood beside the window and the policeman walked back and forth preaching to me but I did not understand most of what he said. In a somewhat raised voice, I said to my father, 'Why don't you tell me what he is saying?' The policeman stopped and looked at me, then at my father to ask what I had said. My father explained that I could not understand German. He seemed to be very nice about it and I noticed even my father seemed more relaxed now. The policeman spoke slowly for my father to translate. 'Just tell your son to get his brother and go to work. It doesn't matter what they will be doing as long as they are there so that I can report to Mr Hengst that they are at work. When I got my orders to come here, I could not say I am not going as there is too much snow. We just have to obey orders.'

I took off straight away to Uncle Frank's for Jan, telling him what an agreeable policeman he'd been. As usual, my uncle was hiding, thinking they were after him. We left for work and made a big fire. About two hours later, we heard the fine sound of horse-sledge bells. As we looked to the road, there was our policeman friend smiling and waving on his way to the forester to report that we were at work. Men standing beside us asked if we knew him. Fortune smiled on us, as usually people were beaten and sometimes taken away to work in some factory or on a farm as a punishment for not obeying orders.

As we walked home later I felt elated inside. Life could have been quite good if all the Germans were like that policeman. It took so little human kindness to spread a little happiness.

On arrival home, I was aware of the relaxed atmosphere in the house. Even my father appeared more lively. That good man had stayed for about an hour. On the wall above our table, we had a picture of the Last Supper, which prompted our visitor to ask my father if he was a Catholic. Father had answered he was very much a practising Catholic. He then looked at a family picture in which my sister, Lucy, was in her robes as a nun and my brother a Franciscan priest and asked if we knew where they were. 'Not so far,' my father replied. The policeman then said that if there was any way in which he could help we were to get in touch. My mother had made a cup of coffee and sandwiches for him and then organized for Uncle Frank to come with a horse and sledge to take him back to the town. She was hoping that if Frank could get to know the policeman, things might be safer for him.

That night, as we all gathered together, we recalled our experiences and how fortunate we were. It seemed my mother's prayers were being answered. Not only had we escaped punishment, but we had someone now to whom we could turn should we need help. I remember commenting that it was advantageous that we hadn't gone to work or we might never have met the policeman. 'Son, I hope you will take it to your heart what he said. You will just have to obey orders,' warned my mother. Obey we did, whatever the weather, and never missed a day after that.

CHAPTER 7

My mother's brother, Leonard, was stationmaster at Rytel, which was the next station after our town. In September 1939, when we were invaded, The Germans had sent a panzer rail wagon packed with soldiers across the border. Leonard received a telephone message about the approaching panzer truck and managed to put it on to a blind end thus forcing it to stop. The Polish forces were informed, but as the Germans refused to surrender, in a short while heavy guns had blown the panzer and the crew to pieces. Had the German authorities found out my mother's relationship to Leonard, the consequences would have been catastrophic.

Our area is much written about. According to history, one of the biggest battles was fought around Krojanty which is about one and a half miles from our village. After the Polish forces retreated, my Uncle Leonard went into hiding about half a mile from his home to a place called Mlynki, where his brother, Johan, had a farm. That was the place I had visited with Bruno when we deprived the dogs of bread and before we faced the firing squad in Rytel. We had a miraculous escape and I do not dare think about what would have happened to us had the Germans known then that it was our uncle who had been responsible for the blowing up of the armoured truck.

The day after the invasion, the Polish forces retreated and the German army occupied the area. My uncle was sentenced to death by a firing squad in his absence. As the search for him began at the station and continued through the evening and on into the night, a German soldier came running up to the farmhouse in Mlynki to warn about the court martial. My uncles at the farm could not believe it when the soldier started speaking in Polish. He explained that his parents were Polish and that it was the least he could do. He said to hurry up and try to hide

Leonard as the soldiers would soon be there to look for him. He wished them good luck before taking off again.

On 3 September a truck load of soldiers went to the farm and the search began. It was a few hours later before they left. What a blessing it was that it had been the German army that did the not-very-thorough search. Had it been the gestapo, the result would have been a very sad one. My uncle was hiding under 25 feet of rye sheaves inside a barn. A few boards had been taken off the bottom of the barn. Sheaves were removed and a small wooden frame built to keep the rest of the sheaves from falling on top of him. Armed with a few blankets and some food, he crept inside. He was able to see the soldiers moving about the farmyard. After that incident we thought it wiser to move him elsewhere and in January we started to prepare a new place for him at Uncle Frank's farm in our village.

A little frame 8 ft. by 8 ft. was built. After two days' threshing, all the loose straw was piled about 20 ft. on top of the frame. Five boards from the side at the bottom were taken off. A piece of wood measuring 3 ins. by 3 ins. was nailed to the boards from the inside and a rope attached for him to pull the boards flush with the rest. Even the nails used were rusty so as not to throw any suspicion on the hideout. My uncle was then taken to his new hiding place during the night. Two men walked in front in case anybody was about and another walked with my uncle. If the men in front confronted anyone, one would light a cigarette. When the coast was clear again, one of us would turn back and we would all set off again.

For most of the way, we could walk through the woods. By 3 a.m., Uncle Leonard was in his new hiding place. He couldn't believe what a nice little den we had prepared for him. 'How long will I have to suffer this?' he enquired, looking rather lost. Had he known the outcome of the war, I doubt whether he would have stopped the panzer truck for all the good it had done. Here we were reaping the bitter harvest of invasion through tears and blood.

New rules were pinned to the wall of the fire brigade building in our village. We didn't bother to read them as we were told about them from customers. There were so many rules. Should we commit such crimes, as they were called, we would be severely punished. The only rule missing was punishment for breathing.

One of the rules was that families keeping pigs should report the number and weight. Pigs sold on the open market were not to exceed 60 pounds in weight. Anyone wishing to kill a pig was required to report the date of the killing and the weight to the police. The person was then required to hand over one half to a given address. The going rate would then be paid to him. A date would then be given when the person was allowed to kill another pig. Anyone possessing a dog was required to report details of their breed and the address where they were kept to the police. As usual, the punishment for disobeying these rules was that offenders would be shot.

We could understand the reason behind the first command as meat was on ration and almost everyone would sell to get a few marks for groceries or some tools. As for shoes or clothing, it was much easier to get those if you had a few pounds of butter or a piece of ham to offer and then the balance was paid in money. If you had the right contact, you could even get a person out of a concentration camp for a leg of ham. However, we could not understand why we had to report all dogs to the police.

It did not take long for us to find out the answer. About a week later, two police cars drew up in front of our house. After a short discussion between the occupants, one car left for the neighbouring village of Klodawa where a lot of German ethnic minority were living. The remaining two men came in our direction. One was the Chief of Police, Radatz, who was feared wherever he went. He belonged to one of our ethnic minorities and before the war had a joinery business in Poland. Radatz entered the shop and asked to see our dog. My mother took him through the corridor into the yard. As our dog ran over to welcome them, the Chief of Police took out his revolver. We now understood. As he fired the first shot, the dog was still wagging his tail, not realizing what was happening. It was only after the third shot that the dog was finally dead. My two younger brothers cried and my father tried to comfort them with sweets from the shop. As for me, I did not dare express my strong feelings as my mother was there.

It wasn't until late in the afternoon that the echoing shots ceased. First it was the Polish dogs (for that was what they called us) and now the real dogs had to experience the masters of our invasion.

In our neighbouring villages of Klodawa and Krojanty there were a lot of German families and their dogs were spared. For some who had taken German nationality but had not taken part in the persecutions, it was rather embarrassing. They had tried to hide the fact that they were Germans but wherever we went and heard a dog barking we knew to beware as the people about must be German. The poor, innocent dogs contributed a little to our safety!

A few days later, Radatz turned up with another policeman at our village blacksmith's. He was a man in his seventies with a family of nine and lived about 100 yards away. As soon as the man came out, the Chief of Police started beating him with a black baton whilst the whole family stood watching and crying. Satisfied, Radatz screamed at the blacksmith, 'That will teach you, you damned dog to write a letter to Herr Hitler. Any complaints you have, you write to me.' We could not understand what it was all about. Later, his older son came to the shop and explained that his father had written a letter to Hitler complaining about the killings and beatings in our communities. He had begged his father not to write. What a sad outcome. Being beaten in front of one's family was the worst fear.

We were fortunate not to have any Germans in our community. At least in daytime we could keep visiting each other sharing any news, all of which was rather depressing with Germany taking one country after another.

Members of the ethnic minority coming to the shop were so eager to tell us news. We would always say to my father when he got the news not to show how he felt but to rejoice for them or we would be in trouble. 'The time will come when the news will be in our favour,' my mother would add with a little smile. 'Then you can show them how you feel but be nice to them now.' After grasping her meaning, my father would say, 'You just leave me be.' Any time my mother got the news that another country was taken, she would smile and say, 'Hopefully you didn't have to sacrifice too many soldiers.' She was a good actress and they always believed her.

My father's favourite visitor was the German forester, Mr Hengst. They would often have long conversations about hunting. My father also enjoyed talking to the policeman who had come to see my brother and me for not working, a Mr Venzell from Berlin.

When we told him about our priest being shot after his release from prison half a mile from his home, he insisted we tell him who was responsible. Eventually, he understood the reason why we could not do this; we were afraid of the consequences. We also told him that, after he was killed, the altar and the whole front of the church were demolished during the night. He turned to my mother, now and again glancing at Father and commented, 'This war is not going to be won by Hitler. They're not only killing innocent people but they are fighting with God as well.' My parents were very surprised to hear him say that and could only look at him. Smiling he continued, 'All we have to do at the moment is obey orders the same as your son had to do after I came to see him that time.' Again he said, 'Trust me. If there is anything at all you need, just come to me. I can help a lot.' He hated shooting the dogs and told Radatz that he could not do it as he was too fond of them. We let him know about his chief and the number of shots taken to kill our dog. He said that for some reason his chief loved shooting and then asked my mother if she would like to be introduced to him as it might be to our advantage. Of course, my mother jumped at the opportunity. How busy we were building our defences - mainly against those we had thought were our own people, but who had turned against us.

As far as Jan and I were concerned, our work in the wood seemed secure enough, at least for the time being. However, hardly a week went by when we could relax as there was always something looming around the corner.

The lady who was in charge of the women's section of the labour exchange, single and lonely, became pregnant. Her second mistake was when she asked my mother to abort the child. Of course, my mother flatly refused, so vengeance was sought. As a result, my sister Maria, who was only 14 years old, was taken to work on a farm where two elderly people lived. She had to work a tractor or horses, and milk cows. Maria had never seen a tractor never mind worked one. After only four days, the old man gave her a note saying he wanted somebody older, not a child. This didn't please the lady at the labour exchange. After reading the note, she gave Maria another job, this time in a bakery in our town. Naturally, we had been worried she might have been sent to work in some factory in Germany, so the outcome was not too bad.

My other sister, Sophie who was 16 years old, was also taken to work on a farm, to do the milking and look after pigs. As this farm wasn't far from home, Sophie tried to please in case she was sent further away. Although there were still plenty of boys of 18 and 19 years of age who could have been sent to do these jobs, this was the woman's way of repaying my mother for refusing to do the abortion. Had my mother carried out her request, it was almost certain that she would have been shot. This would have provided plenty of propaganda about a Polish midwife practising abortions and, anyway, my mother would never, under any circumstances, have done such a deed.

About three miles from where we lived, I knew a girl who was expecting a baby to a German officer and had arranged to have an abortion by a German doctor. On this occasion, it was the poor girl who was executed and not the doctor. Abortion was severely punished, even in Germany.

My sister, Gertrude, knowing what happened to the mentally handicapped she nursed and then having to go into hiding, promised herself she would never work for the Germans. Knowing Gertrude, however, none of us took her seriously. With anything my darling sister said we tended to take the opposite meaning, but she meant it this time, she said. She began starving herself, as well as drinking a lot of vinegar. Whenever we got lemons in the shop, she finished them all. She was fading away before our eyes. Not only was she certified unfit for work, but she almost died. Within a few months she was suffering from tuberculosis.

Every second week now for the past two months, we had been getting an unusual visitor to the shop. He always came between five and six o'clock in the late afternoon. It seemed rather strange, and he was always in SS uniform. He would ask for a pack or two of cigarettes and then leave. One week, as he was leaving the shop, our friendly policeman, Mr Venzell, arrived and the two began talking intently.

Unless Mr Venzell was in a hurry when he called, my mother always invited him into the guest room. Depending on the time of day, she would make him a nice cup of coffee or some scrambled eggs and fried ham. That was his favourite; it worked miracles and was a big comfort to us knowing we had someone we could trust. This time my mother casually asked him about the SS man. Of course he realized my mother was trying to add to her defences and this was a high-ranking SS man. He told us more than we expected. His name was Mr Reinke and he was in charge of our labour exchange as well as the Brusy one, a small town to which he travelled every second week. He even added that he was single and lived alone. Life would have been very difficult had we not had Mr Venzell's friendship. I could see from my mother's face that she was already scheming about how she was going to get my sisters back.

With all the defences we had built up, I ventured to try and get some extra meat. Even with all the rules, one was allowed to buy pigs of up to 60 pounds in weight on the open market but then you were supposed to hand over half of the pig to the authorities. This was not my intention. I contacted a forestry worker I knew well who lived about a mile from us and asked if I could kill some pigs where he and his family lived, as it was rather isolated and seemed safe enough. He readily agreed, provided I killed one for him. That was fine with me.

I borrowed two horses and a four-wheeled cart from Uncle Frank then we made a wooden cover and set off for market. Some pigs were as heavy as 70 pounds and we bought five. We decided to make a start at five o'clock in the morning. I asked the forester to have the boiler ready with hot water and he reminded me that we had to be back for our eight o'clock start in the wood. Being a married man with a young family, I could understand his being rather nervous as the consequences could be serious. Of course, I didn't tell him about the policeman we knew. At the back of my mind I knew that, should anything go wrong, he would probably get us out of the trouble. At the same time, I was hoping not to take advantage of his kindness.

As I rose in the morning, my mother wakened and asked what I was up to and I had to tell her. I could see she was pleased about the four little pigs but very frightened at the thought of something going wrong. However, when I told her about the place where we intended to slaughter them, she seemed to calm down. I told her to tell Jan that I would meet up with him in the wood as there was no point in my coming home after as it wasn't far from where we were working. 'Go with God, son, and be careful,' she said. 'Stay with God, Mum, and don't worry,' I replied. We would never say 'goodbye' or 'see you' when leaving the house. It was always 'Stay with God' with the other person answering 'Go with God'. This expression was so much more emphasized during the occupation.

Everything was ready when I arrived and it was now up to me. The forester asked me if I had done this sort of thing before – I had to admit that I hadn't, but that he was not to worry as I had watched a butcher on many occasions before the war and knew what to do. The main thing was to be accurate with the first blow between the eyes so that the pig would not have time to blink. The rest was easy. I was ready as I instructed my partner in crime, 'Get the boiled potatoes and let one out.' As the poor pig got to the potatoes and settled a little there was one blow from me and she was down and quickly bled. Within an hour, they were all lying there ready to take away. That poor, nervous man was now able to smile and commented that it didn't seem to be the first time I had killed pigs. I reassured him, 'I told you they wouldn't have time to blink an eye, never mind squeal.'

By the time Jan arrived at work, I was waiting and could see the questioning look on his face. But I reassured him that all had gone exceptionally well, much to my amazement. The only problem now was that we would have to take the carcasses home that night. Jan said that he would come with me. Both of our parents were waiting anxiously for us when we arrived home from work. I informed them that everything had gone smoothly, and so quietly that anyone standing outside the building would not have heard a thing. They were obviously very impressed. That was my first successful effort in getting extra meat for us and there were many, many more to follow throughout the years of occupation.

About midnight, we set off to collect our treasures. What a struggle we had carrying about 80 pounds on our backs. We were both puffing like steam engines, but eventually arrived home safely. From then on, we decided, life was going to get better. Between the four pigs, we had almost 170 pounds of meat. It was salted and, at a later stage, a large part of it would be smoked in the cellar smoking room.

Some of the meat was then given to Uncle Frank. Although he had plenty of pigs himself, because Uncle Leonard was in hiding there, it was much safer not to aggravate the police but to report any killings made, which meant keeping to the rules and handing over half of every pig killed.

As both of my sisters had been sent away to work, it was now up to me to go to the wholesaler for our shop's supplies. I always took eggs, butter or sometimes even three or four pounds of meat to give to the office manager. I would neatly parcel these up beforehand and it worked wonders. We didn't stock wine in our shop, but often I would get a case or two or, still more precious, coffee beans that Mr Venzell would call for each time he was in the area. Life was improving week by week, especially as far as food was concerned, but freedom of movement was still rather restricted.

As our priest had been killed and half of our church demolished, we now had to walk about four miles to the town of Chojnice on Sundays, but we felt much safer in that church all the same. There were a lot of German soldiers and officers at Mass and they were very pleasant to us. Whenever an elderly person was standing, they would offer them their seat. It made us feel less wary toward our aggressors. If only the rest of them were like that. At least for the time being, here we were in harmony. It was wonderful what religious belief could do.

I felt sorry for my parents having to walk so far, but that was no excuse to miss Sunday Mass. Sleet or snow, every Sunday we were on our way. That was something the Germans could not take away from us - prayer and hope. I couldn't remember our churches being as packed before the war, as they were now during the occupation, with us praying for England's victory and the Germans for Hitler's. The good Lord must have had some headache deciding who was going to win!

I was annoyed at the way the town was plastered with huge posters. There was one on the wall facing us as we came out of church. It showed an English soldier with dead people lying all around him and he was brandishing a rifle and standing on one body. In big letters were the words 'LOOK, ENGLAND, AT YOUR DEED'. How appropriate it would have been, I thought, if it had read the other way round, 'LOOK, GERMANY, AT YOUR DEED'.

Sundays were very special for us. My sisters, Maria and Sophie, had a day off work so we were together. With all the meat we had, even the smell from the roast made it feel like a special day. Sophie would never complain about her work and tried to console my mother, saying that her boss had promised to get someone else to help her with the chores. Her hands were like leather soles. At night I would walk her to the station. We were very fond of each other: as she boarded the train she would always fight back the tears and try to part smiling. My mother decided that the next time the SS man from the labour exchange came to the shop, she would have a word with him about Sophie. We were entitled to have her help at home as my mother was a midwife and had two sons of five and ten years and my sister, Gertrude, ill in bed. Father had to look after the shop. However, it would be up to the big chief at the labour exchange to decide if we were indeed entitled to this.

It was now May 1940. We had another visit from the SS looking for my brother, Victor, and they searched the house and outbuildings. A few days later, at Uncle Frank's farm there was another big search for Uncle Leonard. Each time the search was over and the SS had left, an atmosphere of fear and uncertainty lingered for a few days after. We were very puzzled why the SS had not checked our place for Uncle Leonard, as he was my mother's brother.

We later heard that there had also been a search at a nearby farm belonging to another of my mother's brothers. We decided that Uncle Leonard would have to be moved further away. The place he was taken to this time was Bachorze, to a family called Januszewski. Their house was well-situated - it was high up and had a good view of the road. The nearest house was about a mile away. On the other side of the house were woodlands with a loch and a stream. What a change it was for him - he had been used to staying in that little hole, sitting or lying down, except at night when he could get out for a few hours. He had much more freedom in his new home. Hopefully, he was going to have a safe stay for as long as need be.

About this time, Gertrude received an unexpected letter from her boyfriend, George, who was a captain in the Polish army. She had met him in 1938 when he was stationed in our area. His parents were Latvians and he lived in the eastern part of Poland near Vilna. Before the war their romance had been quite serious. The letter came from a prison camp. It brought great happiness to my sister and she became a new person. She stopped her starvation diet, and there was a more pleasant atmosphere within the family: Gertrude was now all smiles. Within a few weeks, she was on her feet again and busy making parcels for George. Parcels could only weigh four pounds and the prisoners were allowed only one per month, so we decided to bake wheat bread and then dry it to reduce the weight. But where could we get wheat flour? The only person we felt we could turn to was the German, Mr Rydell, who had a windmill in a neighbouring village. He seemed more approachable than the others.

About two years earlier, by mother had delivered a child to his wife. Off I went with a note from my mother, written in German. Mr Rydell read it, then spoke to me in German - his wife intervened and explained to me in Polish to come back later that night. I informed her I couldn't because of the curfew imposed on us so I was told to leave it to them. The next day, Mr Rydell brought twenty pounds of wheat flour to us himself. Besides paying him, my mother gave him a bottle of wine, a few packets of cigarettes and a quarter-pound of coffee beans. As he was leaving, he told us not to be stuck and just to let him know if we needed any flour. That was the end of our substituting boiled grain or potatoes while making bread. Another important contact had been made. As well as flour, we could get grain for our hens at any time.

During the spring of 1940, Jan and I, as well as other forestry workers, were given the job of planting trees. We worked in pairs. The boy would make a hole with a spade specially made for the job and the girl would put a plant from her box into the hole before it was stamped firmly into place by the boy.

Female company made our present job a real delight, as with all the troubles, we hadn't had time to dream of romance. After a few days of working in mixed company, we had sorted ourselves out, just with looks and smiles, finding a nice partner to work with. The district forester, Mr Hengst, didn't mind us changing partners as long as the work was done properly. He would appear each day for two or three hours. At this time I got to know my future brother-in-law, Eddie, who was the forester for our area. We became inseparable. There were no secrets that we couldn't share with each other through the entire occupation.

We had to cycle about seven miles to work and were always aware of the risk of two of us riding on the same bike, as it was illegal. One morning we had a narrow escape cycling along the main road - a policeman screamed at us to halt. We got off the bike but I didn't understand him and didn't know what to answer. He looked rather menacing, so I called out 'Yes, yes, yes,' and slowly climbed onto the bike. I took off, leaving Jan to follow on foot. He appeared half an hour later. We exchanged smiles while I sensed that he must have thought, 'You're a good one, leaving me all alone.' But there was nothing else I could have done. When we got home, we all had a good laugh although it wasn't funny having to face the police with the threat of being walloped with a baton (they were known to be quite good at using them). We got another bike from Uncle Frank.

With spring well on the way, we could feel and even smell everything coming back to life and yet, at the back of our minds, there was always the knowledge of what was happening all around. We were never sure what the next day would bring. Because of the spring work necessary on the farms, the curfew was lifted. This allowed us more freedom to visit in the evening, but we still had to be very careful of being caught out too late at night. Our ethnic minority were just as eager to catch us and let us know who the masters were. When I planned to visit my Uncle Frank at night, my mother would caution me every time not to stay too late in case of trouble.

France was now almost overrun by the German armies and the Germans were really eager to come to the shop to relay this news to us. With the fall of France now imminent, they were most likely thinking that Germany was safe and that no country could stand up to Hitler. The gestapo made new arrests in our area. Our primary-school teacher was arrested, and the local estate owners. One who was in his late sixties and lived alone was badly beaten and then taken away. One of his executioners had come to see me after my release from prison, boasting that he was wearing the laird's boots. Another landowner, Ignacy Pruszak, lived about a mile from us. He was beaten in front of his family before being taken away. (I have been asked by his daughter, Irene Pruszak, not to forget to mention her father's name in my story.) Another man, who was in charge of the water pumps and whose daughter was married to my cousin, was also taken away. All four were taken in the late afternoon. The next morning Irene and her mother decided to take her father some warm clothing, but when they arrived at gestapo headquarters, they were told that he would not need them any more.

Only a few days later, in our neighbouring village of Klodawa, they took the three sons from one family called Narloch and told their parents and daughter to evacuate their home immediately if they wanted to avoid arrest. They left behind a small farm and a grocery/restaurant business. It was the Volksdeutsche from the same village who then took over the businesses – an elderly couple named Rostowski who had a 17-year-old daughter attending commercial college before the war. I had been in school with the youngest of the Narloch boys.

They were accused of working with the partisans and delivering rifles, which they had supposedly taken from dead soldiers. We couldn't understand why, for that alleged crime, they had not been taken to the Valley of Death, and disposed of straightaway. Instead, they were taken to Stutthof concentration camp near Danzig, but the outcome would be the same. Within a few months, every few weeks, their parents were notified that one of their sons had died from a heart attack until all three had gone. 'Died of a heart attack' was the usual notification, if one received one at all.

Following the last wave of arrests and executions, some of the Polish farmers who had settled in our area from the eastern part of Poland, didn't wait to be arrested. They packed their belongings and simply disappeared. Our neighbour had disappeared like that and within a few days a German was already in his place. The village people were terrified of him. Sometimes we found him outside our window at night, listening for any information about our Franciscan brother. On other occasions, he would walk straight in without knocking and with an impudent smile, ask how we were, then look around and leave again without any explanation. But there was nothing we could do. They were the masters. We really disliked that man, but, of course, we thought it wiser not to say anything in front of our mother. Her response was always, 'Just say a little prayer for him, it will help.' I would have said a very long prayer if I had been sure of a fitting answer!

We suspected that now the grocery business in our neighbouring village was in the hands of a German family, our business would be seen as too much competition, since many of the Polish families from that village were now coming to our shop. Our new neighbour was looking for any excuse to be rid of us and that was one of the reasons he would listen under the windows or burst into the house unexpectedly, perhaps hoping to find Victor.

My mother, however, managed to put a stop to our neighbour's visits and lurking at the windows. The next time Mr Venzell called she mentioned the problem and he promised to do something about it. One day SS Reinke from the labour exchange pulled up in his car and walked across to our neighbour. Shortly afterwards, he came in as usual. No mention was made of his talk with the German, but it had an effect: our neighbour's nightly visits stopped. A word from the SS carried more weight than from a policeman obviously. My mother knew how to protect us.

We still awaited news from Lucy and Victor. Hopefully, one day good news would come. It was soon my turn to be separated from the family for a second time.

CHAPTER 8

Whilst strolling round the town one day, I was arrested and taken to the railway station where another 50 or 60 boys were waiting. One of them was Bronek, the boy I patrolled with in the last two days before the war. We were all taken in a passenger train in the direction of Danzig. Amongst us were two girls who sat in our compartment and who cried throughout the journey. Some of the boys tried to comfort them, but to no avail. The train stopped a few hours later. Terror gripped us – we were in Stutthof, where the feared and talked about concentration camp for our area was.

When we alighted, a number of farmers with horse carts were waiting for us. They then started to point towards us, making their choices. I whispered to Bronek, who could speak German well, to make sure we got together. Just then, a little man with red, podgy cheeks and a Hitler-like moustache pointed at Bronek. Bronek spoke to him before he could point to another. He looked me up and down and then indicated for me to join them. He had a gig pulled by a beautiful black horse which was now covered with white foam from sweating. The farmer had quite a task trying to control the beast. I watched the horse raring to go, and thought that I wouldn't mind seeing the little man lose control, providing the horse took off in the right direction!

Fifteen minutes later we arrived at his farm, where we helped him with the horse before he took us to a cattle byre. There I was pleasantly surprised to find a white-cloth-covered table laden with food beyond my wildest expectations. There was not only meat but an assortment of sausages and cakes. By the time we had finished eating a tall, well-upholstered lady was marching towards us. As I watched her, I couldn't help thinking of the emperor penguin because of the way she walked, paddling with her little hands. Her name was Mrs Vibe.

Bronek told her I could not speak German so she asked him to translate. 'If you are honest with your work, you will be well looked after.' I was surprised that it was she who did all the talking while her husband stood beside her like a midget. She continued, 'You start at 7.30 a.m. and work until 5.30 p.m. There is one hour for dinner. Tea is at 10 a.m. and 3 p.m. If you work in the field, our maid will bring the tea to you.' At that, a girl named Gretchen walked out of the house. She called her over and introduced us. What a beautiful girl she was, tall and black-haired, looking gypsylike, not like the Germanic race that Hitler was going to establish. She regarded me coolly.

Mrs Vibe then took us to our sleeping quarters. They were not good at all – a small room just big enough for the two beds. Next to our room was a pigsty. She further informed us, 'You will call at the kitchen door at 6.45 a.m. for your breakfast and anytime after 6 p.m. for your supper. It is important for you to remember we like to be punctual. There is also a police rule we have to tell you about – you are not allowed to leave the farm premises except on Saturday and Sunday between 1 p.m. and 6 p.m. It is for your own good not to get involved with the police.' Then looking at us she added, 'They are not a nice lot to be reckoned with.' Before Mrs Vibe left I asked Bronek to ask her for the address. Not only did she give me the address but also a writing pad and stamped envelope.

As I waited for the address, I saw another girl wearing glasses with rather thick lenses. She turned out to be the cleaning maid. We got our bits and pieces sorted out and then had a good look round the place. What a place for cleanliness. All the tools one could think of were hanging from the wall, washed. Some were dubbed with oil. Nothing was out of place, except perhaps the two of us.

I scribbled a short note home asking for some working clothes, and praising our new place, especially the food. At the end, I added, 'Mum, it must be your prayers that made the good Lord give me such a good place. The way things are with you at home, I know it will be much safer for me here for the time being. We were told that after the sugar beet harvest is loaded onto the barges, this being the last chore, we will get home again. Don't worry, Mum, I'm OK.'

I gave the letter to the maid for posting. On our first morning, we were up at five o'clock, both aware of how lucky we were. Hopefully, the two girls who cried so much in the train had got a decent place also. Bronek suggested that he would collect our breakfasts and suppers from the kitchen. I suspected he was attracted to the maid, but I was determined to try and keep away from the kitchen as much as possible.

After breakfast, Mr Vibe himself arrived with another two men and introduced us. The foreman's name was Franz and the other one Hans, who first had to milk about twenty cows along with Gretchen before joining us in the field. Our foreman gave me cause for concern. He had a very dark complexion and a rather sharp, determined look. As it turned out, he had a heart of gold. He admitted later that it took such a long time for me to thaw out that he had been rather afraid of me!

Our first job was thinning out sugar beets. What an enormous field we were in. We spent a whole month on our knees and had hardly any fingernails left by the time we were finished. I was rather stubborn when it came to conversation, especially when the maid brought our tea. I would take a piece of bread and my coffee and always tried to sit with my back to the rest of them. Franz, the foreman, was always teasing me about the girl. I could understand a little of the language but not when he or the girl spoke in their own dialect. Bronek spoke very good German as he had worked on a German estate before the war, and I would often ask him in Polish what they were saying. After a few remarks in broad German, Franz would look at me, turn to Bronek and start laughing, saying 'Tell him what I was saying.' Sometimes, he would try to imitate my German and then, pointing at himself, say, 'Me good to you, yes?' then point to the girl, 'Her good to you, too, yes?' I could not help laughing and had to agree with him. He would then add that Bronek, my friend, was not good, he was bad. He was a real comedian when he began, but we were soon happy in each other's company. Our foreman was a kind and honest man.

Our weekends were also enjoyable. We were told we could have visitors at weekends and got quite a few, mostly Polish from the other farms. We were well aware of our good fortune, and not only foodwise: there was little difference between our weekly wage and that of the foreman's. This was most favourable compared to the treatment our friends received.

On Fridays Mrs Vibe would ask us how many visitors we expected at the weekend. We felt we could not give the true number as this would be too much to expect. 'Two or three,' we would say. Besides extra food at weekends, we were given a bar of chocolate and a cake of luxury soap. Mrs Vibe reminded us not to throw any food away should we have too much as food was rationed. Through the week, we would give any butter or meat left over to Franz to take home with him, but from Friday on we left it for our visitors.

On Sundays, we would be asked to get a coach ready, harnessing either the stallion or the mare which Mr Vibe kept specially for Sunday runs with his wife. He would tell us what time he would be back and it was up to us to wait for him. If he said 1.30 p.m. he would be there exactly to the minute: he was a fanatic for punctuality. Each time we took the horse back to the stable, his wife would smile and thank us, and he'd give us five or six marks, which kept us in cigarettes for two or three days.

If he took off alone on a Sunday we knew it was to be his drinking week. Wherever he stopped first, whether at the bar or the hotel, somebody from there would bring the horse and coach back and he would carry on drinking for the next three or four days. He usually arrived back with his face the colour of a red pepper. However, his drinking made no difference to his behaviour towards us. In fact, he became so much nicer each time.

The Vibes had a family of seven boys, most serving in the Air Force from a sergeant to a major, and one or two were SS officers. When they visited, they'd come to see us and talk for a few minutes. Of course, I told them the way things were going at home, and when they left they would give us one or two packets of cigarettes.

Sometimes, I puzzled over the reason for the unusually good treatment we got. Was it because of what was happening on the other side of the public road which ran close to the farm? Alongside the road was a canal and close to that was a concentration camp. We could see the prisoners at work. One lot hauled rubble, bricks and stones with straps around their shoulders. There were about 25 of them to one wagon. Others dug drains and filled them in with the rubble. To me, it was one way of wearing the men down. The work they were doing could have been done in a more civilized and humane way. It was May 1940 and, at that time, they didn't have crematoria or gas chambers so they sucked life out of them slowly by hard labour and starvation.

On one occasion, we were working in the canal itself, driving posts in to make a new walkway for carrying the water we drew from the canal. Shots rang out as we saw a man running and finally falling. Those who had the courage to make a run for it at least found one way of bringing a swift end to their torture. That incident explained the occasional shots we heard. When Bronek went to collect our supper that evening, Mrs Vibe said to him, 'We are very much against what is happening across the canal, but there is nothing we can do to stop it.'

When we weren't very busy, Mrs Vibe asked us to take some of the horses to the canal - usually the stallion and black mare. After a good scrub with a brush and liquid soap, we would ride them into the canal. On one occasion, as we rode in, the prisoners were just pulling out after emptying the wagons of rubble. Franz must have mentioned something about it to Mr Vibe as that was the last time we went to the canal. The horses were scrubbed in the farmyard from then on, with water being carried across from the canal. I think Mr Vibe was trying to spare us the agony of seeing the men working in such a pitiful condition. They were like walking skeletons.

Our next job left me with a handful of blisters. A big field of farm manure had to be spread, taking us almost two weeks. Some days we could hear loud cries from the neighbour's field. Franz told us it was the Polish girls. I was astonished at what happened next. After a few calls and whistles, they left their job in the field and came over for a chat. We tried to persuade them to go back in case they landed in trouble. We asked about the cries, and they told us laughingly that whenever they felt low or depressed, they always had a little cry as it helped. We promised to see them over the weekend.

After work and a wash as usual that night, Bronek went for our supper and came back to tell me that Mrs Vibe wanted to see me. I went over and stopped at the bottom of the four steps leading into the kitchen before she asked me in for the first time in six weeks. The two maids were there, smiling. A parcel on the table was addressed to me and some doughnuts were peeping out from a slightly damaged corner. Mrs Vibe asked me if I'd written home for them, but I hadn't. Bronek translated for me, 'I asked for some working clothes but, as they are my favourite, my mother must have sent them for my birthday.'

'You could have told me,' she admonished. 'Do you think you will still be here for your next birthday?' she asked.

'I hope not,' I replied. She smiled when she said, 'At least you are honest. When is your birthday?' I told her it was on the Sunday and she continued with, 'You know Gretchen would love to make some doughnuts for you.' After thanking her, I assured her I had plenty now. Before we left she quietly said, 'Dominik, you have to try harder to learn German,' and I promised that I would do that.

I was eager to open my parcel before I ate my supper. We had two doughnuts each and they made me feel a little homesick, but there was a letter amongst the working clothes which made up for it. My sister, Lucy, was home after almost nine months and my mother had also managed to get Sophie back home from the farm. That was excellent news. My birthday was going to be a happy one. Hopefully the lady from the labour exchange would leave us in peace for a while. Of course, she would realize she just could not go against her superior's decision and, after all, we had Mr Reinke on our side.

After lunch on Saturday, we got ready to visit the laughing and crying performers. I was glad we didn't go through the village of Stutthof but headed in the opposite direction. It was less than a mile, so should we overstay our visit and leave past six o'clock, we could easily walk through the fields. Some weekends the police would come to the farm and check if we were in. One day the farmer's son, the SS major, was at home on holiday when the police came to check on us. He told them to stop calling and that if we were missing, it was his parents' responsibility - there was no need for them to check up. It was a comforting feeling knowing that the whole family was really on our side.

'Nice to see you smiling today,' we told the girls on meeting up with them.

'Thank you. You know you are the first two boys we have spoken to in the last seven weeks,' they replied as we all smiled. We went to the canal and sat on the bank. How quickly the few hours passed, with all the talk and news we exchanged. They were both town girls and what lively sparks they were. That night when Bronek went for the supper, he told Mrs Vibe about our visitors and that they were coming to see us the next day. She seemed very happy for us.

On Sunday at the usual time, we got the coach ready for the Vibes and at one o'clock took the horse back in again. What a huge dinner we had that day – a special birthday treat. When Mrs Vibe gave us the trays she smiled and wished me a happy birthday. Only the maid, Gretchen, seemed to be rather cool. She must have heard about our two female visitors.

After dinner, we set off to meet our dates and decided to visit Stutthof, hoping to get a glimpse of the concentration camp but always aware of the gestapo moving about. We were tempted to go into the bar for a beer but that was rather risky, and we decided to turn back in case our beer would turn into sour grapes. Our visitors were a bit shocked when they saw our living quarters and our next door neighbours, the pigs, but the food made up for that.

'You know, it is the third time we've been together and we don't know your names,' I said. They then introduced themselves as Halla and Ulla. It was soon time to go and fetch our tea.

Mrs Vibe gave us our usual Sunday chocolate, bar of luxury soap and a mountain of baking as well as 40 cigarettes.

'Have a nice time, Dominik,' she said. I almost felt embarrassed the way she smiled as she looked at me. I replied to her in German, 'Just like at home.' That pleased her very much. As much as I had hoped and prayed for the downfall of Hitler's Third Reich, I often wonder what the final outcome would have been had all the people been treated as Bronek and I were throughout the German-occupied countries. There would have been no complaints against the present occupiers compared to previous invasions. It was something to dream about.

Arriving back with the food, our visitors could not get over the amount we had been given.

'Is it like that every Sunday?' they asked.

'Almost, but not as much food if we have no visitors.' I explained that the cigarettes were a special treat for my birthday. There was a lot of teasing by all of us, but although we were enjoying ourselves I wasn't able to forget the week ahead and all the weeding to be done. Yet it could have been much worse. Those men from the camp who had to pull the wagons would have done anything to swap places. At least we had something to look forward to; in another four or five weeks we would get home again. The girls were upset when we parted; they were taking to working on the farm very hard after town life.

On Monday, Franz, who knew all about our visitors, made many teasing remarks, particularly when Gretchen came with our tea. Franz knew Mrs Vibe had asked me to make more effort to learn German which I did. I even tried to learn a German song. Our work was becoming more relaxed. When the sugar beet weeding was finished, we worked in the garden or in the farm square, cutting sticks or tidying up, although there was nothing out of place. Whatever we were doing, at finishing time, the boss would be standing there waiting for us. It wouldn't do at all to be ten minutes late or early: we had to be punctual.

It was now approaching July. The news we were hearing was still depressing: the French had surrendered and a great number of British prisoners had been taken at Dunkirk. I mentioned to Franz that there would be no men left in Britain if that was the number of prisoners the Germans had taken already.

'Du Hund,' (You dog) he would say. 'You want us to lose the war?' My reply was of course, 'Certainly, Franz, and you are going to.' I could say anything to him. Sometimes he would warn me not to talk like that when Gretchen or the other man, Hans, were present. I said that I wouldn't bother as they wouldn't believe me anyway. He would only reply that I was a wicked, hard Pole! It was a warm feeling to have someone like Franz to trust. He was a good friend to have.

At weekends we had our usual visitors, Halla and Ulla, who always came to our farm. It felt more like a Sunday to them, especially because of the food we were given and which they were usually deprived of. Ulla and Bronek often left Halla and me together after tea. We got on very well, and I was forever teasing and joking with her. The time passed so quickly on Sundays. We often had to take a shortcut across the fields when we escorted them back to their farm so that we could be back before six o'clock. We had quite a race running back along the ditches, not only because of the police but to avoid being late for our supper.

Remembering my promise to learn German, I now went with Bronek for our supper. As I waited at the bottom of the steps, I started humming and singing a few words of the song I had been learning to show off my progress with the language. The two maids and Bronek began laughing. Mrs Vibe came running towards me, calling out, 'Stop, stop, stop singing. Dominik, who taught you that song?'

'Franz, with Bronek's help.'

'Don't listen to them,' she said, smiling a little. 'You are doing fine on your own.'

I suspected something was wrong, but I hadn't realized it was that bad! My sister Sophie sent me a little pocket dictionary. Now I was catching up fast with Bronek. The news from home was encouraging. Now my mother was becoming friendly with Mr Reinke, the chief of the labour exchange, he called every second week for a cup of coffee and some sandwiches. This didn't please our German neighbour - it would be more difficult to report my sisters for not working. It lifted my morale to get letters from home, in particular those containing good news.

Here on the farm, we were preparing for the harvest. Binders were checked, greased and rechecked again. The two crops we had were wheat and broad beans, which were used for feeding cattle and pigs. As the harvest began, some of our boss's sons returned for a longer holiday to help. They took over the binders, with five of us stacking.

Gretchen was now working with us every day. I was surprised at how talkative she became. It was a very busy time with rather hard work, and the weather was hot. We felt shattered at night but with Franz's good humour and the good food, we didn't mind too much. We were well aware that many of the boys from the other farms would do anything to exchange places with us.

As we worked one day, Franz came closer to me and whispered, 'Look,

Dominik, there are British prisoners working with your girlfriend.' That dampened my spirits a little. The Germans had probably spread the few prisoners they had all over Germany and other occupied countries as propaganda.

'Would you like to join the British, Dominik?'

'Not yet, Franz, but once the time is right, I will,' was my reply.

'You are crazy, you Pole!'

After supper, Franz would sometimes come for a bout of wrestling. One night it would be two-one for me, then again two-one for Franz and often we both ended up with torn shirts which his wife would mend for us. Mr Vibe knew we had become great friends and any work that required two men, he'd put us together. Then we talked more sensibly and I would tell him about the events at home when the Germans invaded us and the propaganda that was spread against the Poles. We became even firmer friends. Franz always tried to make excuses about the concentration camp across the canal, telling me how many were against it but just couldn't do anything about it. Then he would repeatedly tell me to watch what I was saying when Hans and Gretchen were present.

Once cutting was finished, taking in the harvest began with three and sometimes four pairs of horses. What I enjoyed most was collecting the horses each morning and returning them at night. We had to take them about three-quarters of a mile so we would ride them, racing bareback just like the Cossacks. Mr Vibe worked with us for the first time inside a huge barn where the entire harvest had been put. After one week's rest from taking all the harvest in, the threshing began. We got extra help for this, a German guard with four British prisoners. I was pleased to see the boys in such good spirits. They were excellent workers, every one of them.

As for me, it was my hardest work ever. I carried bags of grain across the yard and up the stairs into the granary. The only rest I got was walking back empty-handed, but even then I had to step on it as the next bag was filling up. I thought I wasn't going to make it and my legs would collapse under me. I decided to speak to Mr Vibe and ask if I could swap for a day. He agreed and one of the Scots boys took over. I was almost ashamed at the way he worked as he was almost half my size – I wondered where he got his strength from.

I now only had two days each week carrying bags. I really hated that job and the noise from the threshing mill and dust were getting me down. My morale was low. The end of the sugar beet harvest couldn't come quickly enough so that I could get home, and home I would get, even if I had to make a run for it! I was getting quarrelsome with my partner for the first time ever. Anything and everything seemed to be in my way.

At the end of each working day the guard had to take the Scots boys to the kitchen. Mrs Vibe would come out with a basket and give each one chocolate, a packet of cigarettes and a small parcel of food to take back to the camp. The Vibes did show their appreciation to anyone who gave them an honest day's work. My good friend, Franz, must have noticed my low morale. He asked me to come to his home at the end of our garden on the opposite side of the canal. Although it was a weekday and a curfew was on, I took the chance.

As we stood talking for a few minutes, a policeman appeared out of nowhere and my heart sank. Franz and his wife begged him to let me go, but with no success. As we walked past the house, my hands behind my back handcuffed, Mrs Vibe was waiting. Even then he wouldn't give in to her pleas. She called to her son, the SS major, who came with his jacket unbuttoned. I thought it was to show off his rank that he had put the jacket on. The brute stood to attention as the son lectured him. He ordered the policeman to remove the handcuffs and told him not to forget that I was on their property, where I had been visiting their foreman. It was not to happen again. He dutifully obeyed the commands. If Mrs Vibe's son had said to me, 'Kick his backside,' I think I would have put all my energy into it. When I was told to return to my room I thanked him gratefully.

Instead of going to my room, I stepped inside the stable door and looked into the yard trying to work out how it had happened so quickly. I never saw them watching from the kitchen window until Mrs Vibe came over and told me I should always tell them if I wanted to leave the farm when we were not supposed to, and say where I was going and what time I would be back so that if I was not there, they would know where to look. Some of our boys who were caught out walking after six o'clock were taken to the police station in Stutthof and got such beatings they couldn't work for days.

Bronek got a shock when I told him about my experience. He began to spend more nights at home himself. I asked Franz to get a bottle of brandy for us, the first ever, to make up for the bad experience. As we had our little celebration, there was a knock at the door and there stood Halla and Ulla. They'd heard about my near miss.

'Yes, and I'll make sure they won't get another chance to catch me,' I vowed. They then shared a drink with us to help drown our sorrows before taking a short walk.

About ten minutes later Halla whispered that she wanted the two of us to turn back and we let the other pair carry on. It was obvious that she wanted a serious talk. I asked her what she planned to do should she get her release papers and she said she might try for a job in Danzig. I wondered why she didn't intend to go home, but she said that her parents were dead and she had no home to go to. She was still waiting for news of her brother who was in the Polish army. I mentioned to her that Mr Vibe had told me that after the sugar beet harvest was over, he would give me my release papers but that meant I would be sent to another farm. I said I would ask for them and if I was sent to another farm I wouldn't stay long but would make my way home. She wanted me to let her know a week before I left the Vibes, but I assured her it wouldn't be for another few weeks. I suggested she return a little earlier that night so that we could take our time, and in any case, with the crops now cut the police could see for miles. I explained to Halla that the last weeks had really been getting me down and how I had worked like an ox. She tried to make me see how well I was being treated and how lucky I was. Talking it over with her helped a little.

As soon as the threshing was finished, the sugar beet harvest started. This proved a real backbreaker and the weather was getting much colder as well. We were given some extra blankets for our beds. Some nights we were a little tipsy going to bed as Mrs Vibe sent Gretchen over two or three times a week after supper with red wine warmed up with cloves in it. Poor lady, she tried everything to make us happy but we did work for it.

We were also fortunate to have a foreman like Franz. He was such a kind and understanding person. One day Franz showed me a newspaper clipping showing the huge tanks their Russian allies had.

'You would need a ladder to climb into them,' he remarked.

'Surely, Franz, Germany will manage to supply the Russians with ladders.'

'I can't win with you, you cheeky Pole,' he laughed.

I teased him about winning the war and he took it in good part. I let him know how pleased I was to have met him, and wondered what I would have done if I'd had to work beside some dour, grumpy man I'd be afraid to speak to. Franz's eyes sparkled in gratitude. I asked him to pop in for some of the brandy I still had left. He was a true friend. I was counting the weeks now - five or six - when hopefully I would be on my way home.

I received a welcome letter from Sophie. All seemed to be quiet; no more persecutions, no more people disappearing, but there was still no news of Victor. She said they could do with me at home to organize some more meat. Somehow, Jan wasn't any good at organizing anything and it was all left for Mother. It was even Sophie who went to the wholesaler.

I was more determined than ever to go home after my release. We were getting on well with driving and loading the sugar beet onto the barges. It was one of the coldest jobs. It had to be done by hand and the sugar beets were frozen.

One Friday, I gathered up enough courage (my German was getting quite good) to ask Mr Vibe what chance there was of getting my release papers once all the work was finished. He confirmed his promise and said as soon as all the major work was finished, he would talk about it again. However, he did say that I wouldn't get to go home but would have to go to another farm. They were doing this with everybody. He reminded me that I was welcome to stay and that I would have an easy time through the winter. I had already made my decision - home it was to be.

In all the excitement, I couldn't wait until Saturday to tell Halla. I sneaked through the fields to give the girls my news. Halla told me that her boss's daughter could get a job for her in a bakery in Danzig. I thought that sounded promising - not only foodwise but I hoped town life might be better for her. She would welcome it after the experience on the farm but was afraid of going amongst strangers again. If I would stay, she wouldn't bother going. I explained that we had to get away from here and we had to take our chance.

'Surely,' I said, 'you don't think the occupation will last forever with all the oppression and violence imposed on every country? One day the tides will turn in our favour. That's all we have left - dreams and hopes of being free one day. You may take the bakery over yourself one day when the Germans have retreated.' She told me not to talk such rubbish, but that it did sound encouraging.

'The war is not over yet and however long it takes, it will come. One day we are going to be free,' I continued, encouragingly.

I was uplifted now at the thought of going home and counted off every day. My friend, Bronek, decided to stay and I could well understand his reasoning. It would be hard to get another place as good as this one. Saturday came and at one o'clock I was already waiting at Halla's place. As we walked past Franz's home, there he was in the garden. I introduced him to Halla and then there was the usual teasing and joking between us. Halla asked Franz to speak to his boss to try and persuade me to stay. Franz just said, 'You will make it home, or it won't be for lack of trying if you don't.' I could certainly trust him.

At long last, the backbreaking job was finished. The following week, we took the cattle and horses inside. Surely I wouldn't have long to wait now for my release papers. Midweek Halla and Ulla called.

'I got my release papers, Dominik, and the job I told you about in the bakery in Danzig,' Halla told me. I would miss her and the weekends we had spent together, but we had to take the opportunity to get away.

I was expecting my own release papers any day now. When I got back to my sleeping quarters Franz was waiting for me.

'What about coming to my place, Dominik? We will have a little party before your departure. Once it gets dark, I will come for you and we will sneak around the garden to make sure you don't get caught again.' Franz was smiling and said he would tell me why later. I was not to tell Bronek I was going to see him.

When darkness fell and the coast was clear, I made a race for Franz's home. He poured me a drink and wished me success with my plan. He reminded me that if I was not successful, they would finish me off and nobody would know what had happened to me. He also said that if he hadn't heard from me within a month he would know that something had gone wrong and would write to my parents. I was so grateful to him and gave him my home address.

I then asked Franz what he had been smiling about earlier: before he could answer there was a knock at the door. It was Gretchen. Franz said that she knew about my incident with the police and both went on to explain what had happened. The night of the incident, they had planned to have a party just like tonight, only their plan backfired. Of course, Gretchen hadn't planned for the police to catch me and was embarrassed at the whole incident. We spent a pleasant evening together with Gretchen admitting that she would miss me. I thanked Franz for all his kindness. Franz still couldn't understand why he was not able to get on the same with Bronek. I explained that he couldn't help it and that it was through Bronek that I had landed with the Vibes after he spoke up for me at the station. I joked to Franz that there would be no more torn shirts. He was so keen for me to stay, but I had made up my mind.

It was about 2 a.m. when we left. Gretchen admitted on the way home that she had only been trying to get the two of us together. When she saw me, with the policeman, she ran to tell Mrs Vibe. So that was how she had been waiting for us that night. We spent over two hours talking. Whatever had happened to Gretchen! We had hardly spoken a word to each other for five months and then suddenly she was so chatty and friendly. Of course, I was as stubborn as a mule at times, especially with Gretchen, which hadn't helped.

Mr Vibe informed me that I would be getting my release papers at the end of November but should I change my mind, I was welcome to stay and that I would have an easy time during the winter. He mentioned, by the way, that my German had improved considerably.

I told Franz about my release date and wrote a short letter home. I explained that, should I be sent to another place, I planned to make a run for it. I hoped my mother would mention something to Mr Reinke from the labour exchange.

My last day arrived and everything was packed. I was asked to go to the kitchen to collect some sandwiches. Mrs Vibe must have noticed the loving looks I was getting from Gretchen, after all the coolness towards each other throughout the summer. Mr Vibe took me in his gig to Stutthof Labour Exchange and wished me luck. I thanked him very much for the kind treatment. He just gave a little smile in acknowledgement – he never talked much except when his sons came home from the army, and he was quite different then.

When I walked into the waiting room at the labour exchange, a man came to see me and took my release papers. I waited for an hour – nothing. I knocked at a little hatch and was told to wait. I didn't like it and my brain was working overtime. What would I do? I was feeling low. If I thought I could succeed, I would race back to Mr Vibe; but it was too risky. The concentration camp was only about a mile away. I had to watch what I was doing. The man from the office poked his head through the little window, most likely to see if I was still there. I could feel the hatred building up within me again, not only against the Germans but against everything around me. I couldn't help thinking of poor Halla. I hoped she would be pleased with her new job. I had given her 20 marks the night we parted as her pay was very poor.

A little man walked into the waiting room and then into the office. As I had suspected, he had come for me. As we walked to the station, he informed me he was my new foreman and his name was Karl. There were quite a number of people waiting at the station when we arrived. I couldn't help watching a gestapo man accompanied by his wife and two children. As I looked at them I noticed his wife was crying and I thought, 'Oh, you have feelings, too. Well, whatever they are I hope one day you get your share of misery also.'

My escort twice offered me a cigarette but I refused. I told him I had my own cigarettes. I recalled Franz's comment that I was a stubborn Pole and I had to admit I was at times. We got off the train at a town called Tugenhoff, close to the Polish border. We then had to walk about one and a half miles. I kept looking back all the time. Karl asked me what the reason was and I said I was trying to memorize the route so that I would not lose my way when I tried to make a run for it. I was immediately conscious of my behaviour towards him and what I had said, but I could not have cared less. He didn't say a word, just looked at me.

Coming out of the town, quite a good-looking girl came towards us and gave Karl and me 20 cigarettes each. I said to myself, 'You had better take them. Don't be as stubborn as you were with Gretchen.' During the conversation with her, I decided that her people must have a restaurant or hotel. We reached our destination and there I was again at yet another farm, being forced to work for someone against my wishes. I wondered what lay ahead of me.

CHAPTER 9

My sleeping quarters were, again, near the stables and these I shared with Karl, the foreman. He asked me to go to the kitchen with him for something to eat. I thought it must have been out of curiosity, so they could see if I looked as dangerous as we Poles were made out to be.

Our work was mostly feeding cattle, taking in turnips and tidying up. I tried to befriend Karl as I thought I would need his help in planning my escape. As I unpacked, we talked. Karl was astonished to hear about the food we got at the last farm and the special treats at the weekends - all the cakes, chocolate, the soap and the hot wine with cloves in it on cold nights.

'You had better prepare yourself for the change then, Dominik. You are in for a shock.'

Next morning, we went for our breakfast of black bread and a little cube of butter. It was in a big cellar with small, barred windows. We always tried to get back to the stable as soon as possible because of the freezing temperature in the cellar.

By the fifth day, we had still not seen anything of the farmer. The girl I had met the first day was always around. Karl told me that the farmer was on very friendly terms with her parents and did all his drinking in their hotel. Whenever we sat down, be it for a smoke or for our tea, she was there with cigarettes for us and would sometimes pin some silly medals on me. I remarked to Karl that I thought there was something lacking in her mentality. He told me not to worry as she was quite harmless. Sometimes I put my unkind feelings down to the way I felt toward the Germans for sending me to another place of work.

When I was feeding the cattle, I'd sometimes hit out at the big scraggy bull - not that he felt anything, as his skin must have been as thick as most of the Germans'.

One night the girl did not show up and Karl and I had a long an interesting chat. It turned out that his father had died in a labour camp when Karl was in his teens. He was now in his thirties. His father had been in the communist party. I tried to persuade Karl to try for my old job with Mr Vibe. He would then see for himself the treatment I had been given there. I pointed out that the trains were passing here and was I not right in saying we were only one or two stations away from the old Polish borders. Karl agreed and then asked me if I was really serious about planning to make a run for it.

'Oh, yes,' I said, 'my mind is made up. I won't be staying here long.' He warned me that if I was caught I would be sent to a concentration camp. I was aware of the consequences but said that if I planned it properly, it should work. Karl assured me that I wouldn't need to worry about him and he would help if it were possible. I apologized to him for being so awkward when we first met.

I had a pair of long, black boots that were very much in fashion and I noticed that Karl was always admiring them. I promised to leave him the boots and the breeches that went with them. He was delighted with that deal.

We began to plan my escape. The best time for making a run for it must be the day that the farmer was in town, which was always a Friday. The girl usually came to see us after supper. Karl would disappear so as not to throw any suspicion on himself. I would keep the door closed and tell the girl that she couldn't come in as I had a very bad headache. I had everything packed. The train would pass our farm about eight o'clock. Karl would return about nine o'clock and then about half an hour later he would go to the farmhouse to report my disappearance. By that time, I should be in Tchew, a large town across the border.

So far, everything was going according to plan. I got rid of the girl and made my escape as I prayed, 'Please God, let me succeed.' I don't think a greyhound could have caught up with me. It is unbelievable the strength one gets in such a situation. Once in the town, I slowed down to a crisp step not to throw any suspicion on myself. I lost my way and had to ask twice for directions. I eventually got to the station only to find that the train had just left. I was only one or two minutes late. I felt I had lost. I was told the next train would be at six-thirty in the morning. I decided to go to the toilets. Once inside, I slackened the belt on my trousers – there were no locks on the doors, and I would be ready to sit down to avoid suspicion should somebody come in.

About 10.30 p.m. I heard the sound of horses' hooves. It was the farmer himself. I heard him talking to the stationmaster, referring to me, as always, as the 'Polish dog'. I thought my end had come and I could already visualize myself pulling the wagons with bricks in Stutthof concentration camp. Before the farmer left, I heard him asking the stationmaster to report to the police if anyone asked for a ticket to Chojnice (my home town). That was something I had not intended doing – I was going to buy my ticket in three stages.

It was coming on for 2 a.m. I was very sleepy because of the temperature, which was well below -20 degrees. I did press-ups, sit-ups and pulled myself up on a short steel bar which was protruding from the wall. I would shake my head jerkily to keep awake. A headache came on. If I fell asleep, I knew I would freeze to death. There was no sound outside so I decided to try one of the sheds near where the stationmaster lived, about 20 to 30 yards from the toilets.

In the quiet of the night, the crunching of the crisp snow made with each foot step was unbearable to my ears. I made it! I tried one door, then another. At last, I found one door unlocked. I went about eight steps down. All around were shelves holding meat preservatives and a lot of homemade wine. I took a seat on a chopping block and suddenly felt warm. I would have given anything to be back at the Vibes' farm. I asked myself why I had been in such a hurry to get home. I had even tried to apologize to Halla for the way I behaved some weekends because of my impatience. Poor Halla, if she only knew the predicament I was now in. Here I was, wondering if I would make it. I thought, 'If my mother knew, she would have everybody on their knees praying for me.'

About 4.30 a.m. I made my way back to the toilets. I thought that should I be caught by the stationmaster and he saw I hadn't taken anything, he may let me go. I went back to the toilets. How slowly time passed.

The first of the passengers arrived. I decided to come out of hiding about 6.15 a.m., but couldn't go for the ticket myself. I was shivering with the cold. I realized I would have to ask someone who looked trustworthy to get the ticket for me. I studied the faces of the people moving about on the platform. I then approached two men carrying lunch bags on their shoulders and told them the farmer I worked for wouldn't allow me to go home for my father's funeral and I had decided to make a run for it. They looked at each other, then one of them asked me for my money.

As we boarded the train, one of the men saw the condition I was in and told me he would get the next ticket for me from Tchew to Lag. That was the place we had left a few years before the war. We had a few drinks together to help calm my nerves, and then they wished me luck. I thought I was dreaming, but it was reality - I was on my way. A girl sat beside me in the train and what a chatterbox she was! I was glad I didn't need to talk. At the next station, two gestapo sat beside us. It was a blessing the girl was there as she kept them busy talking. I excused myself and took a seat on the opposite side.

After a two-and-a-half hour journey, the train stopped at Lag and I went to the home of our former nanny, Francesca. What a wonderful lady she was. How lucky we were that she still lived there. Poor Francesca had tears in her eyes whilst listening to my ordeal. She was anxious to know how everyone was. I explained how lucky we were compared to other families round about us. The gestapo had called two or three times looking for Victor, but at least we knew that he must be still alive if they were searching for him.

Francesca said that it was becoming a little quieter there but that in the beginning it had been frightening. Many people had disappeared, especially in the town, and you could not ask for them. It was just the same as at home. She explained that things had improved quite a lot since the reserve army had moved in to stay. For some reason, they didn't have much time for the Poles who had taken German nationality since the occupation - the Volksdeutsche. That gave others a little hope or security but there were always some who made up stories against you. Once the gestapo came to visit you, there was little hope - the same story all over again.

I asked Francesca if I could stay for a few days and she happily agreed. I told her I had written home already and that they knew of my plan. I had sent a letter to Sophie to tell them where I would be. 'You know it gives one a secure feeling to know you have someone you can trust behind you,' I said and explained to Francesca about Mr Venzell, the policeman, who was very obliging, and SS Reinke at the labour exchange. I added that I was sure I would get away with escaping from the farm.

Sophie arrived at Francesca's within a few days. I had got the all-clear from Mr Reinke to start working in the wood again. That was great news. It couldn't have worked out better.

'You have no idea what we went through at home thinking you may get caught,' Sophie said, and gave a little parcel to Francesca from our mother to thank her very much for helping me out. I thanked Francesca for everything she was doing for us. Every time we were in trouble we seemed to go to her.

'We have sort of adopted you as our second mother,' I added gratefully.

'Any time, Dominik, you know you can come here,' she promised.

As we set off, I felt wonderful knowing I could get home and that nobody would be after me, thanks to Mr Reinke. Sophie was concerned but relieved.

'You know, Dominik, things will be better again. I feel sorry for Mam, the organizing she has to do. Dad wouldn't go to town to save his life and you know Bruno is not fit. Jan will do anything around the house but don't ask him to go to town to the wholesaler for anything. Even though there are so many people from the town going steadily to buy from the German farmers, Jan just won't budge.' I assured Sophie we would be better organized again. She explained that there was no meat left, and all they had left were the hens.

We arrived home at last, to big smiles all round. I related my ordeal to them, and everybody was surprised that I had attempted to escape so close to the concentration camp. I was delighted to be home again. Even the trees looked better than the German ones!

I resumed work with Jan in the wood. The curfew had been lifted and we felt more relaxed. There was no need to be afraid of being followed - at least this was almost true. Now and again, some crazy, drunken youngsters would beat up people whom they caught alone.

One Saturday, on my way home from Uncle Frank's, I noticed that I was being followed and raced home. They followed me to the house and knocked on the door and my sister Lucy answered. They seemed desperate to get me outside so my mother went to talk to them. Recognizing one of them, she asked, 'Are you not the Saunders boy? What do you want from him? I am going to report you to the SS leader, Mr Meyer.' That did the trick. My mother meant business this time. She did talk to SS Meyer, who in turn promised to talk to the boys. The saddest part was that the Saunders family and ours had been great friends before the war. It was difficult to understand what made people turn against their friends like that. Anyway, my mother's actions worked tremendously well: we never had any trouble from them again.

I found out later that Mr Meyer had a liking for my sister Maria who now worked for a professor's family in the town. Mr Meyer was one of the SS leaders who was organizing meetings and looking for new recruits among our ethnic minority. He liked to call himself a 'political architect'. One day, while having tea in his car, he noticed my sister passing and followed her to the house. That only meant extra worries for us all, especially for my mother. The last thing we needed was for an SS officer or any German to propose to Maria.

I sent short letters to my good friends Franz and Halla telling them about my escape and that I was now safe at home.

The spring of 1941 arrived and we were hard at work planting, which was much better than farm work. I was working with my old partner again. After my narrow escape from the Saunders boy and his two friends, I don't think there was a night when I wasn't home before darkness fell. We looked forward to the evenings now. All together again, we would play chess, draughts, cards and sometimes the three policemen joined us in our games. Through Mr Venzell, we got to know Radatz, that feared chief of police who had shot all our dogs, and another policeman, called Büllert. Büllert was Hungarian by birth with a gypsy look about him, and he was a very decent person. Knowing them and SS

Reinke from the labour exchange, we felt as secure as we could be. Even our ethnic minority had respect for us - they knew that by reporting us, they would be in trouble themselves. It was all due to my mother's fruitful work, always showing kindness and giving a great welcome to everyone.

I killed a few pigs again, and sometimes cycled to the German farms for poultry or butter, which we shared with our protectors.

Workwise, it turned out quite well, too. The Germans decided to widen our existing main road from Germany right through the corridor to the Baltic. That gave some families the chance to earn better money, but at the same time, we wondered why they needed such a wide, concreted road. It was depressing to see the number of Scots prisoners who were working on it.

Our Polish stationmaster wanted to see me one day. He told me there was a railway wagon with supposedly empty barrels for the distilleries, but that there was quite a considerable amount of whisky left in some of the barrels. He knew the connection we had with the police and that it would make it much easier should we be caught. I agreed to do the job.

Everything went without a hitch and I arrived home with ten gallons of whisky. I remember my father laughing when he saw the amount of spirit and he wondered what I would get up to next.

Now and again, we mixed a bottle or two with black-cherry syrup. For some reason, at home before the war, this drink was called 'father with mother'. It went down well with our visitors. Each time Mr Reinke called, he would get a large glass. With a huge smile, he would say, 'What chance is there of getting more? I may come with you to guard the good works.' Between the spirit and the wine I managed to organize, we were able to supply our visitors for almost half a year.

One day in winter, my mother was called out to deliver a child to the head brewer's wife. My mother returned with a gallon of spirit instead of money. We all had a good laugh about it. To me, it was a sort of seal of approval for the spirit I had got but in fact it helped to keep our protectors happy.

The stationmaster of whisky fame was taken away to the concentration camp one day, accused of being in some political organization. For four months, all the village people tried to pull strings and do anything to gain his release. Eventually, he was released, but his job of stationmaster was taken over by a fanatic of about 30 years who was in the SA (Sturm Abteilung – First Nazi Party Members). He started organizing large gatherings which we were forced to attend, otherwise we were accused of being anti-German and would be beaten if someone reported us.

He usually invited some propaganda fanatics to the meetings and they worked themselves into a frenzy telling us about the huge success Hitler had achieved. They would tell of the sleepless nights he was sacrificing for us and order us to scream 'Sieg-heil, sieg-heil'. Some of the Germans were so exhilarated by the news that they had tears in their eyes on leaving. It didn't last long.

On 22 June, Hitler's concrete road became very busy. Endless columns of lorries carrying soldiers and equipment drove by our house and the railway lines were also choked with army equipment. Hitler had now invaded Russia. Of course, we rejoiced at this, believing that the more fronts on which Hitler had to fight, the quicker one would cave in and the tide would turn against him.

After a few days, when the roads had quietened, our Nazi neighbour, Labott, had the impudence to come with a bag of grain for our hens, trying to make friends with us again. He was followed by his little fat wife who had tears in her eyes, and repeated to herself, 'Now we are doomed, now we are doomed. That's the end for Germany now that Hitler has invaded Russia.' Had my mother not been there, I would have threatened to report them for spreading anti-German doomsday propaganda. After listening under our windows and walking into our house unexpectedly in the hope of catching Victor, they were now trying to turn to us again. The rest of our ethnic minority who had spread so much terror and misery also tried to befriend us again.

Our policeman friend, Mr Venzell, who had the same feelings towards the Germans as us, told us how fast the Germans were advancing into Russia and the number of prisoners they were taking. Our morale dropped again. The ethnic minority once again changed faces, particularly our neighbour.

We were ordered to attend the meetings as usual to listen to the propaganda and march and sing, only this time we had to gather on Sunday afternoons as well. After a few weeks, we called these meetings 'The Gathering of Comedians'. Sometimes, we really had some fun and would laugh when the fanatic was reduced to tears with rage. Some of the older Germans were ordered to join in with us, mostly those who hadn't shown enough enthusiasm at being German and tried not to show their German identity to us Poles. There were usually about eighty of us, half German and half Polish. We started off by marching. If there was any dirt on the road, or a pool of water, we circled it. At the other end of the line, others would be jumping over something. People watching us started laughing, causing our fanatical friend to run from one end of the line to the other screaming his head off with frustration. Had it been only Poles, it would have been a different matter: we wouldn't have dared to perform like that.

The best of it was when he ordered us to sing - everyone was out of tune, and some were a verse ahead. We would start arguing that some were singing too high, others too fast, just to pretend that we were trying to be serious. This would only make him purple with rage. Observers standing about laughed their heads off.

With the German invasion of Russia now going very much in Germany's favour, a new wave of terror and arrests began locally. People were disappearing again, being taken from their homes at night and shot. Our ethnic minority were returning to life, but now they had changed their tactics. People were found lying dead but they were never locals so that we didn't recognize who they were. If anyone disappeared from our area, they were always taken by strangers, never by anyone known to us. The dead were stripped of any papers or belongings, making it very difficult or even impossible to identify them.

At night, some of our own people would attempt to bury the dead only to find that they had been removed already. With the success of the latest invasion, they were becoming braver in their cruelty again.

With the German soldiers stationed locally very much on the side of the Poles, we sometimes ventured to a restaurant at weekends for a beer but only did so when we saw some German soldiers inside. We knew we were safe enough then. One Saturday, as I walked into a restaurant with a friend of mine, I saw quite a number of soldiers inside and one of them, who was with a girl I knew, asked us to join them. We were having a great time together until a member of the ethnic minority walked in dressed in SS uniform. My friend got up rather frightened and ready to leave, but the soldiers insisted we stay. I told the girl that, before the war, my friend had been a manager on the estate in the village and that the owner had since been shot by an ethnic minority member.

Some of the soldiers were looking for any excuse to pick a quarrel or fight with these people, especially those in uniform. They were not permitted to drink alcohol and the soldiers knew this. As an excuse to pick a quarrel with them, the soldier offered the SS a drink. Of course, he refused explaining the reason why. The soldier then got up, screamed at him that in a few weeks time he may be fighting for him in Russia and there he was refusing to have a drink with him, and then threw the drink in his face. Not surprisingly, he left the restaurant much quicker than he had entered. I was afraid to walk home after that episode so the soldier offered to walk with us through the village.

As I approached our house, I spotted a four-wheeled horse-cart and six men, including our neighbour Labott. They had ladders leaning against the brick-built monument or shrine, a statue of Jesus and Mary with a metal cross on top. I watched them for a few minutes to let our neighbour know that I could see what they were doing. As one of them hit the cross with a hammer, he called to his colleagues, 'Thank God it is getting loose.' They were now so full of Hitler's success in Russia that God did not exist for them any longer. Most of the shrines in our area were smashed to rubble and our farmers had to clear the rubble away. In places where Catholic members of the ethnic minority also lived the vandals were met with some opposition and had to leave.

In our home town, there is a huge statue of Jesus with an outstretched hand: they did not touch that, as they said he was saying, 'Heil, Hitler'. It was frightening the way they demolished the shrines and it reminded me of my schooldays, learning about the invasion of Mongolians and Tartars (or Cossacks) who murdered the Jews especially and burned churches. The same thing was happening again, this time by a supposedly civilized society. It was like being constantly hit on the head with a sledgehammer and being shown an olive branch and asked to join them.

They started looking for young boys to join Hitler's youth movement. Of course, for the boys it was a dream come true as there was target shooting with live ammunition. If any of the boys failed to turn up for a meeting, they would be asked why - if it was because their father wouldn't let them, some of the group leaders would pay him a visit, beat him severely and tell him not to hit the son back or report them, otherwise something more sinister would happen.

Because of the war with Russia, they tried hard to obtain more manpower and turned to us for volunteers. At our next propaganda meeting, we were told that all of us who lived in the corridor (West Prussia) were looked upon as Germans and could apply for German nationality to join them in their effort to build a new Germany and to free ourselves from American capitalism and exploitation. That only brought us more together and even more against them. Because there was no response and no volunteers, we wondered what they would try next.

September 1941 was approaching. The harvest was beginning but we were not busy in the forestry so Jan and I were allowed a few weeks off to help Uncle Frank with the harvest. It was a pleasant change and the mood was jovial. Each man using a scythe would be followed by a girl tying sheaves. That job didn't last very long for me. Rost, from our neighbouring village, who took over from the Polish family named Narloch a small farm, restaurant and grocery business, asked me to help with his harvest. (I was reminded of the Narloch family and that their three sons had been transported to a concentration camp.) Of course, I had no alternative but to go. Rost and I had a scythe each. His daughter, Trutchen, a really good-looking girl but who had short, bandy legs and only reached to my armpits, and another girl were following behind tying sheaves. Rost himself was the exact image of Groucho Marx: there was no need for any make-up, he needed only a big cigar.

As far as work was concerned, for every swipe of the scythe I took, he had to take three. I was forever waiting for him. It was the easiest work I had done so far. I was beginning to enjoy myself, and at lunchtime, I always got one or two beers or vodkas. Rost's wife, however, tried so hard to act as matchmaker that her poor daughter had to tell her to stop.

When I got home one night, there was an unusually happy atmosphere. A small parcel had arrived with 1,000 marks in it. The parcel also contained a pound of coffee and a note saying 'Everything is fine - Simon'. That was my brother Victor's second name when he was ordained. My mother's prayers had been answered. She had great faith. Because the gestapo had stopped coming to search for him, we had been rather worried, thinking that he had been caught. Now we were really well off with the money he had sent, and on top of that, we had the precious coffee to give to our protectors. Everybody was in a very happy mood. It was as if the sun shone brighter that day.

I told my parents about the German family I was helping with the harvest and how the old lady had tried to play matchmaker between her daughter, Trutchen, and me, telling me how handy Trutchen's commercial-college training was and that one day she would take over the business. Then, looking at the two of us, she would continue, 'It is time, Trutchen, you started to think seriously.' I started to tease my mother, saying that she might find herself with opposition in the grocery business. All I needed to do was propose to Trutchen! My mother only told me to stop talking nonsense and think seriously.

'If you want to propose, then propose to the good Lord and promise him that you are going to lead a better life.'

I found myself in an embarrassing situation. I had no intention of beginning a romance with Trutchen but, on the other hand, I didn't wish to create enemies.

Once the harvest was finished, I thought the mother would ease up, but no such luck. She and Trutchen started visiting us on their way home from town. I didn't mind them visiting, but I was always asked into the sitting room and she would proceed with her matchmaking.

One day I became so angry I could have strangled the old lady. As we were sitting in the room next to the bar counter, someone walked in. I realized that he was the new manager of an estate that had been taken away from the rightful owner who, after hours of torture, had been shot in the Valley of Death. Trutchen's mother went through to greet him. Coming from Berlin himself, it was only natural for him to try and find out what life was like for the ethnic minority before the war. He must have been shocked at what she told him. It alarmed me knowing how easily a person could tell such lies. Her story was, 'We were not allowed to own any properties. We were issued with coupons for clothing and shoes, and ration cards for food. We could not get sugar and sweets at all. Our churches were closed. We could not educate our children.'

As I listened, I thought of the poisonous lies the Germans were being pumped with. That man would go back to Berlin and repeat all he had heard from her when the facts were exactly the opposite. The biggest estate and farms belonged to them, the ethnic minority. The same went for the biggest shops in the town. Her own Trutchen had finished her schooling in a German college of commerce in our town. It was because of people like her and so many others spreading such tales that all the miseries and hatred had been brought against us. By repeating it so often, they must have believed it themselves. As I walked home, I found it hard to accept what I had heard. I told my parents what I'd heard and they just looked at each other, horrified. It was the first time I had seen anger get the better of my father. His reaction was, 'We will deal with them when the war is over.' As usual my mother stepped in: 'You or any of us won't deal with them. You had better say a prayer for her. That may help more. Let us be grateful we are all alive and together, except for Victor, but he must at least be alive if he was able to send us that kind of money. It is not only for us but for our relations as well. We will be able to help more now.'

The connections we had gave me the greatest satisfaction. Sometimes a farmer would come to exchange grain for bruised corn or flour, particularly for baking bread in the town mill. With a few pounds of butter or a piece of smoked ham, you could get more than enough, but then the biggest risk was to get it home. You could be stopped by the police, searched and immediately despatched to the concentration camp. That was where our connection with the police helped: as long as I was sitting on the wagon, the police would just say, 'Heil, Hitler, Mr Stoltman.'

'Heil, Hitler,' we'd echo and pass on. If we were stopped by a policeman I didn't know, the report would be sent to the police chief,

Mr Radatz, but it would be disregarded. Within days, he would come to let us know about it. Of course, we knew what it meant – he was expecting some reward. There was no problem now about greasing their palms.

With my mother's income as a midwife, especially from the German families whom she charged the full fee, and a little income from the grocery business, and now the money we'd received from Victor, we were quite affluent. However, there was always the depressing uncertainty about tomorrow.

Because food was getting scarce, the most severe punishment was always dealing on the black market. The situation was very serious if you were caught, even with only one single pound of butter. Sometimes, people tried to kill a pig and keep the whole carcass for themselves. That was also a serious crime, leading to the concentration camp and possible execution.

I decided to go back to work in the forestry again, but had to cycle five or six miles. I went to work for Eddie, my future brother-in-law, as it was the safest thing to do – none of us were working at the time. It was a thorn in the eye for our ethnic minority but, even though we knew the chief from the labour exchange, we decided not to take advantage of his friendship and be idle.

There was a visit from the head forester, Mr Hengst, who was on very friendly terms with my father through their interest in hunting. He warned my father that I should attend all the meetings where that fanatical stationmaster organized marches and singing every Sunday. For a while, we thought he had forgotten about the meetings when Germany had invaded Russia but, with the success the German army had had, he was coming back to life. I was rather conscious of not attending the 'Gathering of Comedians' and also aware of the consequences should they come for me. They could finish me off one night in some forestry plantation like they had done to so many of our people. Once again, we were performing every Sunday.

I was compensated through my forestry work. I worked with another two men, Poles, who were dependent on their earnings. We came to an agreement that I would share the money I earned between them if they covered for me at work. I would give them three days wages a week and they would get some cigarettes with the coupons. My free time I would spend cycling round the German farms which were further away so I wouldn't be recognized, buying poultry, butter and, now and again, a heavy pig.

We now had the address of where Victor was hiding in Upper Silesia and started sending parcels to him, mostly of cured meat. By now, we were greasing so many palms and helping Victor and Uncle Leonard with meat that we were always in need of supplies. I must have been one of the biggest law-breakers on the black market. I often killed a heavy pig at home in the late evening while the police watched the house in case of unexpected visitors coming for some messages.

Just when I thought I was well protected, I received a letter to call at the labour exchange. I was sent to work on a farm again. I was so sure that I would be left to work from home but something had gone wrong. I found myself again in Germany, about twenty miles from the border. What now?

CHAPTER 10

On my arrival at the farm I learned that an elderly couple called Wegner lived there with a son in his late twenties and two boys about my own age of 22 to 23 years. I couldn't understand why such a small farm should require another hand. One of the boys came from our neighbouring village and I was rather surprised to learn that he was a German. We knew that many had changed their nationality, but some chose to keep the fact a secret. He had received his call-up papers to join the army and the other boy was going to the army as well. No wonder I just couldn't get on with them.

At breakfast one morning, I started teasing them saying, 'You must be proud to have the privilege of fighting for your fatherland. Make sure you make yourself worthy of the German uniform, now that you have changed your nationality.' Willie Wegner, the farmer's son, who was in the SS, called from the other room, 'That's enough, Dominik.'

'I meant it well, Sir,' I replied.

'You just leave them be. They don't need any speeches from you.' The two boys and I slept in one room. After a few days, one of them left. The other boy stayed with me for another two weeks but there was very little conversation between us. I got the impression he would have liked a fight with me but was afraid that I was a bit too much for him to tackle.

There was so much friction between us that I decided to cycle home at weekends to ease the situation, otherwise something untoward would surely have happened. As I arrived in the centre of town on my first visit home, the area around the church was like a beehive. There were a lot of SS men on the church steps arguing with some Wehrmacht (army) officers. To my horror, I soon found out what was happening. They were commemorating the day when the Polish army, retreating through Bydyoszcz, had been fired upon by the civilians and in retaliation, on recapturing the area, had taken a large number of men to the outskirts of town and executed them. Now, to commemorate that occasion, they intended taking two men at random to be shot. They were obviously not content with the number of innocent people they'd already taken away and shot every month, leaving them in the woodlands for us to bury. Now, to create even more of a disturbance, they decided to invade the church.

That was a mistake as every Sunday there were hundreds of German soldiers, including some high-ranking officers, who attended Mass. As the helmeted SS walked in carrying rifles, the Wehrmacht officers told them that if they did not remove their men immediately they would send for soldiers to arrest the lot of them. As onlookers, we were hoping for a fight between the army and the SS. We believed it might snowball into something bigger, but no such luck. The SS dispersed after the threat of arrest. It was clear there was no love lost between the army and the SS.

Life seemed less anxious with the army staying in the town. We could go to the restaurant or café without any fear and the soldiers seemed very eager to make friends with us. An SS man would not enter a café or restaurant where there were groups of soldiers sitting. Some of our Polish families were so grateful for their friendship they often invited the soldiers to their homes and they, in turn, were eager to accept. We took advantage of the chance to talk more freely, telling them of the way our ethnic minority members were treating us.

I remember one of the soldiers who came from Cologne, after hearing the experience we had with the SS at the church, told us that they had similar experiences at home. My father's reaction to the argument between the SS and the Wehrmacht in front of the church was the same as mine – he also was disappointed it hadn't come to blows. My mother, on the other hand, praised the brave Wehrmacht officers and, as usual said, 'Pray for the SS', but I don't think I could have found a suitable prayer for them.

I dreaded the idea of returning to the farm. My sister Maria was also trying to get away from the professor's family because of the treatment she was receiving.

Back on the farm, the job I least liked was the milking. I was being kicked, my greasy hands were sticking and there was sometimes more milk on me than in the pail! Some mornings, the daughter Lucy would help me. We were quickly on very friendly terms. Her husband was at the Russian front. The poor, lonely women were all showing severe symptoms of love starvation. Somehow nationality didn't matter to them. At night, as she passed my room, she would whisper 'Good night' at the door.

A girl from Berlin was visiting a neighbour. Late at night, she would parade in front of our house, always with a stick behind her back and her elbows behind it so that she could show off her boobs better. She'd always whistle a well-known song, 'Come back, I am waiting for you, you belong to me.' I always thought, 'If only the SS would be half as pleasant, we would get on better and life would be less worrying.'

One night instead of whispering 'Good night' as usual, Lucy decided to open the door. Before I had a chance to say anything, she closed the door behind her. I told her that if her brother, Willie, found out he would shoot me.

'Are you going to tell him Dominik?' she asked, smiling at me because she knew I wouldn't dare. Anyway, Willie was away at one of his weekly meetings. I reminded her of the tension between Willie and me but she replied that if I tried a little harder I would be able to stay. The work wasn't difficult. I started laughing... There was the whistling again outside. Lucy indicated that if I was nice to her she would keep me warm and help me with the milking as well. She knew I hated that job. I promised I would try to get on better with her brother.

It was beginning to get bright by the time Lucy left me. As soon as I was alone, I took a hard gulp of tea made from tobacco which I had prepared a day or so before. It tasted ghastly. It was my intention to be sick so that I could get a doctor's certificate stating that I was not fit for hard work, but I was not prepared for the after-effects. I had taken too much tobacco tea and was forced to lie down. Everything was going round in my head. I checked my pulse which I could hardly feel at first.

Then I felt a few really hard thumps. I had a frightening sensation as if my heart was trying hard to pump but could not push the nicotine liquid through my veins. 'Please God, let me survive,' I prayed in my panic. Now I could feel my pulse becoming more regular. I had made it, although for a while I really thought I was finished!

Half an hour later, I felt as if somebody had thrown a bucket of water over me. I was wet with perspiration. Shortly before starting time at 7 a.m., I went downstairs to tell them I did not feel well and asked if I could see the doctor. Willie agreed. I suspected that Willie must have telephoned the doctor as I didn't get much sympathy from him.

He gave me two days off work as I really was in poor shape as a result of my tobacco tea. I realized later what I had done: had the doctor found out, it would have been the bullet for me. To camouflage my scheming, I offered to help with the milking and cutting and stacking sticks in the shed. In the afternoon, while helping with the milking, Lucy thanked me with a big smile, believing I was trying to make friends with Willie. Poor, dear Lucy; if she only knew what was going through my head. My intentions were to make Willie so tired of me that he would send me home. Eventually, I succeeded but he made me pay for it. Because of my own stubbornness, he almost succeeded in finishing me off.

One afternoon, after my two days' sick leave, Willie and I went for a load of potato shaws. I was building the load while Willie was forking. I was then asked to take the reins and take the load to the farm for cattle bedding. As the field was rather steep, I decided to steer the horses at an angle. Within seconds, most of the load was on the ground but I just carried on with what was left.

Coming through the farm gate, I broke the gate strainer. That was the final straw for Willie. I was ordered to loosen the horses and take them to the stable. Suddenly, I felt a sting at the back of my head followed by a burning sensation in my head as I tried to get up. I put my hand on my head and felt the wetness of blood. I realized only too well what had happened. As I looked around, there was Willie foaming at the mouth and Lucy and her mother trying to restrain him from doing any further harm. Had it not been for Lucy and her mother, I would surely have been knocking at the pearly gates and maybe arguing with Holy Peter to let me in. However, I thought Peter was busy enough with all the Germans from the battlefronts knocking at his door and all the innocent civilians the Germans were sending to him. The good Lord must have decided my time wasn't up and that I was doing a good job making them angry.

'Go to the pump, you damn Polish dog and wash yourself,' Willie shouted.

As I washed myself he stood there miscalling me for everything under the sun. I was frantic now and I thought he may go to the house for his revolver and shoot me. Had he tried that, I don't think even my mother's prayers would have helped me. As usual, it would have been 'one Polish doggie less'. That was their favourite name for us. Of course, I was aware that I had brought it upon myself.

After cleaning myself up, I went to my room, leaving the mother and daughter talking to him. Two women from the council houses had arrived for their daily milk and the whistling lady from Berlin was looking on from the road. The farmhouse stood close to some council buildings. I was reassured a little, thinking he wouldn't dare shoot me in front of all these people. I could feel the blood trickling down my neck and thought they would offer me a bandage for my wound. As I walked to my room, I made up my mind I was going to make a run for it that night. It was the night Willie went to his SS meeting.

Upstairs, when I had changed my clothes, I could not believe the number of bruises I had on my back and arms. I was now aching all over and had a strong burning sensation in my head. I packed whatever I thought was worth taking with me. All I could do was wait for the appropriate time. I could hear them downstairs arguing with Willie, trying to persuade him not to go to his meeting in case I ran away. In the end, he went, telling them to telephone him should I leave the farm. Once he had left, Lucy and her mother came upstairs with some warm water to wash my wound. Poor Lucy. I guessed she wanted to talk but being unable to with her mother present we just exchanged a few sorrowful glances. After all, it had been Lucy and her mother who had stopped Willie from beating me while I lay unconscious.

After they left, I waited until there was no more talking. I was worried that Lucy might call in on her way to her room. That would certainly have put an end to my escape plans. She had told me earlier that she would come to see me every time Willie was at his SS meetings.

All was quiet as I crept down the stairs and past the kitchen door. I closed the outside door. Just a few yards to the left and I would be inside the cattle byre. I could hear somebody following me. What now? At the end of the byre, I opened the toilet door and went in but made the mistake of throwing my bag into the pigsty and the pigs began to pull at it. A light was switched on. As I sat in the toilet, I could see the shadow of the old man bending over to take the bag from the pigsty and then almost running back to the house.

My life was more precious than my clothes so I took off. After crossing the road, I went into a steep, ploughed field about 300 yards long. It is amazing the strength and speed one can exert when one's life is at stake. Greyhounds wouldn't have had a chance to keep up with me! I tried to keep midway between the River Brda and the road which ran almost parallel to the borders and into Poland, always on the alert for any sound and looking back.

Suddenly, I noticed two lights quite a distance behind. I went down on my belly and lay in a field of green corn which the farmers used to cut for their cattle. I could hear Willie talking and swearing. Not daring to think what would happen if he got hold of me, I waited until they were a good distance away, then made another run for it. Now I was almost behind them. As it was pitch dark, I had to be careful to keep a reasonable distance from their bicycle lights. Running and concentrating on the two bikes, I nearly bumped into two men cutting oats. This was something I hadn't expected so late at night. About 30 yards away from them I lay down to wait.

I was terrified that they would continue cutting and meet up with me. Before leaving, I had put on my swimming trunks in case I had to wade through the river. I pulled my trousers down in preparation. However, the men stopped to load their horse wagons about 15 yards away from where I was. As I waited, the two bikes passed back again. What a relief! Once the field workers left, I had the night to myself and could relax a little.

I kept close to the river for the last two miles. As the terrain was all peat and bog, quite often I sank up to my waist and deeper in mud. At long last I could see the bridge and my homeland. About 400 metres from the bridge lived a family I knew. It was now three in the morning. Knocking at the door, I was given soup and bread before I took off again, and I felt safer as I continued on. There were only fifteen miles now between me and my home, all woodland except for the last half mile where there was a ditch. Because of our German neighbour, I had to wait for darkness to fall again. I could see my sister going in and out of the house. When it was dark, I made a race across the road and listened under the window in case they had any visitors.

When I opened the door, my parents, sister and brothers just looked at me in astonishment. Before telling them of my experience, my wound was properly cleaned and patched up. My father found it difficult to believe that I could have covered such a distance in so short a time.

We decided that I would go to Uncle Frank's for a day while my mother went to see the chief of the labour exchange. The news was good; I was told to stay at home and not to hide. Should anyone come for me, I would be taken to the police cells, but this would be quite safe as we knew the police chief. Mr Reinke promised to write and complain to the farmer telling him that he wouldn't get any more labour from his area after the treatment he had given me. Of course, it was only all the palm-greasing that made it so easy for us. Otherwise, I would have been sent, for six months at least, to what we called the concentration camp, but what the Germans called the training unit. Whatever the name, very few returned from it.

The news at home was rather depressing, hearing about the way the German armies were successfully continuing their advance into Russia. This knowledge made the gestapo and the ethnic minority even braver. There were now rumours that all our farmers were to be taken to the concentration camps and their places taken over by Cossack families who were very much pro-German and whose sons were fighting alongside the German army.

I returned to work in the wood again with Eddie and the same two married men. The arrangements were as before – I would share my earnings with them and take two or three days off to buy butter, poultry and pigs.

Life went on. So many more arrests and forced evictions took place.

1940. My mother Leokadia   *My father Bernard*

My sister Lucy

1939. My brother Victor, Ordained in August of that year

1942. My brother Johan in prison in Magdeburg. He was later to die saving children from an unexploded device.

My sister Gertrude

Bruno - my brother who was imprisoned with me when the war broke out.

My two younger sisters, Sophie and Maria

January, 1945. Lance Corporal Dominik Stoltman as a Polish soldier in Scotland

My two older sisters, Lucy and Gertrude.

Sophie's Wedding Day, with sisters Maria and Gertrude. She married my close friend Edmund.

Irene who, with her family, hid my brother Victor for five years.

CHAPTER 11

My Uncle Leonard, who was responsible for destroying the armoured truck, was arrested with another man and taken to the Stutthof concentration camp. Later, the second man was set free, only for us to discover that he was an ethnic minority member who had infiltrated the organization for the sole purpose of betrayal.

After three months' searching, going from one SS office to another where everyone was looking for bribes, we finally landed in Danzig, at the head office for the Stutthof camp. Eventually when they released my Uncle Leonard he was advised by one officer who had received most of the bribes to seek a good hiding place to ensure he wouldn't land with them again. How considerate they became once their palms were properly greased.

In the camp my uncle had been assigned to a job clearing woodland. They used to call it the disposable squad who eventually ended up in the gas chambers but first had to work clearing tree stumps. They were given very little food to eat before the final sentence came. The work allocated was both physically and mentally destroying.

Working with him were a lot of Russian women whose lives ended there and who were so easily replaced by others. A good many of the people included in the disposable squad were members of political organizations and most or our priests landed there from West Prussia, which the Germans called the corridor. From East Prussia came many German priests, teachers, and anyone unlucky enough to have neighbours bearing a grudge against them. Included were numerous German families who were suspected of being anti-Hitler.

Through the hatred built up against us by our ethnic minority they had arrested so many people that there was insufficient accommodation to hold all prisoners at Stutthof. To ease the situation, some were sent to Germany. They included a large number of priests and those arrested and sentenced to permanent imprisonment, or as we knew it 'extermination'.

Between 1940 and 1941, from the Baltic area and the corridor alone they had arrested so many that after lengthy interrogation they had to release about 2,000 because they had no space for them. The unlucky ones who were in the disposable squad but unable to work any more due to starvation were taken to a place called the 'Stink Barracks' – the end of the line for them. The next move was to the crematorium or gas chamber. It was frightening and so depressing to listen to my uncle's many tales. It was the first time that we had been told what was actually going on in the local concentration camp.

So many people who came out alive refused to talk about it, for fear off landing back there. As it was, we were lucky to get our uncle back. I was reminded of my own successful escapes.

A friend of mine from the village, who had simply disappeared, arrived at our railway station six months later, joyful and emotional but weak through starvation. As he stepped onto the platform, he simply collapsed. He had to be carried the last hundred yards into the house. When I visited him, I could not believe that a person in his condition could still be alive. He wouldn't say a word about Stutthof and what was happening there.

But the most cruel thing was to come. While still recovering, he got a visit from some SS official to sign as a volunteer for the German army. Of course he did this rather than go back into Stutthof. After his training he was sent to Russia where he was killed. Some volunteer! We learned from his sister that the condition of his release was to sign as a volunteer for the German army.

Rumours were now going around that all young boys would be asked to sign up as volunteers, referring to Polish families who opposed the German nationality. I decided to wait and see until the time came. Meanwhile, we were busy ourselves, trying to find a safe place for Uncle Leonard.

My mother knew dozens of places deep in the woodlands, which had once belonged to her grandfather who had been a big landowner. The area contained many lakes, small streams and a winding river. The place couldn't be more suitable. Now we had to find a reliable family. Eventually, we got a place for him on a farm where he managed to stay to the end of the war. What a coincidence - their name was the same as ours, Stoltman. So often there were surprises, and never a dull moment for us.

My youngest sister, Maria, told me secretly that she had made her mind up to run away from her place of employment. The reason was that the professor's family had two daughters almost the same age as my sister. With my black-market contacts, I could get anything in the clothes line for Maria. As a result, my servant sister was much better dressed than the professor's two daughters. One morning when she cleaned all the shoes for the family, the girls threw their shoes at Maria to be cleaned again. That was enough. She cried whilst telling me about it. What now, Maria? Well, we both agreed the only safe place to go to was to our nanny, Francesca.

Early Sunday afternoon, pretending I was going to see Eddie, the forester, I went to see Francesca, taking her some smoked meat and other things, including money. She was delighted to see one of us again, never thinking about the punishment she could be dealt for harbouring fugitives on the run from work. The minimum was six months in the camp each time. She was more than happy to house Maria.

It was arranged that Maria would stay at home for the weekend then on Monday would go back to work. In the afternoon Maria was always sent into town for some messages - this day instead of running her errands, she went to her SS friend, Smith, who took her to Francesca. After a few days he called on us to tell us how things had gone. My mother was there, shaking her head. She could not believe how we had planned it all and that a high-ranking SS official was helping us with the escape, though because of that she felt more reassured.

As for myself, I had tried to attend all the meetings including the marches and singing with our crazy fanatic to avoid any more trouble. We were expecting a visit any day from some SS looking for my sister but nothing happened. Then one day Mr Büllert, the Hungarian policeman, came with a little package telling us the professor's wife had taken it to the police station and was demanding that the letter be opened and at the same time accusing my sister of stealing some items. The police chief, Mr Radatz, told Frau Professor Müller, 'Please be careful of what you are saying. I know the family personally and if I were to repeat your allegations to Frau Stoltman you could be accused of slander. As for the items you brought and the letters which I can't open, they will be delivered by one of my men to the girl's mother immediately.' He seemed to enjoy telling us about it more than we did listening to him. Of course it meant a little reward – a few pounds of smoked ham here and there – but that was the least of our problems.

Had some higher authorities discovered the corruption a lot of the police and SS, and my family, would have been thrown into a concentration camp. But there was not much fear of that. They were all hungry. At the end of it all, it would only have meant bigger bribes again. Somehow, the bacon, poultry and butter passed to them were more valuable than our lives.

We had one or two good, honest men amongst us, for instance, Mr Venzell, the Berliner, who was the police chief's deputy, and Mr Büllert, the Hungarian. All the community in the village felt at ease if any of them were on inspection. When they were leaving for home those two were loaded with meat, eggs, butter, anything. But it wasn't just because of the bribes; they were popular from the very beginning.

A new priest was once again in residence in Brusy, a little town about five miles away, and we were all of the opinion that it was thanks to an Italian family named Guliano who had a big business conserving and drying mushrooms and employing a high number of people. Because of the priest's arrival from Germany, the convent in Brusy was reopened. This was the convent my sister belonged to and she was allowed to go back with other nuns on condition that they would work for Guliano, which they accepted. He seemed very helpful to the nuns, being a Catholic himself.

Having the German priest, we bravely managed to rebuild our own parish church which the local Volksdeutsche had broken up and another priest was installed. That was a big help, especially for the old people who, until then, had to make long treks to the town every Sunday. With small concessions like that, people were so eager to believe that things were going to improve. There was always something in store for us though, and this time it was something quite different.

Each family got a letter to attend a meeting; any not complying with the orders would be severely punished. We soon found out the purpose of the meeting: any family with a son fit for the army and who had not been in the Polish forces, had to sign up as a volunteer in the German army. We were called Class 3 Germans, but how incredible it all seemed. It was ridiculous: even the Germans must have been aware of our opposition to German nationality after the treatment we had received - all the beatings, shootings, concentration camps. Now, when the situation was becoming worse on the Russian front, they were asking us to enlist as volunteers and not signing meant internment for the whole family.

I felt I would not sign and preferred to join the partisans. My dad said that as I was over 21, the decision was mine and he would not be asking me to join up. My mother was quite upset, begging me to sign and promising to pray that nothing would happen to me.

Before our turn for an interview came, I told my mother, 'OK, I'll sign. Don't worry.' She almost cried with relief. The atmosphere around us was one of shock. Coming out of the office, families would gaze around unable to express in words what they felt as the truth was difficult to accept.

We were called into the office where some high-ranking SS officers sat behind a long table while other personnel checked our names against a list to see if we were all present. We were called in together - my parents; Jan, who was in the Polish forces; Bruno, who had survived all the prison camps with me earlier, my two younger brothers, Stanislius and Franc; Gertrude, the vinegar drinker who nearly poisoned herself in order not to work for the Germans; and my younger sister, Sophie. Maria, of course, wasn't there as she was still with Francesca.

To verify that the list they had was correct, they asked about Victor, the Franciscan, who was still in hiding. When we said that we did not know of his whereabouts, they could only stare at us and talked amongst themselves for a while. They even knew more about my mother than we did. They knew that my mother came from a titled family. When they came to Jan, they started teasing him. 'How come the Polish army took a man like you into the army? Your left arm seems to be shorter than your right one.' Of course, there was nothing you could reply. Eventually they came to me. Yes, I was the right specimen the German army was looking for. After signing some forms I was given one of them and told to get a photograph so I could obtain a German passport. I would be a Class 3 citizen. What an achievement! Little did they know that I was going to join the partisans within the next few weeks.

Suddenly they noticed that Maria wasn't present. They asked if we knew where she was, but we just said that we had no idea. If they had only known of the SS man who had helped her flee . . .

After we got home, my mother still kept thanking me for signing up. I now realized myself that it was the only thing I could have done knowing my actions would save my family from the dreaded concentration camp.

Back at work in the forestry, there was little conversation between the workers because of the tense atmosphere. Up until then, we had convinced ourselves we were safe with the good news coming from the Russian front being so much in our favour. Even the Volksdeutsche tried to become friendlier yet again, hoping to encourage us to join up with their fighting men. How changeable they were. As the German invasion of other countries was moving forward, they were throwing the news at us from all directions. It seemed incredible that within such a short time the German army had almost reached Moscow.

We began to see our dreams of freedom fading once more. But come September/October and on into December the news heard was in our favour. We were not hearing it through the Germans but via the partisans who had their own secret radio stations in the woodlands.

Food must have been getting short in Germany. Polish families, especially the farmers, were getting many visitors from Germany. Relations whose husbands were already fighting on the Russian front turned up. The news they brought with them only confirmed what the partisans were relaying. Things were really going our way now.

1941 to 1942 was the hardest winter we had in Poland for many years, with the temperature -41 degrees. Each house had straw mats on the windows to save fuel, and paraffin lights throughout the day. In spite of all the frost, we still had to work in the forestry. We would gather together, sometimes about 20 men, and make a big fire to sit around. It was impossible to work with the hard frost and the deep snow, but we had to be out.

With all the relations visiting from Germany, Uncle Frank's sister, Helen, came from Stadthagen. Most of the people had come in the hope of getting some food, but it wasn't easy with the restrictions put upon us, especially about killing pigs. We all looked forward to speaking to Helen to find out what life was like in Germany. It was only natural for us all to gather round for conversation.

After telling her of all the innocent people in our area who had been shot, her comment was, 'We need Lebensraum,' which meant, 'we need room for expansion.' We were aghast and looked at each other in disbelief. Born and bred in Poland, how could she have made a comment like that? Within a few days, she went back rather disappointed about our attitudes. In the eyes of Hitler's followers, he was God. With regards to my own Christian feelings I did not voice them in front of my mother, nor did my father who shared my feelings. But my mother's response was always, 'Pray for them,' as if feelings of hatred did not exist only love and compassion.

One day, Aunt Helen's son came to visit us on his way to the Russian front. After that he visited regularly - he had fallen in love with Maria, and my sister felt the same way, too. He promised my dad he would come with Russian tea once he called again on leave. About three months later we got a letter informing us that he had been killed. He was a very nice boy, about 24 years old. My sister shed quite a few tears. As for me, I am sorry to say I could only think of Helen's previous comments about needing room for expansion and that it was time for her family to start making the room as we had made enough already.

It was now March 1942 and another little surprise awaited us. All the men in the Polish army were asked to take working clothes and report to the labour exchange. Three days after Jan reported, we got a letter from him sent from Magdeburg, southwest of Berlin, telling us that he would be working in the factories or on the land. The number he got for us to refer when writing to him was 3499. We were rather relieved with the news that he was alive and well. What confusion! Here was I in the process of becoming a third-class German citizen and the rest of my family were still Poles. Now my brother was in a prison camp because he was in the Polish army. I decided to try and delay my German citizenship as long as possible by not sending off my passport photograph. Since being asked to sign up for the German army, I was acting braver, for example going to a restaurant or a café at night not so much for what I could buy there, but to show our ethnic minority that I could visit the same places as they visited.

The Germans were constantly searching the woodlands for the partisans with special equipment. Quite a number of Polish soldiers who came from the German prison camps had joined the partisans, believing the occupation would not last much longer.

By April 1942, our ethnic minority were getting rather worried, in fact, very worried, because of what was happening on the Russian front. One family that had been responsible for the deaths of three boys in a concentration camp simply disappeared one night, leaving their farm and heading for Germany. Another man who took over a bakery from a Polish family killed himself. They became conscious of their earlier crimes to the extent that they started taking their own lives. Of course, the ethnic minority and the Germans would listen to the radio through the night, picking up English broadcasts giving up-to-date information. Sometimes it would take a month or more before we'd get the same news through the partisans in the underground movement. That news was mostly in our favour now.

One day, the SS man who helped Maria escape called to tell us it would be safe for her to return and that he would go with her to the labour exchange. However, when Maria did return we were told by his office that he wouldn't be back for another two weeks but had arranged with the police that Mr Büllert would go with her. What VIP treatment my sister received in his presence. We expected her to be sent to another job but instead she was told to go home.

A few days later, my mother received notice that she might be transferred as a district midwife to a place close to Lucy's convent. We were quite happy with that piece of news. There were no Volksdeutsche and no German families at all in that district because of the very poor soil. The Germans were not interested in scraping a mere living out of the ground. The forestry where my friend Eddie was the forester was only twenty minutes walk away. Best of all though was that we would have two houses to run. My dad with his shop was needing someone to stay and help him. Bruno was exempt from work and Gertrude was now in real trouble by contracting tuberculosis. It was Maria who stayed with Dad to help and look after them all, including my two younger brothers. Sophie and I would go with our mother. That way there was not much danger of any of us being taken to work for the Germans again.

We really looked forward to moving and waited for the order to come. With the news always now so much in our favour, we were even approached by our friendly SS that Victor could come home from his hiding place but we decided it would be better and safer for him to stay wherever he was. It must have been a safe place because of the money he was sending us. We, in turn, kept sending him parcels of food so we let things stand as they were.

My Uncle Leonard had a good hiding place as well. It was just a matter of helping them with food. We firmly believed we would have little trouble as the news continued to be so much against the German force.

Then one early spring morning, whilst still dark, we heard numerous vehicles drawing up outside. As we looked through the window, we could see the black uniforms of the SS as well as the police. Slowly they started moving into the village, leaving their vehicles behind. What was it all about? Why were there so many SS and police? We all got dressed and waited to see what would happen. It was the first time I had noticed my mother really worried, so much so that her head was shaking with nervousness, but there was nothing we could do but wait. After all, they were our masters.

There came a light, repeated knock at our door. My mother went to answer it as she was the best able to talk to them. It was Bernard, one of our local farmer's sons, who had managed to slip away and he was able to tell us that whole families were ordered to get dressed (farmers only apparently). They were not allowed to take anything but clothing with them. They were to prepare a pair of horses and wait beside the horses and wagon for further orders.

While Bernard was getting the horses ready with his brother, Leon, he decided to make a run for it and succeeded in sneaking through the fields and into our house.

There was another light knock on the door. It was Auntie Maria, Uncle Frank's wife. Her face was scratched and bleeding and she was in a terrible state and crying. Frank had taken off to the woodlands. Because of our relationship with some of the local powers, who knew our connection with the couple, their escape was ignored.

About eight o'clock that morning, the farmers around our village got orders to board their wagons and start moving out. They were joined by another column of horse-wagons from a neighbouring village. It was a sight I will never forget. Some of the boys and girls wept, others had their heads down, not wanting to see what was happening. I tried to give a friend of mine a packet of cigarettes as he passed but I was prevented from doing so. Others, when passing our house, gave a little goodbye sign, trying to force a smile, and most likely wondering what their destination was. Would they ever see their homeland again?

The news travelled fast that day. We were all very concerned about what was going to happen to them. They were taken to a goods station in our town and ordered to board cattle wagons, and they were taken to a prison camp called Potulice, about 40 miles south. It was a camp that was managed by the commandant of the Stutthof concentration camp. The Germans were busy extending Stutthof camp but meanwhile, because of lack of room people were sent to other camps, but still under Stutthof management.

The farms, meanwhile empty of people, were guarded by the SS to discourage any pilfering, especially of livestock.

About midday, we noticed a long column approaching our village. As it passed our house, we stood aghast at the sight before us. The wagons were overflowing, and on top of their belongings families were sitting, mostly children and the elderly. A man holding a large framed picture sat on the highest spot of the wagon. Some had a picture of Hitler, some Himmler or Hess, all the heroes they believed so much in; even Goebels the propaganda minister who was giving them all the good news they were wanting to hear. We called him the 'Minister of Lies'.

It was easy to see by the way they were dressed and their facial features that they were Cossacks; those who settled nearby came from the Ukraine, on the border with Romania.

When they came to our shop for their groceries, they appeared friendly enough. Some of our people said that if only they had replaced the Volksdeutsche, life would have been more pleasant as they seemed to keep very much to themselves. We could sense there was not much love lost between the Ukrainians and our Volksdeutsche.

Thus began a weekly collection by the whole community of any spare food such as a loaf of bread, which would be eight to ten pounds in weight, smoked ham, pork dripping. Early in the morning we would have the whole pack on the bikes and take off to Potulice, where our local farmers had been taken. It was a sad meeting; someone was always weeping. They still couldn't get over the shock of what had happened to them. Their only crime was that they didn't have a son at the right age to enlist as a volunteer, as they expected me to do. The families lived in huge tents similar to those in Nuremberg where I had been forced to stay with Bruno. The surrounding fence was eight feet high, and five feet from that was another ordinary stock fence where the guards would march back and forth. As long as we were able to give our parcels to them, we thought they would survive the internment.

On one of our usual visits we noticed there were more guards than usual. When we attempted to hand over our parcels, we were stopped and warned, 'Nothing to be handed over. Any attempt will be severely punished.' Of course, we obeyed. We knew only too well what it meant. We were so taken aback, we were near speechless. I could not help thinking of the despair of the people inside. It reminded me of when my mother was pushed away when she had come with food to us at the transit camp. We waited for a while hoping the guards would move away but they remained there twenty yards from each other, staring at us. Eventually we left for home, where we related our story.

The following Sunday we took off again only to experience the same disappointment. How we hated them for all the things they were doing to us. Our only consolation was the news from Polish Radio London telling us that they were aware of the situation in Poland. We were also told that once any volunteer reached the front, they were to cross over. We would then have the chance to join the Polish army to fight our common enemy. That was something my mind was always occupied with – escaping from the German army from wherever we landed after our training.

I noticed that German transports *en route* to Russia often stopped at our station. It would be no problem at all to disappear should I find myself in similar transport. Then again, should it be France, Belgium or Holland, there was bound to be a family that would manage to hide me. I would just have to wait for the right opportunity. After all, my mother did say when she asked me to sign up, 'I promise nothing will happen to you. I'll be praying for you.'

CHAPTER 12

At long last, my mother got a letter about her transfer. The Germans gave us a place in a farmhouse where the farmer had been ordered to vacate some rooms. First of all, my mother tried to get back Sophie, who had to work on a farm. She was entitled to have someone to take any messages or calls in her absence. I was very pleased to have my sister back as we had always been very close. When she did return, her hands were as hard as leather but she never complained; she would rather have a little cry, hiding in some corner. We never had any secrets . . . and what a wonderful cook she was!

Once again, we were all together and my brothers, Victor and Jan, and sister, Lucy, were reasonably safe elsewhere.

I had new hunting grounds for my meat supplies and now a chance for some fishing. The farmhouse we lived in was about 80 yards from a river and another mile from a good-sized loch. The fish were collected each week from Sinclair, the fisherman, who kept them in a holding cage built in the river. My mother delivered a child to his wife and, as usual, her method was to take from the rich and give to the poor. Mrs Sinclair was one of the poor, with a big family that my mother took under her wing.

Mr Sinclair wasn't allowed to sell any live fish but I sometimes went fishing with him. In the middle of the boat there was a box with holes to allow a fresh steady supply of water and while taking the fish out of the nets to put into the box, Mr Sinclair casually said, 'How easy it is to kill fish; just a hard squeeze on the gills.' That was enough for me. Most weeks I would go for one trip with him and the bigger the catch was, the more squeezing I did. I paid him treble the price so everyone was satisfied. Even my dad was pleased the way things had worked out. He always kept telling me to be careful with the fish I was getting, but then the police were getting their share too! We were forever getting warnings from our police about anyone who informed on us.

The village councillor had a farm, restaurant and grocery shop and was a great friend of my mother. He knew her from childhood, when her grandparents still owned their large estates. He would offer my mother a gig to go for a picnic ride through their now lost estates, three miles away from where we now lived. At these times, my father would come to spend the weekend with us. This was always a special occasion, but mother preferred to stay at home. She didn't like to reminisce about what they had once had though Dad enjoyed the outing and Mam would eventually be persuaded to join him on these picnics.

We all agreed this was a wonderful place to live in. You never had the feeling that the Germans were watching you. We were all one happy family. The only German we saw while working in the forestry was our district forester, Mr Hengst. Eddie would warn me when Mr Hengst would be visiting his district to make sure that I'd be at work that day. He would always keep on at me to wear working clothes, telling me Mr Hengst just wouldn't believe that I came to work smartly dressed.

I was absolutely amazed that places like this existed in our country. At that time life was so good. Walking home at night, sometimes I felt like jumping and running in circles just from sheer joy but I tried to restrain myself in case someone seeing me would think I had gone crazy.

Often at night, while walking home, I would think about the advantages of living there; it was as if God was trying to compensate the community for its poor living by keeping our enemies away. Yet, sadly, only a few miles away from us, in a small town called Brusy where my sister Lucy was now, many people were being taken away during the night and shot in the woodlands on the outskirts of the town, and only because our ethnic minority disliked them. A few silly lies were sufficient for an execution. In Brusy, they still seemed to be very much in love with their Hitler and his one-thousand-year Reich. The only day we went there was on Sunday, to go to church. After Mass sometimes we visited Lucy in the convent, close to the church. It was a depressing place where many said that the sun just disappeared and forgot to rise again. How lucky we were to be in the place we were living now, where my mother worked as a district midwife and having the two households to run. We were sure that there wouldn't be much chance of any one of us being taken away again to work for any German family.

Eddie, the forester, lived quite close to us. There was hardly a day when we didn't see each other: if he was busy through the day, he would call at night so we could share any news. If the news was of particular interest, on occasions Eddie would call as late as 11 p.m. or midnight. As my bed was close to the window, he would give a light knock and produce a miniature bottle of vodka. After the dram, the news we shared always seemed more exciting.

Eddie's house was ideally situated for any meeting we had. It stood on a little hill with a view of woodlands to the east, and to the west was the main road, so any strangers could be easily spotted. Usually, we met at Eddie's house on Saturday or Sunday. A lot of people would gather, some being my old school pals and others I hadn't met before. One time I was aware that something unusual was going on. It wasn't just to meet for a drink and even though Eddie was courting Sophie, he would not reveal anything. I decided to wait and see.

One day, the two of us went to the restaurant owned by Mr Jankowski, my mother's friend. His son, Clemens, joined us. We were always given VIP treatment and ushered into the lounge bar. Though it was already very scarce, Clemens or his sister, Elli, would generously give us drink. When Elli left us, Eddie rather quietly and seriously brought up the subject of my last visit to his house and it seemed I was now going to find out what all the mystery was about. 'I was asked by certain parties who know you to ask you if you are prepared to join us, the partisans,' Eddie explained. 'You do understand what I mean?' All I could say in reply was, 'Yes, Eddie, I do understand.'

I sat for a while speechless, not because I did not want to join but I felt honoured to have been asked. At last I had a purpose in my life. I would be able to contribute something towards the freedom of my land. I was aware that taking this step could cost me my life, but that was the last thing that worried me. I promised myself that should the time come when my life was in danger, I would make sure it would be at great expense to our common enemy. After a while, I turned to Eddie with my answer,

'Yes, I am ready to join any time and I am grateful to those who believe in my conviction and have asked me to join.' Great relief showed in Eddie's face after my seeming to take so long to answer. I explained that it wasn't uncertainty, but that I had been so overwhelmed and pleased I just lost my tongue. We shook hands as Eddie said, 'You will hear from me again. Let us talk about something else now before Elli comes back.'

On leaving the restaurant, we had to go through a section where people bought groceries and who was behind the counter but Franek, my cousin, who was a teacher. At that time Elli and Franek were courting with Mr and Mrs Jankowski's approval. Of course, Eddie knew now why we were given VIP treatment when I explained who Franek was.

That same evening, I asked Eddie and Clemens to come round for a beer and a game of cards. My mother was content as she loved to see us having our friends in the house, providing she approved of them. She'd take over the kitchen, making sandwiches and doing anything to please us. Often, she would ask before friends arrived if I had enough beer. With Clemens coming, it wasn't just beer, as he would always produce one or two bottles of wine from his father's restaurant.

While enjoying our drinks, the door opened and who should appear but Maria, who stayed with Dad but who often visited at the weekend. Poor Clemens, on seeing Maria, he was instantly smitten – for him it was love at first sight. It was so obvious it was almost embarrassing. When I turned to look at Mam I thought that she was just as excited as the poor boy: I could almost read the signs of approval on her face. I wish I could have said the same about Maria. In the midst of confusion, poor Clemens took his comb out and started putting it through his hair – the little he had. Eddie whispered quietly, 'Put your comb away, Clemens, you may break it.' Sophie intervened with, 'Don't be so rude, it is what you have below that counts!'

I was very pleased the way Sophie and Maria came to his defence, not to mention my mother. Even though I was very fond of Eddie, the difference in behaviour between Eddie and Clemens, especially in company, was like comparing a wet stormy night with a sunny day. Clemens was always very polite. It was a pleasure to be in his company.

It was 2 a.m. before we decided to call it a day. After Eddie and Clemens had left, Mam mentioned that she was upset at Eddie's comment earlier, but then she never did approve of the courtship between Sophie and Eddie due to his general behaviour and manner. As for me, I was very much on Eddie's side not only because Sophie loved him but because I couldn't see anything wrong with him.

Before Maria left, we prepared some food parcels made up mainly of meat. I organized this not only for Dad, or rather Maria's household - a comment she loved to hear - but also for our protectors, the police and SS and, of course, for our wholesaler from whom we received a lot of foodstuffs without any extra ration cards. It was a constant palm-greasing exercise. Money was being sent to us from Victor in Upper Silesia where we, in turn, sent a steady supply of meat parcels, not only for him but for his friends who were paying him. The only worry we had at present was for my sister, Gertrude, who was suffering with tuberculosis. It took almost three months before my mother got her on her feet again. What made things worse was that food parcels sent to her boyfriend, George, were being returned. He was assumed to be dead. Gertrude had hardly recovered from her illness when she went back onto her starvation diet. There was nothing anyone could do but watch her fading away.

It was spring again, and we got a new supply of forestry plants. I asked Eddie to tell me when planting started so that I could work with my favourite female partner again. It was more like having a long holiday which lasted about six weeks. I did see her most weeks throughout the year but I was always worried Mother would find out as it just wasn't done in those days unless your intentions were honourable.

Now we would be together again each day, neither expecting much more than a close friendship as long as we could stay together through the occupation. My mother even made a comment to Sophie about my late nights having stopped, which made me more conscious than ever and left me feeling more guilty.

The only person who benefited from my late nights was an old man named Lesner who was employed by the farmer on whose farm we now stayed. It was heartbreaking to watch that poor soul doing his chores round the farmyard. He was in his early fifties but looked more like eighty. He would look sideways at you as he couldn't straighten properly – his back was bent due to years of hard work. That poor soul reminded me of the hunchback of Notre Dame. His clothes were in rags as well.

Within a week my mother and I between us had him dressed from head to foot in better clothes. In fact, he was better dressed than the farmer's son or the farmer himself. The good relationship built up between my mother and the farmer was very much affected because of the way they treated him.

Any night I got home late, to make up for my guilty conscience I would make up slices of bread with butter and sausage and take a pot of coffee to his sleeping quarter. He lived no better than a dog, with only torn blankets and a bed of straw.

The first time I went to see him we had a long chat. He cried, telling me how frightened he was of my family. He thought that we were an SS family, most likely being told this by his employer. The most heart-rending thing about him was that for him his main compensation was that they had promised to bury him once he died. It made me think how grateful and content some people can be for such small rewards while others would walk over dead bodies to achieve the impossible.

Arriving home after a day's planting, I was told of a letter we had received from Upper Silesia: it was an invitation for my mother to visit a family. We knew straight away that it was a family who was hiding Victor. What bliss that letter brought! My mother was quite overcome. There was a photograph enclosed of a girl who would wait for my mother on her arrival at the station. What a beauty! I kept going back to the photograph just to have a glimpse of her. I said to myself, 'God must have taken an extra day to create a beauty like her.' That photo was to have a lasting effect on me.

My mother asked me if there was any chance of getting some meat before she left for Silesia. Eddie had recently told me about a family who had a pig for sale. They lived in his isolated area of the forestry, which was handy. We called the place, for some unknown reason, 'New America'.

So off I went with Eddie one evening and he introduced me to the family, a middle-aged couple and their attractive daughter with long, auburn, wavy hair. In no time at all, they produced two dainty plates with honey and a glass of wine. I looked at Eddie questioningly. He started spooning his honey and taking sips of wine so I did likewise. The two combined had a wonderful flavour. The wine was non-alcoholic with a rather bitter, herbal flavour. It reminded me of bible lessons when Jesus, on a visit, was welcomed with similar hospitality. We soon got down to business.

The girl took me to see the pig and what a monster it was! I guessed he weighed about three cwt. so I told her my price. I noticed the rather surprised look on her face as she thanked me very much. Her parents were delighted when she told them what I had offered, as I was paying three times what they could have got from the Germans. We had to reassure them that they had nothing to worry about selling it to me.

We arranged the day when I would kill the pig, and as we left I saw a man hiding behind a tree. Eddie explained to me that every time anybody came, he tried to hide as he thought the gestapo were coming for him. Poor soul, how afraid he was of the gestapo. He was the pig farmer's brother.

Eddie returned with me to our house. My mother was more than pleased with the deal I had made in getting the heavy pig, but every time I bought one from a Polish family, the first thing she would say was to make sure I left a piece of meat with them, which I always did. I never did when buying a pig from a German family. I told my mother teasingly about the beautiful girl I had met but she only told me to behave myself as she handed me a letter.

On opening it, my heart sank. I passed the letter to Eddie, whose face dropped on reading it. 'No doubt there will be one waiting for me at home,' was all he could say. It was a request that I report for a medical to determine what unit I would be assigned to in the German army.

For the rest of the evening it was as though a bomb had dropped. We had a few beers and sat around saying very little, with Sophie and mother trying to think of something to do to take their minds off the news. Silence had fallen in the house and Eddie and I could only look at one another. Yes, I had enlisted as a volunteer as my mother had asked me to in order that my family was spared the horrors of the concentration camp. I told myself that the day of reckoning was near.

Eventually, Eddie asked me to go to his place. His parents lived with him, working the land that went along with his house as a forester. On our way, we stopped at Clemens's place for a beer. As usual, Elli took us to the lounge bar. We agreed not to say anything to Clemens unless he mentioned first that he had received papers for his medical.

After a while, he joined us as he usually did and was even more generous with the drinks because of his fondness for Maria. Frequently, he asked, 'What's wrong with the two of you? You're unusually quiet.' I think he must have suspected something as several people in our village had received the same papers.

We eventually left for Eddie's home and talked through the night about what we could do. We consoled each other that it wasn't the end of the world yet. After all, it was only a medical and just maybe we would fail the examination. It was up to us to see that we failed. I remembered Mam and Dad talking about the First World War and how Mam had gotten Dad out of the German army with tablets she provided him with. As a midwife she knew what she was doing, only in my case it was different. Now my dear mother was armed with prayers. Yes, I had a lot of faith in my dear mother and her prayers but I decided I had to put in a little effort myself if I wanted to succeed.

'You know it will be the bullet for us if the doctors find out that we tried to make ourselves unfit through drinking some poison or suchlike,' Eddie remarked.

'Yes, Eddie, I am aware of that, but then surely it is up to us. We won't talk about it but just get on with it.'

We left the subject there and when I got home it was about 5 a.m. To cheer myself up, I made some sandwiches and coffee then visited my old friend, Lesner, hoping to at least make someone happy. I told Mam where I had spent the night, at the same time noticing she was reacting differently. Now, it was me who was trying to believe everything would be all right. She admired me for the way I tried to comfort her.

After breakfast, as it was Sunday I visited my dad and accompanied him to Mass. We talked about my medical and I told him what I was planning to do to make myself unfit. His first words were, 'Watch what you are doing - the consequences could be disastrous, not only for you but for all of us.' To appease him I promised I would try to come more often for a game of cards. He loved to spend a night playing cards but he did have good company in the boy who had escaped the evacuation of farmers earlier on. He was a proper comedian. When he talked about the injustice, he would say to Dad that when Hitler dies, he would get a special place in heaven as nobody would argue with him about entry. When it was time for me to go, I mentioned about the large pig I had managed to get hold of.

I spent a short time with Gertrude who looked to me for sympathy but, somehow, I couldn't bring myself to give her any. She was like a skeleton and still she didn't eat. We all suffered because of her. 'It's time I was off, Maria. Look after the family.'

'She's a good cook,' Dad called out to me. 'Just make sure we have something to cook.'

'I'll make sure, Dad, that you will have enough.'

I left to meet Eddie as arranged. As soon as I got near the house Eddie was there waiting with the door open which made me think at first that I was late. It was rather dark inside, but I was soon to learn the reason why. I was asked by a person I did not recognize if I would be willing to join the organization that used to be called 'Partisans' and if I would be prepared to give total obedience once I was called upon.

'Yes, I am,' was my reply to both questions. I was informed, 'Our password will be "wanderer". If changed, you will be notified.' With one hand on the cross and my right hand up, I was sworn in. To me, it was a rather solemn moment. Now I knew I definitely had a purpose and a chance to do something for my country. The rest of the men were sworn in then departed. Eddie and I tried to talk, but somehow after the solemn ceremony we just didn't know what to say so I decided to take my leave also.

As I cycled home, I thought of all the miseries caused because of one man - Hitler. I remembered once hearing a comment, 'You should have been drowned at birth,' a comment I detested so much, but as regards

Hitler it would have prevented so much cruelty and heartache. It wasn't only Hitler, though, but also his generals and other followers. Some of them were so eager to execute his wishes.

The same applied to ordinary folk, especially our ethnic minority, who contributed so much to all the misery and degradation. I was still trying to accept what was already happening. Here I was now, sworn to join the partisans, and at home I had a letter to join our persecutors. How unbelievable it all seemed. I was determined that wherever I landed after my medical the Germans wouldn't have much joy from me as a volunteer soldier. I could only wait and see.

As usual, when I got home I made sandwiches and a pot of coffee and went to see Lesner in the barn. This became my routine each time I arrived home late as I knew he would be waiting up for me. Poor man, he managed to smile occasionally now and seemed a new person. In the morning, we tried not to talk about my medical in the house but whenever my eyes met Sophie's I felt sorry for her. She was badly affected by it.

Mother decided to postpone her visit to Victor until after my medical, which was still another three weeks away. I tried to persuade her to go but to no avail. She wrote to Victor explaining why. I remember, before I had got the letter for my medical, making the comment that if I got a call-up to join the army I would disappear underground, which meant joining the partisans. I knew that that was the reason for my mother's postponement but I promised her that I would go for the medical.

Meantime, we concentrated on getting the pig killed as soon as possible. Once I was away our supplies would suffer as there would be nobody to take over. It would mean leaner days again, not only for my immediate family but also for Uncle Frank who was in hiding with his wife and Uncle Leonard. The latter looked like the wild man of Borneo, just a mass of black hair on his face, his eyes barely visible. He never ventured outside after his experience in the concentration camp. We had just managed to get him out in time as he looked so terribly thin. I think even the gestapo would have run away from him now, seeing his face with such a mass of hair and two black sunken eyes peering out.

Each weekend, Eddie asked me to go with him on his errands. There was always something to be done for the scattered groups of men hidden in the woodlands. One particular weekend, with Eddie's help, I decided to kill the pig. We arranged to do the job on Sunday afternoon. As before, when we arrived, we got our little plate of honey and the herbal wine. The farmer's brother was once again hiding from us. It was such a lonely, forgotten place there was more danger of being attacked by a wild boar than being bothered by the gestapo.

Eddie enquired if I'd brought a drop of vodka to celebrate the kill. It was the custom at home that every time a pig was killed and all the work was finished, with the first meat cooked and eaten one would have a drink or two of vodka. Answering Eddie, I said, 'Yes, I did bring some vodka and I only hope that you are going to help me.'

'You must be joking. I wouldn't know what to do,' he remarked. Iris then said she would give me a hand and that I didn't need to instruct her as it wasn't the first time she had done this sort of thing.

'You needn't worry about me, I will know what to do at the right time,' Iris said.

'Well, Dominik, you've got the right partner now,' Eddie said.

'More than I can say for you, Eddie.'

I went into the pigsty with Iris who was carrying a basin and a pail for the blood. She smiled and said, 'You just knock the pig out properly and the battle is over. I hope you are good at it but you look strong enough.' She almost had me blushing. 'I will keep tickling her on the belly and she will stand quieter,' she continued. She certainly knew how to go about it. I lifted the axe, waiting for the right moment. With one quick chop the beast was down and soon it was bloodless. We praised each other for our good work. I asked Iris if she had put salt in the pail to stop the blood from curdling and she had.

'I notice you are not just beautiful but brave as well,' I complimented her.

When we returned to the house, we noticed them all waiting at the window. On seeing us they smiled knowing the job must have gone well as Iris was carrying the blood. After a cup of coffee, we had a vodka and then got down to the biggest job of cleaning and cutting up the meat. When I turned back I was startled to see Iris following me. It was the first time that I had really enjoyed killing a pig because of her company. I didn't think either of us would have minded if the operation had lasted a few days longer as we enjoyed each other's company so much.

I had a specially made carrier on the back of my bike and by the morning, I had all the meat transferred to our house. The farmers had seemed very pleased with the deal, which included the twenty-pound piece of meat I had left behind. It had been a job to persuade them to take it: in return they asked me to dinner and I accepted. Eddie commented that I should say thank you very much to him for getting the pig and then getting Iris and me together. Poor Iris started blushing as she said, 'Eddie, what would we do without you?' As usual, every time we killed a pig, there were so many palms to be greased. Everyone was waiting for a piece.

My mother and I decided to take another three or four small pigs, each 60 to 70 pounds in weight, which one could get freely on the market. It was all because of the uncertainty about how soon the Germans would enlist me into their army if my own plan failed, although I was determined that it would succeed.

You could almost sense the heavy atmosphere in the village. There were so many boys my age in the same situation. What made things more alarming was the number of Germans with radio detectors roaming the woodlands looking for partisans. After joining them I was made very much aware of it. I still had ten days to go before my medical. I told Eddie that whatever happened in a day or two, he wouldn't see me at work for a week. I was not to worry as Eddie would cover for me at work. I hoped very much to succeed with my plan.

For the next three days, whilst at the planting, I kept complaining of headaches to avoid any suspicion later on. My planting partner was very concerned for me. She was even accusing me of having a secret girlfriend. She was right in a way, but it was the photograph of the girl we had been sent that made me become less fond of her and more determined than ever to fail my medical.

I started my starvation diet on the Wednesday. On Friday morning of the following week I was due for my examination. My diet involved chain-smoking. I must have smoked a hundred cigarettes a day and I chewed and swallowed the butts whenever I was on my own. They had a revolting taste. I barely ate any food and I was drinking gallons of vinegar diluted with water so that there would be no traces on my tongue. At night, Eddie came to see me and to make up for my starvation diet we went to Clemens's for a few beers and vodkas.

Each day Eddie arrived at nine o'clock and his first question would be, 'How are things progressing, Dominik?'

'Fine, Eddie. Everything is going according to plan.'

'Boys, you will poison yourselves. I can't see you going on like that and lasting until Friday,' my mother intervened, distressed.

Sophie was behind us though as she said, 'Don't worry Mam, everything will be all right.' Eddie didn't tell me what he had chosen to do to fail his medical. He appeared healthy enough, though, if he was on a special diet.

It was my third day now on that detestable diet. We went to see Clemens who was very pleased to see us. The first thing he said was, 'When is Maria coming to see you?'

'Sometime this week, I will let you know.'

As Clemens went for our order, Eddie whispered, 'Make him happy and tell him Maria was asking for him.' Of course, I couldn't do that. It was very much the other way round. I wished it was true, as the whole family liked him very much.

When we left to go home, I was startled by what happened to me. My legs had turned to jelly and I couldn't walk. I realized it was my new diet. We were in tears with laughter. 'You must have a different pair of legs tonight, Dominik,' said Eddie.

'I think Clemens tried to immobilize me, Eddie, with whatever he put in my drinks.'

Then with Clemens's and Eddie's help, I managed to struggle home. I was surprised Eddie had not been affected the same way, assuming that he was on some sort of starvation diet as he had proposed. For the last three days I stayed at home.

In the afternoons, I would now go down to the river about 80 yards away, undress and lie down in the water with my head resting on a little mound of grass. I would stay there for three or four hours. On the day before my medical, as I made my way up to the house, I collapsed a few yards from the door. Eventually, with Sophie's help, I got into the house. My mother just looked at me not saying anything, but within myself I was sure my plan would succeed. I ate a small piece of bread and I could almost feel my tummy singing praises with satisfaction.

In the evening, just in case I couldn't complete the cycle journey to the town the next day Sophie and I went home to Dad's place, as this meant less cycling in the morning. I could see that Dad was very much in favour of my effort. Even Mam gave me some tips before I left her. If the doctor should ask during my examination for any illness in the family I was to say that my father had had heart trouble and tuberculosis. Also Bruno was not fit to work. That was something I was grateful to her for.

The dreaded day came. Eddie came to our house about two hours before we were due to leave. That morning, I had a normal breakfast. We arrived at our destination and the atmosphere inside was one of ghostly silence. All undressed in the corridor and we were called in in alphabetical order.

As Eddie's name started with 'K' and mine with 'S', we arranged to meet in a café later on. At long last, my name was called out. As I walked in with another two boys, I saw a long table behind which sat high-ranking officials who watched and listened. Then there were a few clerks who were writing down comments made by the doctors. I was pleased with the doctor I had. He was an older person in his late fifties and quietly spoken. I was asked to stretch my arms sideways. I could feel sweat running down from my armpits to my feet. Next, I had to stretch my arms forward, then bend up and down. By the third time, on trying to get up, my hands began shaking and my knees wobbled. I just managed to get up. The doctor observed me, then quietly said, in sympathy for me, 'Enough, enough.'

I thought my heart would burst with glee as I said to myself, 'I got you, I got you, you monsters.' Then with the stethoscope, he listened to my heart beat. I had to breathe in and out and I could hear my lungs making a noise like an old smiddy bellows. Questions and answers followed.

'Do you smoke a lot?'

'About ten a day.'

'Any illnesses at home - your parents?'

'My father has heart trouble and TB, and my older brother has been s semi-invalid from childhood.'

'What's wrong with him?'

'It is his heart and nerves and he has a speech defect.'

The doctor turned to his superiors at the table and said, 'Such a developed body and yet healthwise completely ruined.' Then to the clerk he made a few remarks and at the end I could hear him saying, 'Fit for light work only.' Then the three of us in the room were told we could get dressed and go home. As I went into the corridor, I hopped like a kangaroo for the joy I felt. Those watching me must have been thinking I was away with the fairies. As I dressed, I said to myself, 'You have made it, you have made it.'

I hurried up in order to reach the café as arranged with Eddie. I ordered a few pieces of cake and a coffee and how sumptuous the food was after my starvation diet. As I sat waiting for Eddie, a young and attractive girl walked in. As she sat down our eyes met and exchanging smiles, I realized who it was so I went over to speak.

'Hello, Halla, how nice to see you. What are you doing here?'

'Don't worry, Dominik, I wasn't looking for you.'

'What a pity.'

'You don't expect me to believe that, do you?'

'Yes, I am very pleased to see you, especially today.'

'What's so special about today?'

'I have just had my medical for the army.'

'Poor you.'

'Oh, I didn't pass. It is my poor health.'

'Not again, how did you manage that? Sorry, I shouldn't ask.'

'Just poor health, just poor health. Sometimes, it can be a great advantage for survival.'

'I believe you, Dominik.'

'How is Bronek? Is he still with my old boss, Mr Vibe?'

'Yes, he seems to be very pleased with the place but all the boys on the farms around Stutthof got the call for a medical. They will all be taken away into the army. By the way, Mr Vibe got drowned in the canal. One night, after a drinking spree, he decided to take a short cut not knowing the icebreaker had been through the canal and with a hard frost and sprinkles of fresh snow he just disappeared. Poor man, he was a good soul. You know, Dominik, when you ran away after your transfer, we didn't think you would succeed. Bronek told me that Mr Vibe went a few times to Stutthof concentration camp and made enquiries thinking that you would end up there.'

Eddie then arrived at the café so I introduced each to the other explaining Halla was the beauty I had met whilst working on the farm at Stutthof.

'Pleased to meet you. I can't believe you would go with a boy like him,' said Eddie.

'You are right, sometimes I wondered myself,' admitted Halla.

'We were good company for each other. You know you even stopped all the crying in the fields,' I said. 'It must have been all the chocolates I was saving for you.'

'That's what it was, Dominik. I have to admit we were good friends,' said Halla smiling. 'Oh! I almost forgot to tell you, Dominik, I got married. He is a baker. That's the reason I am here, to look for a job for him.' I congratulated her, and hoped she would be successful with her enquiries and that we would meet again. We parted on good terms after chatting further.

We set off for home in a happy mood knowing we had nothing to fear about joining our persecutors. I felt sympathy for the rest of them who were fit enough, but there was nothing to be done. If we were found out, nothing would save us from the bullet. With problems like that, it was everyone for himself.

Arriving at Dad's home, before I had a chance to say anything, Maria put her thumbs up to indicate a 'Yes'. Her face was all smiles when I said we'd made it. Dad came with beer for each of us. Even Bruno joined us. Dad related how Mam had got him out of the German army in the First World War with the tablets she had sent him. Like father, like son! Only I did it the hard way. What a lighthearted atmosphere. It was as if the war had ended for us anyway.

A few hours later, we took off to tell my mother and Sophie the good news. Cycling home, I couldn't believe the energy I had.

Again at home, we went through the whole performance - me standing in front of the doctor, the doctor's comments after his examination.

'I never believed you would succeed, Son. Hopefully, we will manage to stay together now. If only Gertrude would stop starving herself. If she doesn't she won't last much longer,' was my mother's worried comment.

We were preparing now for Mam's visit to Victor. I went on a buying spree round the German farms to get some butter for Mother to take with her. We sent a letter to the family telling them of the day Mother would arrive so the girl could meet her. We were rather concerned for Mother, wondering how she was going to manage the heavy cases loaded with meat, butter and pork-dripping. She reassured us that that was the least of her troubles. As for the German police control at the station, it was quite safe and because of my signing as a volunteer she was able to obtain a Third Class German passport. It meant her luggage would not be checked.

At the station there were two exits - one for Germans and one for Poles. The Poles were thoroughly searched but nobody took any notice of how many cases the German-passport holders carried. Poor Mam, she was so excited about her visit. It was to be her first meeting with Victor in nearly three years.

I was back to work planting. The only thing that changed during Mam's absence was the extra parties we held. In a way, it was an excuse to celebrate my medical success, only it happened almost every evening and also the news we were getting regarding the Russian front continued to be in our favour. Even Uncle Frank would visit us more often from his hiding place. He told me about his sister living in Stadthagen, Germany. She had now lost her third and last son, aged 19 years, in Russia. I could see he felt sorry for her now despite the comment she had made on her visit to his house about making room.

I felt the need to speak and said, 'Uncle Frank, I can understand how you feel as it must be heart-breaking for her, but then they died for something they strongly believed in. She wasn't moved at all when told about the killings of innocent people in the concentration camps. You know yourself when Hitler or Goebels speak at any mass gatherings and ask, "What do you want, cannons or butter?" you hear one loud scream from the German race of "Cannons". Well that's what they are getting now. That's what they asked for.' Uncle Frank responded, 'I suppose, Dominik, looking at it that way, there is no way out.'

'No, there is not, Uncle. Look at the way they are treating the Russians in the camp near our town. You see them standing there. They don't deserve such inhuman treatment. It is so tempting to give them something to eat but you would be doomed if you got caught. I wonder what is going on next door. They had had a few visits from the gestapo. There is a young man who calls now and again but if he doesn't stop his visits, they will catch him. It is not often you see the gestapo in this village. It must be something serious.'

We drank quite a few vodkas and beers. Sophie made us a nice meal and, as usual, we made a small parcel with meat for Uncle Frank when he left.

'I am glad about your medical, Dominik. You know you are a big help to us. Look after yourself,' were his parting words.

'You too and best regards to Aunt Maria. Make sure you come again next week,' I said.

'Thank you, Dominik, I really look forward to my visits here.'

We did feel sorry for him, for only being in that silly organization he had had to lose his farm and go into hiding, but we thought that the gestapo were too busy now searching for partisans to be bothered with him.

Shortly after Uncle Frank left, Eddie arrived and, being Saturday, we went off to see Clemens. Sophie joined us to celebrate our medical success. Because of Sophie's visit, Elli joined us, too. Later that night, Maria arrived and what a party we had. Clemens's parents joined us once they closed their shop – I think to show their approval of their son trying to court Maria. I only wished Maria had been a bit more interested in Clemens, not that she would show it. It must have been his shiny, bald head and red, podgy cheeks.

We mentioned our medicals for the first time. The outcome they already knew, I guessed, because of the jubilant mood we were in. Then about 1 a.m., seeing Mam was away, we continued the party at our house only to break it up and get ready for church.

Every Sunday afternoon, we spent half an hour with Lucy at the convent, just beside the church. When told about my success, Lucy commented, 'I knew you would succeed. We all prayed for you in the convent.' She was so like Mam, believing my success was only because of their prayers. Still, I almost believed it myself.

'It is time you prayed a bit more yourself,' Lucy criticized. I defended myself by saying, 'Well, I was praying today in thanksgiving. By the way, I am in church each Sunday.'

'Yes, but stop visiting the girl who lives beside the convent. I know all about her. She is a bad lot and, if you won't, I will tell Mam. Promise you won't see her anymore,' pleaded Lucy. She was referring to a girl I had met only once on a previous visit so it was not difficult for me to promise Lucy that I wouldn't visit her anymore. Sophie and Maria started laughing.

I did not mind about having to make the promise to Lucy as my interest was now the girl in the photograph who was to meet Mother at the station. We took the train home and Maria carried on to my father's house. We ate a tasty dinner before Eddie called and we went for a long walk along the river.

It was a wonderful feeling to know, at least for a while longer, I was safe. You could forget at times that a war was in progress but there was always something to remind us that more was to come. The Germans were desperate for cannon-fodder, and now they turned to us. Most of the boys that were with me for their medical had already received their call-up papers for the army. Most were surprised that after only two weeks from the medical they had to go. Many people wondered why I was still at home. Our only comfort came from the underground radio.

The news from Polish Radio London was telling us they knew we were being forced into the German army and, whenever the occasion arose, we should cross over and join the Polish army. It was the only hope there was after joining up but success wasn't always easy to find. It depended so much on the unit one was assigned to. So far, I was still at home and we could only play the waiting game.

We were expecting Mother to return any day now and were anxious to hear her news. One day Sophie came to my work place asking me to come home straight away but she would not say why. As I opened the door, Mam was waiting there, smiling happily as she said, 'You had better go through and have something to eat.' My dinner was already on the table along with a big bunch of flowers. Then I noticed a head hiding behind the flowers. As the person got up, I couldn't believe it: it was the girl in the photograph. We were introduced and I must have been blushing like a red pepper as I tried to control my emotions.

We began eating but when I stopped, Sophie, sitting beside our visitor, asked me why I wasn't eating.

'I'm not hungry. I just want to have a good look at you.' I replied watching Irena.

'But you can't, Dominik,' commented Sophie. 'I'll move the flowers aside.' That made things even worse. I was completely lost and confused. Later I went to the kitchen and took a stiff vodka to help me regain my composure - it worked.

Mother began to tell us about her visit and praised Irena and her parents hiding Victor from the gestapo. Through Irena, my brother kept in contact with his Franciscan brothers and with people who, after the invasion of Poland, had taken German nationality to protect their business and property. They were helping people like Victor and some of the underground organizations.

The gestapo were so anxious to trace Victor because of his sermon in the early 1940s when he spoke out against the German regime and of how they had started killing our priests and demolishing our churches. Even then, before the gestapo came to the monastery looking for him, he was warned by one of them to run and hide.

While my mother was visiting Victor, she was very distressed at what was happening to the poor Jews. They had to wear a star on their backs and were not allowed to walk on the pavements. She brought some photographs of people, including Jews, who had been hanged in a town square. They were left hanging there all day as a warning to others. It took my mother some time to get over what she had seen and experienced. In our area, the gestapo, with the help of our ethnic minority, had cleared every town and village of all Jews and old Polish intelligentsia.

I was very pleased that I could see mother's approval of Irena and my fondness for each other. That made me immediately happy. It was the end of my late nights again except when I was on my errands searching for butter or some other food. We were very much aware of how we were being chaperoned by Mam. It was still the old custom that when a daughter went to a dance, the mother went with her to make sure she kept the right company. If the boy danced with a girl who was not chaperoned, she was considered a bad lot, and the boy was, too, and it would be talked about by many in the village.

For some reason, during the German occupation, that custom was fast disappearing. The only time we had by ourselves was going to Clemens's place for some groceries. How I wished the road was longer. Sometimes I would even hide matches in the house so as to have an excuse to go back again to the shop. Irena asked me what I'd be hiding next.

'Anything and everything to be with you Darling,' I replied. Our excuses were so obvious that some days even Mam would say, 'Is there anything we need?' I was ecstatic when Mother told me that in two months' time I would be going with some supplies to visit Victor.

The dreaded day came for Irena to return home. Unfortunately, we weren't able to give her any meat parcels to take with her as it was forbidden for Poles to have meat. As she had to go through a checkpoint at the station where she would be searched, the risk of being caught was too high. It wasn't worth the consequences.

When I arrived home from work one day Uncle Frank was there. Sophie handed me a letter and I noticed from the looks they were giving me that something was wrong. On enquiring where Mother was I was told she had been called out to deliver a child.

My heart sank when I opened the letter and saw that it was a call-up paper for the army – and I had thought I was safe with my category – but I still had one trump card to play. I confided to my uncle that I was not going.

'You know what is going to happen to your family should you disappear,' he said.

'I know, and I won't do that. Just listen carefully. The day we had to sign as a volunteer, I was told to send a photograph to an address I still have. They would then issue me with Class III German citizenship. Well, I didn't send a photograph off so I am still a Pole. We can make up a letter to say that I am still treated as a Pole but as soon as I receive my German nationality, I would be willing to join.'

'What if they check up on you?' asked my uncle.

'You will write another letter to where I was to send the photograph telling them I was called up for the German army but refused to go, and that I am still waiting for my German nationality papers.'

'Have you got a photograph?' asked my uncle.

'No, we are not going to send one; just play ignorant. Once they write back asking for it, then we will send one.'

Uncle Frank smiled as he said, 'I am amazed but I think it will work.' It was a blessing Mam was not there: it would have been hard to persuade her to let me have my way. Uncle Frank wrote the first letter and another one was posted three days later asking about the passport. I figured that by the time they replied explaining the reason and asking for a photograph, then my sending one, and finally them forwarding the hated passport, my date for the army would be well gone.

We promised not to say a word to my mother as that would have been too much for her. We wished each other good luck after I thanked him for his invaluable help and I promised I would keep in touch with him about any post I got.

Next day, I went to work as usual but I was particularly nervous. As we worked close to the road, I was alert for any cars stopping in case they were looking for me. They were fearful weeks during which I dwelt on my visit to Irena and Victor, while not knowing if and when anything would happen and feeling the blasted Germans forever on my back.

My mother could not understand the change in my personality lately. It was partly because of Irena but the main reason now was for my safety. Running away from a farm was dealt with by the local police and SS whom we knew but now I was dealing with the army personnel. Often at night I would go to Clemens's place just to sit in the corner in the lounge bar alone until Eddie arrived. As it was open throughout the week,

Clemens's 12-year-old sister, Frances, would sometimes keep me company. At that time there was no school and she always asked to hear ghost stories. I gave Eddie all my news. He thought I had a very good chance of getting away with my scheming.

I was quite curious to know why Eddie had not received call-up papers. When I asked him about it he replied, 'Because I had been in the Polish army and should not have even been asked to attend a medical. Next time you're in my house I'll show you the letter they sent me explaining they had made a mistake and that I would not be called up.'

After the shop closed, Elli and Clemens would join us, mainly to discuss news about events at the Russian front. When we were on our own, Eddie told me about the German transport on its way to Russia being derailed due to the work of our group. It was encouraging news. Not only our unit but also other units were becoming more active. The better the news, the braver the underground army became. Of course, we had losses as well. To date, our unit hadn't suffered much.

Then arriving home one evening I learnt that the gestapo had arrested a young man who had been secretly visiting our neighbour. I was terrified, thinking he might belong to the same unit as myself. I took off to see Eddie as soon as the coast was clear but he told me there was nothing to worry about and that the man did not belong to our unit. After a few days of torture he had died. He did tell them though about one underground bank but when the gestapo checked it had been vacated. A note had been left for them saying they had to leave because of a damp problem!

Two weeks passed slowly and I still hadn't heard anything about my refusal to join the army. Finally, I received a letter explaining the reason for not getting my Class III passport and was asked to send a photograph. My mother liked the tone of the letter. If she had only known about the letters Uncle Frank had written for me earlier. I waited for a few weeks before I called at the office in our town armed with a photograph. Eddie came with me for moral support. On telling Eddie, 'I am a proper German now,' he consoled me saying, 'Don't worry, Dominik, it is not the end of the world. It is what you are in your heart that counts, not on the paper.'

He tried to persuade me to go to a fortune teller who was supposed to be very accurate, and eventually he succeeded and off I went. She was rather sinister-looking. When I met up with Eddie later, I accused him of telling her everything about me but he swore he had not said a word. She had been so accurate about most things; for example, that I was sending parcels to someone and later would go to the same place. Yes, I was getting ready to visit Victor who was in hiding and we were sending parcels. But more important, she told me that I did not have to worry about being taken into the German army before June 1943. She asked me to come back after that date. How wonderful it would be if she proved to be correct.

I was now preparing for my visit, which I was looking forward to so much - not only to see Victor but also Irena, who was so much in my thoughts. Because of all the food I was taking, Sophie was coming with me. To be on the safe side, Sophie took Class III identity so we could both go through the German exit at the station and avoid any control. At long last we were off.

CHAPTER 13

After travelling all night we arrived at Katowice in southern Poland. I could not take in the number of people begging for food, from young girls offering themselves in return for very little food, to old grannies.

After hearing from Mother about the people at the station, we had taken with us small half to three-quarter pound pieces of dripping to hand out to the elderly. Tearfully, they thanked us. We had to tell them to go quickly as we could have been in trouble if the Germans noticed what we were doing.

Once again, we boarded a train and after another two hours' journey arrived at our destination – Dombrova Gornicza. Here, again, we went through the exit for Germans and this time I was even dressed like one. I had long boots, breeches and a Tyrolean hat. The exit for Poles was heartbreaking to see. How thoroughly they were searched: every little item was taken away from them unless they could prove the goods had been bought with their ration cards.

Irena and her brother, Jan, were at the station to meet us. What excitement all round. When we left the station and were on the street, it was painful to see such solemn-faced people, especially the poor Jews who were walking a good distance away from the pavement, almost in the middle of the road. What an existence, and what was still awaiting them? I realized how differently one reacts on hearing such stories, when it's taken lightly, to actually seeing these people with almost no facial expression moving slowly along the road. I thought, 'They must be alive if they are moving.' I understood why Mam would not talk much about it.

At long last we reached their house, where a joyful reunion took place. We tried not to show our surprise on seeing Victor as Mother had warned us that he had put on so much weight. His whole body was swollen because of lack of exercise and fresh air. What was more important at the moment was that we were together again. We celebrated with a glass of Hungarian red wine.

When we unpacked later they were surprised at what we had brought with us. Victor said laughingly that the supplies we had taken would do until after the end of the war.

'Well, my dear brother, there must be some rewards for me having German nationality,' I said, and we all acknowledged that with another glass of wine. After exchanging news, we all went in to Victor's room. It was rather small, containing his bed, a small couch and table and his pet miniature poodle. We talked into the late afternoon.

Later on, we joined Irena's parents, Mr and Mrs Jesionek, for a cup of coffee. They were very amused by my experiences of how I had managed so far to avoid the German army and about my black-market butchering. Then Victor showed me how he managed to cheat the gestapo when they searched for him in his small room.

To me, it was a puzzle as I just could not see where one could hide in such a tiny room. He took the bedcover off. The mattress which was about three inches thick was one big padded lid, Victor slipped into the box and Mrs Jesionek lay down on top pretending she was ill. The whole procedure took under one minute but my brother said he just couldn't have done without their help. Mrs Jesionek was very composed when the gestapo came, she lying in bed and Victor below her in the box.

While I was there, they were considering taking the Class III German nationality, hoping that that would make them less suspicious. They were aware of the consequences should anything go wrong - the punishment would be execution by hanging for hiding a fugitive.

When we went with Irena to do shopping in the town, I realized again how lucky we were to be living in the country area. Here we would have to wait for hours in a queue for bread and meat. Often when your turn came there would be no meat left. Yes, you could buy anything from our German farmers who believed so much in Hitler's victory, and they knew they could charge almost double. On the other hand, any Polish family keeping any animals at all just gave up or brought to the gathering point what was required and kept the rest for themselves. They were keeping to the rules. In 1943 to 1944 particularly, the Polish farmers were eating more meat than before the war, as they didn't want the German marks, or only enough to buy sugar and salt.

I wished Victor was able to get out at night for exercise. He had a friend, a Jewish doctor, who was also in hiding and at times he would make special arrangements to visit him to help with the medicine. It was always at night and although it was risky to go out, as they lived on the edge of town near woodlands, this made it easier to go the short distance to where the doctor was in hiding. He didn't look at all like a Jew as he was tall and blond. Victor introduced me to him with a comment, 'That's my brother who supplies us with all the goodies,' and he smiled and said, 'Yes, that's a big advantage to me - as well as the fact that the good Lord gave me blond hair. I don't look as suspicious as the rest. I hope you will manage to keep supplying us with food as we haven't got any ration cards here. As for money, we manage somehow.'

I promised them, especially the doctor, that as long as I was safe and at home, the supplies would continue. How well they managed with the contacts they had. They had plenty of money, gold, spirits, cigarettes and cigars, and this was often traded for food which was very much harder to get because it was an industrial area.

I had looked forward so much to my visit and seeing Victor and Irena who had changed my life completely. Being here had a big effect on me. I didn't care much if I went out or not. I was so conscious of what was happening around me, especially to the Jews who had to walk in the middle of the road. This did not happen in our own town. Of course, the Germans had made a clean sweep of the town at the very beginning of the invasion and all Jews had been executed in the Valley of Death.

Victor asked us to visit someone in the Franciscan monastery in Panewnik to which he belonged. He always kept in touch with them. What a wonderful place. As we entered the magnificent cathedral we could hear singing, so magical was the quiet harmonization. This was a different world with no bother from the Germans. What a pity my brother had spoken out against them in his sermon, otherwise he too could have been here. They were almost self-supporting.

There was a huge area of straight beech trees, 60 to 70 feet in height. The ordained monks lived in small villa-like bungalows. Since the war began they were no longer allowed to go on missions and preach sermons. Most of their time was spent in prayer and pastimes doing anything that would make extra income for them.

On our way out, I whispered to Irena, 'You know, I could join them myself.'

'You can turn back,' said Irena.

'Well, Darling, I thought somebody has to look after you and I'll be the happiest person if you will let me.'

'You know I would like that.'

At long last, we had a chance to be out alone. It was almost unbearable how my mother had chaperoned us, in spite of her approval. That was why Mam had sent Sophie with me. Victor laughed when I told him about our trips to the shop and the excuses I had made just to be with Irena. We must have been the happiest couple on earth, especially because we knew that our parents approved of our courtship.

We arrived back in time for tea in Victor's little room. My poor brother found life hard, not being able to get out except at night when he could open his balcony window to get some fresh air. He loved to play the violin with Irena playing piano but that had to stop because of the people living below who started asking questions. He had a special instrument that he placed on the strings to deafen the sound, but in the end it was safer to give up playing altogether.

Before the war, he gave violin lessons to students. For his birthday at the end of term, he was always presented with a violin, which he would send to me. In the end, we had five violins at home. We could have started a string orchestra.

In the evenings, Victor and I spent a lot of time playing chess. Then on the third and last week, we had a surprise when Victor asked us if we would like to go to a holiday resort. It was almost as if he was trying to make up to us for his miserable life. Of course, we were jubilant. We decided to go to the Beskidy Mountains southeast from Katowice on the Czechoslovakian border. We travelled to a very small station named Zwardon. First, we had to book into a hotel. Unfortunately for us, every hotel was packed with skiers but Sophie and Irena were as determined as I to find a place to stay.

After a little snack in the hotel we tried the 'Highlanders' but had no success at all. The only thing for us was to find out the time of the last train home. We noticed an old sign 'DO NOT TRESPASS - CZECHOSLOVAKIAN BORDER'. We decided to cross it - at least we could say that we had been abroad!

Back in the train we felt rather disappointed but as a consolation we were sitting together and the lights were out.

'I'll leave the two of you alone. You can do a little smooching,' said Sophie, thoughtfully. It was the longest time yet we had spent together with no one else around.

Back again at Irena's house, Victor tried to console us by saying that we had so much time in front of us. In spite of our disappointments that day we had had a lovely time together. The last few days were spent making plans for our next visit and what Sophie and I were to take back home with us.

Victor was getting a large amount of money from his friends who had taken German nationality and from the Jews who were in hiding with Polish families, in exchange for food. We couldn't use it all as there was so little to buy and it was worthless lying in the bank. He started buying gold bars and valuable jewellery which we planned to take home after each visit. It was like building a new nest for after the war. Of course, I was pleased the way things were going, not only for Victor but also the help given to us. In turn, we could help others, especially through my mother. With some of the poorer families, when she was asked to deliver a child, instead of charging a fee she would help them with money and food. At the same time, I could not help thinking about the poor people there, the working classes, the Jews who were made to walk on the road. But then it was always the same throughout the country during war time or peace time - the same people would always suffer in various ways. Yet over and over again, one hears, 'Blessed are the poor and oppressed for they shall inherit the Kingdom of Heaven'. I was sure that the majority would do anything for more comfort with their families here on this earth and take pot luck in the Kingdom of Heaven.

Before we left Dombrova Gornicza it was agreed that Irena and her brother would make a return visit to us in the near future. Seeing Irena again was something to look forward to.

We were persuaded to go to the cinema which was about a hundred yards from the house. Off we went to see a nature film, my favourite, about Africa. We were in a great hurry to get to the cinema in order to have a few hours alone. The introduction to the film showed a group of topless African women dancing in fine rhythm, causing their breasts to swing freely. Poor Irena was so embarrassed by what she saw that she wanted to leave. I followed her out and we spent the spare two hours just walking around and gazing into shop windows. I knew she felt herself degraded by my watching them with keen interest.

Back home, Victor gave me a beautiful ring to give to Irena at our departure at the station. He had managed to obtain the ring from a Jewish friend also in hiding. As Irena knew this friend was a jewellery dealer, he had wanted to keep his visit to deliver the ring a secret which was why we had been persuaded to go to the cinema. It was in appreciation for all the times she had taken risks acting as courier between my brother and his numerous friends in hiding. As her boyfriend, Victor thought I should be the one to give it to her. He knew what a pleasure it would be for me to do this. Despite his own difficulties he had unselfishly wanted to please us both in some way and he had succeeded. In my excitement the morning couldn't come quick enough. I promised Victor that as long as I was at home they need not worry about food supplies.

The parting was rather sad for us all at the station next morning. I took Irena's hand and placed the little box containing the ring into it. Sophie and I watched her. She was so happy she hugged me and Sophie and tearfully we tried to comfort each other that shortly we would be together again. We said our farewells before the train took Sophie and I off into the distance.

It was late at night when we arrived at our station. There was an unusually large number of soldiers standing very much on their own. They must have been wondering at the unwelcome looks they were getting from civilians. It turned out they were volunteers from Spain. You poor lot, I thought, if you only knew what lay ahead of you ... but then if your fanaticism for Hitler is that strong, you deserve it. The Russians showed no mercy for prisoners, especially volunteers. There was more cruelty at the Russian front than in any other country conquered by Germany. To the Germans, the Russians were subhuman and they were treating each other's prisoners as such.

We were home once more. As the days passed we often talked about Victor and how lucky he was to have that family, not only because they had moved house because of him but because they were risking their own lives as well. As for me, I was back to work in the forestry. On days off, I would visit my father or remain at home. I became such a loner that even Eddie and Clemens were rather baffled by the change in me. My only trips were to buy food from the farmers or accompany Eddie at weekends when we visited some of the group leaders of our underground organization.

A friend who belonged to our organization and who lived deep in the woodlands had a small still where we often made whisky to give to the people who were already hiding underground, just to break their monotony. As for myself, I often told Eddie I would be happier disappearing underground if I could be sure that my parents would be left alone by the Germans.

Periodically, someone would be arrested and accused of spying for the Russians. It was a miracle how we had managed to exist so far without detection. Eddie kept reassuring me there was nothing to worry about. Then one of our men, who had also been forced to join as a volunteer into the German army but who had also joined the partisans on the same day as me, was picked up by the gestapo at the station on his return to his unit after his holidays. At times like this, it was hell for two or three months, always wondering if your turn was next. That boy was taken to Danzig for execution.

Towards the end of 1942, we were told to attend a meeting. We were asked to hand in any old woollen articles at a certain collection point. Of course, we had to give something in order not to be blacklisted. All wool was to be used for clothing soldiers on the Russian front. The ethnic minority were now trying hard to become friendly with us once again. One day, while on a cycle ride with Eddie, we met Alfons who had called to see me on my arrival home from Nuremberg Prison, proclaiming his total allegiance to Hitler. As we drew nearer to him, in unison we called

'Heil, Hitler Alfons.'

'Shit Heil, Hitler,' Alfons answered back trying to force a smile.

'Alfons, I could report you to the police for that comment, and you of all people in SS uniform. You know you could be shot for it. It would be rather difficult to explain yourself, especially speaking in Polish which you yourself forbade me to do in front of my father.'

He was unprepared for my reactions and we just left him standing there.

'The brute! After all he did to our people. It wouldn't surprise me if he was now prepared to join our underground if he was asked. He will be sorry to leave his big farm once the time comes for him to flee,' was my reaction.

They were much better informed of the events at the Russian front, as they had radios. The little news we received sometimes came via the underground. The German summer offensive on Caucasus had failed and Stalingrad was Hitler's next major worry. He was even sacking some of his generals.

Near the end of November, news was coming in that about a quarter of a million German soldiers were surrounded. There was an air of jubilation throughout the village as we contemplated the good news.

Irena and her brother, Jan, came for a two-week visit. First thing Eddie said was not to take too many days off work and I promised him I wouldn't. If I did, I'd do it the legal way. My intentions were not to miss too many days but I needed to find an excuse while Irena was visiting. I took her brother, who was 15 years old, into my confidence and he agreed to help me. I went to the stick shed to cut some kindles, taking a carving knife with me. Just as we planned I opened my right hand, put the point of the knife inside just above the second finger and pressed the point hard in, then turned my head away. I then instructed Jan to hit the knife with the stick. I had a gash an inch and a half long. To this day, I still have the scar.

Bleeding, I ran into the house where Mam put a bandage on before I cycled to the doctor. My hand was freshly bandaged and I was given ointment and told to take a week off work, just as we had planned. To make sure it didn't heal too quickly, once home I took the bandage off secretly out of my mother's view. I put on paraffin, any rubbish, salt, dirt, just to slow the healing process.

The second evening, Irena, Sophie and I went to Clemens's for a beer. As soon as we were out of the house, Irena gave me a big hug and a kiss to thank me for arranging time off work and as Sophie didn't know what we were talking about, we had to tell her about the plot. She was amused but we agreed not to say anything to Mother.

When Eddie arrived and saw my hand, he burst out laughing knowing I'd been up to something. I gave Eddie the line from the doctor and said, 'One week off, by the way. There will be another line next week.' He correctly assumed Irena was staying for two weeks. We had a good laugh that night over the affair. It was marvellous being with Irena again, often going for long walks or visiting my father. Poor Gertrude was still in bed trying to delay her recovery to avoid work. She asked me about the boots I'd promised my sisters.

'Everything's in hand, Gertrude. Next week, they will be ready. More to the point, when are you going to wear them?' I asked. Sophie and Maria were pleasantly surprised about the boots and I was pleased to tell them, 'Yes, it was supposed to be a present for Christmas. Mam knows about it, only the last payment had to be in meat. That was the agreement. I would like you, Maria, to come with me that day. As usual, I will carry an accordion and you a violin case.' It was always the same, if anyone wanted good quality material or the boots for the young ladies which were so much in fashion - first of all one had to pay double the price and part of it was paid in eggs, butter and meat and the other half with money.

My sisters couldn't believe their luck in getting their boots at long last. On that long-awaited day, we packed into the accordion case fifteen pounds of meat and ten pounds into the violin case for Maria to carry. When we descended from the train I nearly had heart failure. Beside the ticket controller were two railway policemen with an alsatian dog. There was no other way out. We couldn't get to any other exit. I thought perhaps the good looks of Maria and Irena would distract the attention of the policeman.

I whispered to Maria to go first followed by Irena and I would follow last. Maria handed over her ticket, the Irena. Before I had my ticket out, one of them said to Maria, 'Why don't you give us a tune to cheer us up?' I hastily promised them a tune next time as we were in a hurry. There was no reaction at all from the dog. Most likely the dog didn't know what meat was as it was in such short supply.

Outside the station, before getting into a taxi, we looked at each other with wide grins. It was the first time that we had encountered railway police with alsatian dogs. Usually it was town police with whom we were acquainted. Coming back with three pairs of boots would be just as serious a crime. We decided to walk the six kilometres home.

There was great excitement at home, especially for Dad who had more fun watching my sisters. Even Gertrude forced herself up out of bed to try her pair on. We all wondered if she would ever wear them. I told Dad about our experience at the station. We all agreed there would be no more travelling with accordion and violin by train.

We walked to the village station to catch the next train home to Mother. There stood a goods train filled with soldiers. The sliding doors were open. The floor was covered with straw and you could see, looking at the majority of them, that their morale was low. I nearly felt sorry for them. They must have been aware of the situation on the Eastern Front, in spite of Goebels's propaganda. I thought, 'If you only knew that once you arrive on the Eastern Front, most likely your next trip will be the Siberian coal mines.' Even the Cossacks who took over the farms from our own people sometimes remarked to Dad that they hadn't wanted to come here but were forced to and that they had had much better land at home.

The Cossacks were really in a bad position the way they looked to the Germans for support, every able man fighting for them at the front. It was only because Hitler promised them a Ukraine free from Russian and Polish domination after the war. Even the Germans, when speaking about the Cossacks, did not have much time for them. They almost disliked them as much as the Poles did. A Cossack on the Russian front was shown no mercy. They were really in a bad way. They didn't know where to turn to at times. The poor Cossacks were aware that one day they would have no place to go.

When we arrived home that afternoon, I prepared for my doctor's visit. The bandage was removed while I washed all the dirt out in soapy water, put on the ointment and rebandaged ready for the next day's appointment. Next morning, I boarded the train with Irena in the hope of getting another week off. We were together again and how happy we were just to hold hands. There was never any need to be intimate. I never believed pure love could be such bliss, so wonderful. We were just like two kids with a big lollipop and holding on to it hoping it would last forever.

Yes, I did get one more week off. We went to church for a few minutes – or should I say I had to – to give thanks for the week I got off. Next we visited the nuns in the convent where Lucy was to give them a meat parcel. They depended so much on us. It pleased me to see that the nuns were so fond of my girlfriend.

On our trip back, Irena asked me if I believed in what the fortune teller told me. I was very much aware that up to June 1943 I was supposed to be OK. I never forgot it.

After Irena returned home I hardly missed a day from work. It was now approaching Christmas and it was a happy one for us all as the news we were getting from the Russian front was still to our benefit. Early on Christmas morning, still in bed, we were listening to somebody singing 'Silent Night' outside in the garden. I looked through the window and there to my surprise was my friend, Lesner, who I visited late at night with sandwiches and coffee, standing knee-deep in snow singing and watching the window to see if I could hear him. What a wonderful present! Mam, Sophie and I got up, took Lesner into the kitchen and had breakfast together. Mother had two pairs of socks for him. Later, the three of us set off by train to be with Dad.

We didn't bother much with presents. Our best gift was the good news coming from the Russian front and the fact that we were all still alive, even though Jan was in a labour camp in Magdeburg, near Berlin. At least he was receiving all our parcels.

Spring again, 1943. We were back to planting trees. I left the female partner I used to work with. Even Eddie was getting on to me about the way I behaved when in the company of girls.

'Dominik, you are becoming a recluse and turning into a real woman hater. What's wrong with you?' he asked.

'Not altogether, Eddie, I will still keep you company depending on where we intend going. I hope you won't spill the beans to Sophie about me.'

'Don't be silly, that's your life.'

I knew I was not very attentive and showed a lack of interest in girls but Irena was so much on my mind.

Eddie and I had a lot of outings, always visiting someone in our underground movement who, like me, was for the moment not in any danger and had no need to hide. We spent many pleasant evenings just chatting, sometimes about what we were going to do when the Russians started fighting on our soil.

In April 1943, I went back to visit Victor and Irena. My poor brother looked worse than when I first saw him; much more bloated. I felt really sorry for him but he was in good spirits knowing the occupation was nearing an end. One evening Irena came to our room and blushing she gave me a ring with our initials engraved on it. It was a 30-gram gold signet ring. I just stood there until Victor prompted me to give her a squeeze. I valued that embrace more than the ring. I knew it was Victor who had bought it for her to give to me.

After two blissful weeks, I was back home again. Only then did it dawn on me that I hadn't seen any Jews marching in the middle of the road while on my visit. It was obvious what their fate had been!

Arriving home from work one day there was a letter waiting for me. They wanted me to join the army on 23 June. I felt the earth moving from under my feet and suddenly I was lost. Sophie could only stare at me with tears in her eyes. I looked at my mother and on seeing her expression reassured her, 'Yes, Mam, I'm not going to hide underground. I will go as promised.'

'Son, I promise nothing will happen to you. Have trust in God. I will pray for you.'

'I know, Mam. Just don't worry. I promise I will go,' I repeated.

I cycled over to see my father who reacted differently. He didn't depend so much on prayers but more on actions. Dad knew I was sworn in to the partisans and said, 'Well, Son, you are 21. I am not going to ask you to go. Whatever happens to us, the decision is yours.'

'I will go, Dad. I will survive whatever happens,' was all I could reply.

The 23rd of June was still two weeks ahead. A few days later, my mother told me she could still obtain a large pig for me to kill as there wouldn't be anyone to organize it once I was away. I didn't go to work any more. Every day someone would call to cheer me up. In a way, I could consider myself lucky, at least my call-up date had been delayed thanks to Uncle Frank and his letter-writing. Lots of the boys who had attended the medical on the same day as me had already been killed at the Russian front.

The dreaded day arrived. Sophie and Maria accompanied me to the station. What an atmosphere! There were quite a few SS strolling around who must have been wondering what kind of volunteers we were, all speaking Polish and singing Polish songs. I had to tell my sister, 'Please go once the train comes.' There were enough people crying already at the station, and with good reason. All the oppression and deaths, and now they were asking us to fight for something we despised so much.

When the train eventually arrived, we said our goodbyes quickly. 'Tell Mam not to worry,' I reminded them. Perhaps that was easier said than done.

CHAPTER 14

I landed in the Scharnhorst barracks in Lüneburg, south of Hamburg. We got to our quarters about 2 p.m. and there were 12 men assigned to each room. I was on the first floor.

They were huge blocks and the place was almost like a village. After the long trip, everybody opened his food parcel from home containing smoked sausages, smoked ham, etc., and began eating. Suddenly, a German corporal positioned at the door of each room, started screaming at us, 'Out, out, everybody out.' What chaos with men and food flying everywhere. Once outside the sergeants surveyed us. After four or five minutes, we were shouted at again to get back inside the barracks.

I noticed there was a big sausage ring missing from my parcel and everybody else was in the same boat. I found the incident very amusing and I couldn't feel anger. I could only laugh about how clever and quick they had been. It couldn't have been the first time that they had done such a thing to their new recruits. Of course, meat was so scarce, being rationed, and to them it was a great treat.

The following day, we were issued with uniforms. Although we were asked our boot size, uniforms were just thrown at us from two different piles, whatever they thought the right size might be. Some of us looked like ballerinas, the uniforms were so tight, whilst others were turned into clowns with their loosely hanging uniforms. A few days later, we were sworn in. Instead of repeating the words after the officer, I was saying a little prayer. What an army we were, not one German amongst us except our instructors and officers.

As the weeks went by quite a few boys were sent home again as they were really in poor health. I almost enjoyed the training and tried to do everything as well as possible. I kept telling myself that one day when I succeeded in going over to our allies I would make a good soldier. One thing I detested was the names they were calling us and it was very degrading.

One night I went for a walk inside the barracks' perimeter. I met Bronek who had been working with me on the Vibes' farm near Stutthof. It was like meeting a long-lost brother.

'So they got you, too, Bronek,' I said.

'Yes, the local police came to see us on the farm with forms to sign. Some couldn't read German and didn't know what they were signing.' I suggested that we celebrate our meeting.

'Only if you have money as I am skint,' he replied. The drink was on me and we drank champagne. That was the only drink available. We got two drams of vodka and schnapps on rations every ten days but champagne, which was rather expensive, one could buy anytime. He asked what we could do about our present situation but I told him we could only obey for now.

'You just watch me, I will get out before our training is finished,' he vowed. His words were to come true. We parted in a very jovial mood and arranged to meet the following Saturday again.

A few days later, I was amazed as Bronek had managed to arrange a swap to join my group through his group leader, who must have been delighted to be rid of him. That changed the life of our group of 36 men very much - at our expense. When we were issued with rifles our group leader would show us how to take them apart and reassemble, and was forever reminding us never to point a rifle barrel at anyone. But there was Bronek already pointing it at him. Anything we were told not to do, he would do.

Next day, our group was out marching and Bronek was ordered to put a gas mask on and run around as punishment. This was very exhausting but it didn't change Bronek's attitude. Sometimes, when marching through a village where trees were overhanging the road and laden with fruit, a warning would come from the officer or group leader. 'If anyone dares to pick an apple, he won't look at fruit again.' There was Bronek again hanging on to a branch.

When a group leader could not get a man to obey, the whole lot would be punished and that man would be visited while asleep by some of the boys who would put a blanket over his head and give him a good hiding. In Bronek's case we stuck together. No one would dare to hurt Bronek.

The food could have been better. It was always thick, floury soup and bread, very rarely potatoes and meat. With the bread we got a little cube of butter, just enough for one slice. It was nourishing enough, like feeding hardworking horses oats and oats again. We did receive food parcels from home, though, which was a big help.

Almost every second week, I got a small parcel and about 100 marks from Irena and Victor. The Germans were very much aware of the parcels we received. Sometimes, we had unexpected checks of our lockers, supposedly for tidiness, but they were more interested in what food we had stored away. They would just look at each other at times. They even told us not to forget to share our food with our comrades.

The first time my locker was checked over, they admired Irena's photograph, which I had pinned inside the door. There followed a conversation with a sergeant: 'Grenadier Stoltman, I can't believe you have such beauties in West Prussia. If she should visit you, or any one from your family, they can stay with my wife.' On his way out, again. 'I meant it, Grenadier, what I said.' I replied, 'Thank you, Sir, I'll remember.' That was the beginning of a pleasant and friendly relationship between the two of us.

His name was Sergeant Flack. He had been wounded in Russia - his left hand was artificial and he always wore a leather glove. He was a rather good-looking man; tall, slim and blond and a real soldier, different from the rest. Most of the young instructors we had were proper pigs. For each room of 12 men we had a corporal and they lived together, three to a room.

One Sunday, one of the corporals was on his own with his girlfriend. I was called in as usual and thought it was for some messages. As soon as I entered the room, he shouted various orders at me such as, 'Under the table, out, under, out . . .' His girlfriend was laughing and found it all very amusing. When I got back to my room, it was the first time since I don't know when that I had a little cry. I felt so degraded and filled with rage. How I hated that man! I only wished that we would get together at the front line and my first bullet would be for him. I don't think Bronek would have obeyed his orders.

When Bronek, after a long drill, was called by a corporal and told, 'You are a silly ass. Repeat it,' he would repeat it and say, 'You are a silly ass, Corporal.' We would all laugh as the corporal raged with anger,

'Not me.'

'Yes, Corporal, not me.' repeated Bronek.

Then the corporal would say, 'I'm a silly ass, repeat it.'

'I'm glad you're admitting it, Corporal,' and on it went.

I started to drink vinegar again in order to get out of the army and now I knew why Bronek was trying his best to get out. Sometimes, we had a long march through the night, coming back at three or four o'clock in the morning. We usually got extra rations, two thick slices of bread and a cube of margarine, but that stopped because of the shortage of food. When everybody was in bed, Bronek would get up and go into the corridor and shout, 'Fetch your extra rations,' and then he would return to his bed. From each room, one boy would go, only to return empty-handed after an hour waiting.

The funniest episode was when Bronek was on duty, which was every twelfth night. The corporal and the sergeant would come helmeted to inspect that everyone was accounted for and also to check for cleanliness. As they came near the door Bronek stood to attention, and would make his report,

'Room No. 10 - 11 men in bed - dust equally distributed - cobwebs hung up!'

'See you later, Grenadier,' he was informed.

'Yes, Sir.'

Everybody sighed, 'Oh, no Bronek,' whilst some swore or laughed at him. When they had finished inspecting all the other rooms, the corporal would return and quietly order us all out into the corridor, still in pyjamas. We knew we would be given strenuous exercises. We had to watch and follow the corporal's finger - up, down, up, down. All one could hear was, 'ssh, ssh, ssh, ssh,' and an almost ghostly silence.

After an hour, we would return to our beds covered in sweat. I could not believe how Bronek had changed and I admired his courage. When we worked on the farm we were not very close, although we had shared a room. There had always been a little friction between the two of us then. I respected that man now. What endurance!

If I went for a drink inside the barracks, it was always with Bronek. Each time we would empty three or four bottles of champagne. Even our corporal instructors would start talking about me, wondering how I could afford to be drinking so much champagne. It was thanks, of course, to my darling Irena and Victor, for they were sending me money.

One day our Sergeant Flack came to me and said, 'Thank you, Dominik, for the nice parcel.' I knew at once what it was all about. I had written home about him and his offer that any visitors could stay with his wife. The parcel was a little thank-you from my mother.

We were free on Sundays to do our own thing. I was quite shocked when I attended Mass, as from the time the service began, the Hitler Youth Band would march round and round the church playing as loudly as possible. Other days, especially during our last month of training in September, we were free from 6 p.m. onwards and were allowed to go out. Still, some of the corporals would send us to the kitchen to peel potatoes. There was little we could do about the matter.

One evening, I had to go with Bronek. There was a regular squad of girls peeling potatoes and some of them would start throwing peelings at us, simply to make contact. On our way back to the barracks, I said to Bronek, 'Next time I am asked to go, I will get my hair shorn off. That will show them what I think of them. Fancy doing it yourself, Bronek?' He thought I was crazy but dared me to do it.

I didn't have long before my next order to peel potatoes was given. We had a hairdresser in our group. That same night I got my hair cropped as short as he could make it. In the morning, as usual before breakfast, we had to line up for fingernail inspection and so on. I noticed the sergeant's face reddening and all the boys were grinning. I was called for everything under the sun. Now and again, I had to say, 'Yes, Sir, yes, Sir.'

'You are a disgrace to the German army.'

'Yes, Sir.'

'You look like a Russian prisoner.'

'Yes, Sir.'

As soon as we got outside the barracks, we were given such a drilling. It went on all week and the boys started complaining, 'Why did you have to do it, Dominik?' They stuck by me all the same.

The best day of all was when we went target shooting with live ammunition. Our spirits rose only to fall again at the finish of practice. There were five of us whose aim was deadly accurate. Then rumours went around that we may be taken first as snipers. From that time, I could not shoot straight despite all the drilling I got. I was all over the target. For some reason, I was taken to be trained in heavy machine gunning which I didn't mind for as far as I was concerned it was something I would have more experience in once I went over to the Americans or British.

During the last weeks, we were trained in case of gas warfare. That was some experience. It was held inside the barracks. First, we got hard drill with gas masks on. One's chest was painful with breathing. Then the gas alarm was given and we were chased into the huge room with glass all around us. Some of the boys had fixed their masks so that they didn't need to breathe through the filter. Within seconds, they were clawing at the doors as gas filled their lungs. We were not allowed to touch the gas mask once we had them on. We were watched through the glass. On being let out, what a drilling some got for not fixing their masks properly.

Bronek started pretending to take fits. While we were marching, he would fall, clutching his chest. Each time, they would leave one man behind to look after him. Eventually, he was taken away from us. His acting had paid off. Nobody had suspected him of play-acting.

The last few weeks he was still with us on training. Bronek would be asked to go and beg for sandwiches as food was getting poor. What sandwiches he would bring back; sausages, cheese, smoked ham, etc. These were obtained from the surrounding houses. Not one of them did we get ourselves as they were quickly eaten by the group leaders. The best organizing was done through the night. Again, Bronek would volunteer. We would get plenty of fruit like apples, pears and plums but Bronek always had two or three hens and sometimes rabbits as well. These he would give to our group leaders who lived inside the barracks in married quarters. We scored on such occasions as we didn't get any drill at all. The atmosphere was very friendly on such nights.

One Saturday afternoon, as I gazed out of the window, I spotted Sophie and Maria. I ran next door to the officer and sergeant who were on duty to ask for permission to go out. On asking where my tunic was, I apologized as I'd forgotten in my excitement. They agreed to let me go as they knew my sisters were visiting me. I ran out to greet them excitedly. I was proud of them; the way they were dressed so smartly. They had on the long boots I had obtained for them. I took the heavy parcel from them and put it away in my locker. They were not allowed inside the building.

We then went to visit Sergeant Flack who offered me room for my sisters. He and his wife couldn't have been nicer. I almost forgot I was in the German army, considering the friendliness. We left a little parcel with them before we went into the town. I heard all the latest news.

Everything was fine at home. Some of our ethnic minority members were regularly coming to our shop to renew friendships. The best news of all was that the Russian front was only 150 miles from the Polish borders. Surely it wouldn't be long now until we were free again. The most incredible news concerned my brother, Jan, who had been in the Polish army and was now in Magdeburg labour camp. All the men there had been ordered to join the German army but they all solidly refused. Luckily, nothing was done about it. It seemed the Germans were just as desperate for labourers.

That night, we went to a restaurant where we were surprised at the large helpings we were given - potatoes, vegetables and generous slices of black pudding. After one big bite, my sisters looked at each other then offered me their portion which I readily accepted as I was hungry. After taking a bite myself, I had to leave it as any more and I would have been sick. It was horse meat and blood, a sort of black pudding. I took Sophie and Maria to their lodgings.

Next day, before our morning call, they were already sitting on the lawn waiting for me. The young lieutenant in charge called out that I was excused and whispered that I was to give his best regards to my sister, the blond one. I nodded in agreement.

We went for a long walk into the town again, talking about the training which was now skiing. That meant the Russian front. I assured my sisters, 'Don't worry. By the time we are finished here, the Russians will be fighting on our soil. I won't get lost.' We were promised leave before we were moved anywhere.

'Whatever you do, don't say anything at home about skiing and what it means,' I said.

Hamburg was being heavily bombed now. It must have been terrifying there. They sent some of the German boys from our camp to help clear the bodies from the streets. It must have been some experience for them as it really affected them badly. To me, there was no comparison to what they were doing to us Poles – thousands of Jews gassed and burned every day. I felt it was time they had a taste of their own medicine.

'By the way, Maria, the lieutenant at the morning call was asking for you,' I informed her.

'Just tell him to treat you like a brother-in-law already and once Hitler wins the war, tell him to remember me,' was her reply.

I got the message and we all started laughing. In the late afternoon, we went to the station where we promised each other no emotional farewells.

After buying their tickets, most of the money they had in their purses was left with me. I had almost eight weeks' pay in advance.

'Remember, as I always said at home, nothing will kill me, only a heavy axe and in the front line they don't fight with axes. I am looking forward to my leave and to seeing you and Irena. It shouldn't be too long now. Tell Mam if she manages to get a pig or two, I'll kill them for you during my leave.'

'You can be sure Mam will have something. Give our thanks to your sergeant's wife for the nice sandwiches.'

'I will. Goodbye.'

Oh, how sad I felt when walking back to the barracks. What a struggle I had to hold back the tears. I couldn't get inside the barracks quick enough. I still hadn't opened the parcel from Sophie and Maria. I went to the wash room, gave myself a splashing with cold water and then went to the canteen for a quick drink. That didn't help much. I only started reminiscing, which made me more homesick than ever.

It was the next evening before I opened my parcel when we all had a treat. It was the custom for most of us to share whatever we got from home with the exception of a few who would feed themselves from their parcel which remained inside their lockers. We would joke amongst ourselves for someone to put a blanket over their heads in case we saw what they were eating from home.

A call came through the microphone for me to see the lieutenant. When I walked into his room, he was grinning shyly as he enquired, 'Grenadier, do you think your parents would mind if I were to visit them?'

'I don't think so, Sir,' was all I could reply.

'I really fell for your sister. Do you mind?'

'Not at all, Sir.'

When he asked me to mention something to my sister in my next letter, I said I would.

As I walked out, I thought that that was something my parents could well do without. Straight away, I wrote a letter home explaining what was in front of them. I asked them to treat the visitor nicely, otherwise he could make life difficult for me. I was sure they could handle the situation well after Maria's comment during their stay.

Life was easier now as we had very little training, mostly skiing, but once during training, one of the boys tried to shoot his finger off - anything to get out of the army. He was very lucky he wasn't court-martialled. He was saved thanks to Sergeant Flack, who had already been to the Russian front, and who prepared the report somewhat to the boy's benefit.

Finally, the long-awaited news came. In four days, we were off on our leave. Two days before our departure, we had a long march through an unknown area. We stopped in woodlands at a place where sand was excavated for a glass factory. As we waited above the sand mine wondering what would happen next, an order came for us to get into a single line, twenty yards from the edge. Then came the next order, 'All ready, run to the edge, jump down and shout, "I'm going for holidays",' The slope must have been 60 feet deep and very fine sand. What a funny experience.

After jumping, we turned to watch the cowards who ran to the edge, stopped and with a shaky voice shouted, 'I'm going for holidays,' but didn't jump. Eventually, some had to be persuaded with a gentle push.

We hadn't laughed so much during the whole training as on that day. Some even made the comment, 'After 40 days in the desert when Jesus was tempted by the devil to jump from the rocks, he had a choice, but for us there was no way out.' We got our leave.

It was exhilarating to be back in my own land. There were some very happy reunions, first with my family and then on visits. Two of Mother's brothers were ordered into the German army: Johan, the oldest at 47 years, and Bernhard, 40 years, had to go. It was ludicrous to think that they had been called up while their brother, Leonard, after destroying the German truck and spending a few months in a concentration camp, was still in hiding.

I went to visit Victor and Irena. Now in German uniform, I could take more food than ever without any fear that I would be searched. I was teased about my hair-cut although it was now about one and a half inches long.

Irena had had to take a job in an office. Between myself and Victor, we decided that I would go to her office and get her a few days off during my stay. Of course, since I was now in German uniform I could ask for some privileges. There must have been twenty people working in her office. On arrival, I asked for the Office Manager as Irena looked on puzzled. A man approached me dressed in the SA uniform of the Nazi Party and we exchanged our 'Heil, Hitlers'. I began my prepared speech. 'I'm here for two weeks' holiday before going to the Russian front. Could you possibly give my girlfriend, Miss Jesionek, a few days off?' He readily agreed and gave Irena two weeks' leave and wished me good luck. Another 'Heil, Hitler' before I left.

We had only walked as far as the corridor before we remarked on our luck as time off work was difficult to get. We then agreed it must have been because of the strength of our love. We skipped home lightheartedly. Victor and her parents couldn't help being amused about the outcome of my office visit. But Victor was rather worried about the possibility of my going to the Russian front. There was not much hope of saving one's life by running over to the Russian side. To Stalin, we were just as big an enemy as the Germans, and more so, being in German uniform.

Irena went back home with me so we could spend the rest of my leave together. A few days before my departure, Mother still had a little job for me - to slaughter a big pig. I scored, being able to take some cured sausages back to the camp with me.

My dreaded departure date came. All was packed. Sophie, Maria and Irena went with me to the station. We had almost three hours to wait. We were surprised at the number of SS who watched us. I was more than ever aware, being a member of the underground movement, that they were probably looking for someone to arrest. Just to break the uneasy silence, Maria told us about the visit of the lieutenant who had stayed with them for three days.

In an instant, the mood changed as music came through the station microphone, a sad-sounding tune about a homeland. Those travelling had taken something to drink from home so we reached for the bottles. It was a strange atmosphere. Some of the people wept while some were boldly outspoken. We were not alone, but standing together in support, all because we were being forced to do something against our will. The SS moved in amongst us to disrupt things but to no avail. The train arrived and we all stood on the platform. Finally the whistle blew and as we were boarding the train someone called out, 'We'll return to a free Poland.' That was too much for the SS who charged at us trying to catch the man who had shouted those brave words. Within seconds, we were in the train and off. What a fright we all had.

We were once again in our barracks. Now fully trained, life was easier. Even our instructors showed us a little respect whilst awaiting postings. October 1943 came and we were all checked for our equipment and issued with some new items including our iron ration which was a small tin, like Heinz baked beans, with instructions that it was only to be opened on orders from the commanding officers. We were then marched to the railway station and onto the train.

We arrived at another barracks on the outskirts of Hamburg. There was not one German soldier amongst us. I sent a telegram home, 'I'm off to the Russian front.' We kept singing Polish songs only to be interrupted by some of our superiors telling us to sing German songs if we wanted to sing. That didn't make much difference.

We were four days in our new quarters when I was called to the entrance of our barracks. Oh, God, I couldn't believe my eyes – there was my mother. If only I hadn't sent the telegram.

'Oh, Mam, why did you have to come here?'

'Ssh, Son, I just wanted to see you.'

I knew that even my wonderful mother must have been aware that there was not much chance of survival going to the Russian front. We spent three hours together. Her next train was in the morning.

I tried to get a bed for my mother. There was a bombing raid over Hamburg and I kept thinking it wouldn't be long now until we were free. I knocked at one door and a lady answered. Before I had a chance to say anything, she called out to me, 'Heil, Hitler'. I called out, 'Heil, Hitler,' in reply but my poor mother greeted her with, 'Blessed be the Lord Jesus Christ,' as she would have done at home. The door was quickly slammed in our faces. I pleaded with Mam to say, 'Heil, Hitler' otherwise we wouldn't get a bed for her that night.

At the next door, I stood in front of my mother as I quickly said, 'Heil Hitler, could I get a bed for my mother? I am going to the Russian front.' It worked before Mam had a chance to greet her. Farewells were said again and my mother once again reminded me, 'Trust me, Son, you will survive.'

'I believe you, Mam.'

'Go with God.'

'You, too, Mam.'

Back I went to the barracks a mile away. Next morning, we were all called out and everything was again checked. I was in trouble this time. I had used up my iron ration but only to substitute it with a double-sized tin of meat from home. My name was taken before I got back on the train.

It wasn't long before we realized that we were travelling in the opposite direction to that expected. We saw Bremen, Oldenburg, Amsterdam – 'hooray', we were in Holland!

En route through Holland the Polish recruits had been dropped off at various stations two or three at a time along with about a dozen German soldiers. It was obvious they didn't trust our kind to be in the army. I landed with a unit and remained there until the following year – September 1944.

CHAPTER 15

My postal address was Bergen, which was about twenty miles north of the Belgian border on the shores of the North Sea. We were located in bunkers under the ground. I was the only Pole in my group of 12 Germans, but I did come across quite a few Cossacks. They stayed in their own group under their commanding officer, though I did become friends with them much to the awareness of the Germans around me.

From the time of my arrival, I was very conscious of our lieutenant in charge. His name was Schulze and he was blind in one eye over which he wore a black patch. He definitely had something against me but I didn't know what.

A week after my arrival there, I was taken away by two soldiers. No explanation was given. I became terrified, thinking they had found out that I had been working at home with the partisans. My knees were turning to jelly. After half an hour travelling in the lorry, we stopped and I was taken into an office. The charge was read out to me and a two weeks' prison sentence with strict rationing was the outcome - all because of my having eaten my iron rations before the journey. Relief flooded through me.

I was locked in the attic of the house used for offices and given bread and water only. In the morning, I was taken out to do my toilet for half an hour. That was something I could not do as ordered. I knocked at the door after two or three hours when I needed the toilet and what a drill I got. I could hardly get up the stairs to my place. I never knocked again but instead, when necessary, I used the sink in my little attic room. I took the chair to the sink and ran the cold water, praying they would not get the smell.

After two weeks, I was returned to the bunkers. I really felt so lost, so lonely and homesick. We had some Dutch men calling at the barracks to do repair work and I got friendly with one of them. One day he asked me if I could supply them with some rifle ammunition but as they were searched on their way in and out, it was up to me to take it out. On my days off, when I went into town, I was to give the supply to a driver who would put an unlit cigarette in his mouth as a signal. I did it as arranged quite a number of times. But one day, two young German boys from our bunker were sent to execute some Dutch people in Amsterdam. I decided there would be no more ammunition. I didn't want to lose my life for a few silly rounds of ammunition.

Instead, I turned back to starvation and to drinking vinegar, hoping to get out of the army. For our main meal at midday, we would all come from various bunkers to a big dining hall, about 100 in number. I ate the same as the rest but back in the bunker I went to the toilet where I put a stick in my throat and vomited all the food out and then drank vinegar. Within a week, my face and feet began to swell and I was admitted to the sick bay. Not being able to get more vinegar, within a few days I was declared fit again so it was back to the bunkers and my diet.

Eventually I was told by the doctor, 'Grenadier Stoltman, I wish I was as healthy as you.' I had to give up my diet. By now, one needed to be half-dead to get release papers from the army.

From the news point of view, I was lost. There was nothing, absolutely nothing I could find out. The Germans would listen through the night, glued to the radio as I pretended to be asleep but I was unable to hear anything. They wouldn't tell me what was happening either. On duty visits to the Cossacks who stayed about a mile from us, I noted they were also tuned into the radio. They didn't worry if the German soldiers saw them although it was strictly forbidden.

At nights, we would go on patrol in twos. One patrol we were very nervous about was when we checked on the Cossacks. About 100 yards from their bunkers, we would start talking loudly so they could hear us. Often, before asking for the password, we had to go flat on our bellies as they were very quick to shoot first and then ask for the password. Apart from these incidents, they were generally very friendly.

It always made me homesick listening to them playing their balalaikas, a small stringed instrument. You could sense the sadness and longing in the music - yes, longing for freedom. I was helped at times by mail received from home and Victor and Irena. All were very pleased I hadn't landed at the Russian front but in Holland.

On a very stormy night, whilst on duty beside the sea, that fanatic of a lieutenant came to see me. Before I had a chance to report to him, he screamed accusations at me that I had been sleeping on duty. Next day, I was called before the commanding officer who read out the charge to me – 'Sleeping while on duty, endangering the life of your comrades and the safety of the German Reich. Anything to say?'

'I was not sleeping, Sir. In that storm with frost one could die of cold if one slept.' The lieutenant approached as I defended myself and he just screamed at me that I had been sleeping.

'Are you saying the lieutenant is a liar?'

'No, Sir. I'm saying I was not sleeping. It would be hard to stand and sleep in that stormy weather, Sir.'

'Are you aware that you could be court-martialled?'

'Yes, Sir, but I was not sleeping, Sir.'

I could see the commanding officer felt pity for me. We all knew that he did not have much time for the lieutenant.

'Is there anything in your favour that you can tell me? Your situation is serious, Grenadier.'

'I don't know, but I am still under the doctor.'

'You mean now?'

'Yes, Sir.'

'Grenadier, that may save your life.'

'Thank you, Sir.'

'I will try my best. You can go now.'

'Thank you, Sir.'

On my way back, as I walked along the sand dunes, I watched the American bombers, just little silver specks in the sky. My spirits rose. I knew the end must be near. The German fighters didn't even bother to engage them. One bomber was hit by the German heavy guns. The pilot bailed out but no effort was made to save him.

Everyone in the bunker was waiting to hear the outcome of my interview with the CO until one day when I had to report to the lieutenant. I was ordered to put on my battledress tunic minus belt.

'Consider yourself lucky, Grenadier. You have been sentenced to three months' strict imprisonment at Den Haag.' I managed to scribble short letters to my parents, Irena and Victor saying that I would be on manoeuvres for the next three months and although I was allowed to receive letters I could not send any.

Accompanied by two guardsmen I was taken in a small truck to the railway station. I tried to speak to them but they only looked at me. This was the first time I had ever been in a military prison and I was curious to know what life would be like inside. The prison layout was of long corridors with cells on both sides and in the middle of the doors were little round coin-like discs covering peepholes.

Along with six others, I was searched on arrival. In front of me stood two German officers, one of them a major in his early sixties with a deep ruddy complexion. For some unknown reason, I felt sorry for him. The search was conducted by a young SS member. I was then taken to my cell which contained a wooden-framed bed about eight inches high, slightly higher at one end to act as a pillow, a small table 24 inches by 30 inches, a chair and a bucket. On the door was a list of rules. I was in no rush to read them as it couldn't be any worse here than in Nuremberg prison at the beginning of the war.

One rule I didn't like was 'YOU ARE NOT ALLOWED TO LIE DOWN THROUGH THE DAY UNTIL AFTER YOU HEAR EVENING CALL. YOU ARE TO STAND TO ATTENTION EVERY TIME YOUR CELL DOOR IS OPENED.' I decided I'd better behave myself.

Our first prison ration consisted of a thick slice of black bread and a cup of brown water – supposedly coffee, but it didn't taste like it. A loud scream of 'Bedtime' indicated when we could lie down. To my dismay I hadn't been given blankets. I was tempted to knock on the door but then thought 'Don't, it is not a hotel you are in; it is supposed to be strict prison.' My bones got sore as I tried to get comfortable rolling from one side to the other during the night.

At last, morning came and every door was opened. We were marched out with our buckets. We had to wash in a long, metal trough with cold-water taps only. Breakfast was the same as the night before and midday was bread yet again. The next day, we were given the same food. 'Good Lord,' I thought, 'it is worse than my Nuremberg imprisonment.' After breakfast we were taken out into the prison yard, hands behind our backs. For one hour we walked in a monotonous circle closely watched by guards. About 30 yards away from us, hundreds of prisoners were walking about. For whatever reason, they were not so heavily guarded as the rest of us. There must have been nationalities from all over the world, from Mongolians to Hindus to black people.

On our third day, I got a slice of bread and a cube of margarine, an improvement of sorts. Later, instead of marching in the prison yard, we were given buckets and ordered to clean the corridor. After a few minutes' work, it seemed everything around me was moving. I was lightheaded and dizzy. Here at least I had a chance to talk to my partner doing the same job. Midday came and we had cabbage flavoured with caraway seeds and bits of meat which tasted delicious. Supper again was a thick slice of bread, cube of margarine and a blob of jam. That night, I was handed two blankets, a pillow and a mattress. I slept like a log with all my comforts. In the morning, all bed gear was removed and the two bad days began again. Yesterday had been what they called a good day (one in three), now followed a repeat of the first two days there.

To be honest, I was pleased with my present situation as it was an improvement to being in the army. If I could be sure of getting another six months for bashing one of the SS guards on the nose, I would have done it. It was the sight of the revolvers they carried that prevented me.

Most of the guards were quite decent really - except for one. On opening the door in the morning, he would kick the bucket and then call you for everything under the sun, blaming you for soiling his feet. That meant cleaning over and over until there was no smell left in the cell.

Six weeks into my sentence, things improved a little. We started working outside our own prison building, especially round one block that was full of young SS German boys. They were all serving prison sentences. Sometimes they would throw us a piece of bread and were quite friendly.

When we first arrived, we were warned not to look into the open cells at the end of the corridor to the right. What could be the reason for this? As we approached the cells there was no need to turn our heads to see inside. The wooden doors were open revealing another metal-bar door. Some of the men had a desperately pleading look in their eyes, others just stared into space. One in particular had the expression of a wild animal. Demented, he held onto the bars ready to pounce if given the chance.

While at work, we learned that these German soldiers were waiting to be court-martialled, which often resulted in a death sentence. For this reason the wooden doors were left open so the guards could watch out for any attempted suicide. Those already sentenced to death were kept in other cells along a corridor we often had to polish on Saturdays or Sundays. From there they were taken for execution. I just couldn't get the look on their faces out of my mind. Suddenly, my attitude towards the Germans changed. I lost my hatred of them. How many innocent lives were lost like that just because of one fanatic and his followers?

The prison was gradually filling up. I was put into a cell with a Russian in German uniform. He was a true Mongolian, with a flat nose and squint eyes but was very pleasant. After work each day, he would always have small bits of bread. Every piece would be put on a small table and he would share them with me. The guards would come at night only to annoy him making gestures that he was crazy and make monkey-like noises at him. When they left, he would cry with rage.

During our last few weeks, instead of cleaning corridors at the weekends, we were allowed to walk for two hours within the prison square. In that square was a group of twenty Hindu soldiers. It was a pleasure to watch them. As their superiors talked to them, they stood to attention. Their faces wore expressions of bravery and self-possession. Immaculate in dress, they never talked to anyone outside their own group.

I was into my last week now and my bones were no longer sore. I was acclimatized like a proper jailbird. I wished I had another six months to serve. The only thing I missed was mail from home. I knew my mother would be suffering more by not getting any news from me.

On my day of release, I was given a sermon from the governor about how serious my offence was, sleeping while on guard duty. I was tempted to ask them to keep me for a further six months if they thought I deserved more. Instead, I found myself heading back to my unit to serve the Führer and the glorious Third Reich.

On the train, I was aware of the strange looks I was getting from the Dutch civilians as I was travelling without a belt and a rifle. In Holland at that time, it was compulsory for a German soldier to carry a rifle and ammunition. I was given a great welcome from one of our boys who was on guard duty. Better still was the news he gave me - the one-eyed fanatic, Lieutenant Schulze, had been transferred. Life was bound to be easier for me.

On entering the bunker, I got tidied up and went to report to my new commanding officer, 'Grenadier Stoltman back from serving three months' sentence in Den Haag, Sir.'

'At ease, Grenadier. Well, your three months are over. I have read the report and what happened was unjustifiable. Anyway, once the holiday blockade is lifted, you will be the first to go on holiday as compensation. I hope that will make up for the three months.' I was glad to be told that.

What a bundle of mail was waiting for me with money in each letter to help with my supposed manoeuvres. Life changed for us all. It was like one long vacation under the new CO. The Cossacks would join us for a game of football or a wrestling match. They were rather small but what strength they had. There was nobody who could put them down and most of them were only half our size.

We still missed hearing what was happening at the front line, although the Germans listened nightly to the radio. Glancing at their faces, I guessed that on both fronts things must not have been going very well for them. Sometimes, at midday, the wireless would be switched on for news from Berlin and someone would call out, 'I can tell you the news myself.' Before he had a chance to say anything more, another would call out, 'According to plan.' The official news broadcast from now on was, 'The front line was being pulled back, according to plan.'

Even now, there were still some who believed in Hitler's secret weapon that was going to win them the war. Among the Cossacks, one could see quite clearly that they were very worried at the way the war was progressing. They believed and hoped so much in Hitler's victory in order that they would have an independent state free from both the Russians and Poland.

We were allocated a new job. With the help of a very powerful water jet we drove heavy wooden piles into the ground along the shoreline. Another squad would follow and attach mines, platelike in shape, to the top of the piles. Once the tide was in they were completely covered.

One day, I was called to the CO's office and asked, 'Grenadier, would you like to be my batman?' I was delighted and said so. My luck was in. I had to clean his bunker and get breakfast and supper. Most of my time was spent with his dachsund, Max. He would eat any dirt he came across and then roll around in it. That meant bathing the dirty little brute three or four times a day. Often I promised myself that once more and I'd drown him... but then little Max had his uses.

We were friendly with a few Cossack soldiers, who were usually on duty at the entrance to our camp. Ten yards from the camp gate was a nissen hut packed with bags of biscuits, similar to dog biscuits. If any of my Cossack friends were on duty I would get in touch with them. As usual I would take little Max for his walk. The guard on duty was only doing his duty with more alertness than ever! I would go to the far end of the nissen hut where one of the corrugated iron sheets was loose. I would fill my pockets and share the biscuits out that night.

With my new dog duties and all the money sent from home, I often went to a restaurant and took a corner seat and listened to music which made me feel homesick. Even the Dutch drinks couldn't cure that. I was always pleased to see how few of the Dutch would talk to us soldiers. At home we wouldn't have dared to show such coolness but then we had not even been allowed to enter a restaurant at all before the German army reserve had been based in our area.

There were times while sitting in my corner, I longed to make friends with some Dutch people. If the occasion arose and I had the chance to escape I could have hidden with a Dutch family. It would be seen to be suspicious though, even dangerous, to try with all the soldiers and officers about, especially as I was not long out of prison. The Germans must have been aware of the Dutch animosity. They made it so obvious how they felt, it made me feel very uncomfortable.

A day came when my CO told me to start packing as in two or three days I would have my ticket home for a fortnight's leave. I smiled broadly on hearing the news and he appeared to be just as happy. I don't know what it was, but we all took it as a great privilege to serve under him.

Because he was allowing me to go on leave first, I wondered if he had some closer connection with Poland. We had men who were older and/or married and there was I, the first to go on holiday. I often pictured myself at the front line with the opportunity of making a run for it to the American side but coming across my new CO lying wounded. I knew, without hesitation, I would have abandoned my plan of escape and stayed with him whatever the outcome.

A few of the older men complained about my going first on leave. I could well understand their feelings. Some of them were in their forties and with families. Maybe my CO knew I was not as keen as the rest of them to fight for their fatherland.

On the day I was due to leave, my CO asked me, 'Are you going to tell your parents the truth about your prison sentence?'

'Yes, Sir, I will, only I looked on it as more of a holiday than a prison sentence after serving under that Lieutenant Schulze.'

He wished me good luck and a pleasant holiday for which I thanked him.

I had never looked forward so much to going home as I did then, especially as I could listen to all the news. How much longer were the Germans going to hold out? Surely, it must be months rather than years?

CHAPTER 16

No one at home knew I was arriving. It was too short notice for me to write. I met my sister, Maria, in the village and she told me that Mother was with them for a two-day visit. We decided that Maria should go home first and mention that somebody had seen me at the station. It would have been too much of a shock for Mam for me to have suddenly appeared at the door. I arrived 15 minutes after Maria to a great welcome. It was fantastic to be home again, my mother all smiles, with a tearful look of adoration.

I told them about my time in prison. My mother admonished me for not telling them the truth earlier but what would have been the point when they would have worried so much? As it turned out, Mam cried daily when she had been told three weeks ago. I went on to explain how I felt.

'It wasn't that bad. In fact, I wouldn't have minded spending the rest of my war days there. I was jailed for sleeping while on duty, which I hadn't been. From the time we landed there from Hamburg, I knew the lieutenant was out to get me. Being in prison has been a good experience for me. There were people there of all races but the majority were German soldiers, young SS boys and German officers. What was distressing was to see these boys awaiting the death sentence. I really lost all hatred, sorry Mam dislike, against the Germans. Mam, I even started praying for them as you do.'

'Now, now, you just pray for yourself, you need it all but if you do mean it, it was the good Lord's doing never to bear a grudge against any of your fellow men,' was my mother's response. I couldn't help but smile and think what a wonderful world it would be if everyone could be like her. But in those days of war we needed more than people armed with bibles. We needed action as well as prayers.

That afternoon, we took the train to Mam's place. It was great to see Sophie again, my favourite sister. It was good to know we were all together again, at least for a while anyway.

Later, Clemens arrived and we greeted each other warmly. When asked if I was going back I said, 'Watch what you are saying - you will spoil your good name with Mam if you try and make a deserter out of me. Mind you, I have a rifle and live ammunition with me which would be a help to the partisans. Since I left my unit I've constantly thought that if I knew my parents would be left in peace my decision would be made in seconds!'

'Oh, Dominik, I shouldn't have said it, you had better go back,' Clemens said.

'Clemens, you are a mystery to me. How did you manage to evade conscription?'

'I'll tell you one day.' To this day, I still don't know.

A while later, my good friend, Eddie, called and welcomed me home. That completed our gathering. I told him I was home for a fortnight.

'The way things are progressing, Dominik, there may be no need for you to go back.'

'I don't think it will come that quickly,' I responded.

'With your rifle and your training, you could help us a lot,' said Eddie. My mother interrupted, 'You had better stop talking that nonsense and don't look for trouble.' I assured her Eddie was teasing and I would be going back. Clemens changed the subject by saying, 'What about coming to our place for a beer? Elli is looking forward to seeing you, also the rest of the family.' I said I would go along the next day but Mother urged me to go out and enjoy myself and take Sophie with me as there was plenty of time during the next fortnight to be in her company. As we were leaving, I stopped behind for a few seconds, put my arms around Mam and stressed the point, 'Mam, don't worry, I am going back to the army.'

At Clemens's place, his parents joined us along with Elli and her younger sister. It was a very happy reunion. Their son was in France with the German army. I had a chat with Elli.

'How did you land in prison, Dominik?'

'Well, Elli, I had so much experience in everything, I was curious to find out what life was like in prison.'

'Knowing you, I believe it. You got very thin, Dominik.'

'That's the special diet we were given to keep fit.'

'You won't get lost, Dominik?'

'I'll make sure of that, Elli, and if I do, it will be on the right side.'

I felt sorry for all the boys who had gone to the Russian front directly after their medicals. There was no way one could face Stalin's army and say, 'I'm a Pole.' You would be the first to get a bullet, sooner than a person of German nationality.

Eddie told us a joke about Stalin, regarding his cruelty.

'Did you hear about Stalin's dinner party with Roosevelt and Churchill? They had roast duck for dinner. Stalin took the duck in his hands and started chewing. His companion said, "Use the knife, Stalin, use the knife." Stalin grabbed the knife, got up and whispered, "Which one?" It seemed appropriate. As for myself, I felt confident I was going to make it now. I had always been terrified at the thought of being sent to the Russian front.

We agreed to have a party before I left. A few days later, Mam suggested that I should go to visit Victor and Irena. There was nothing I longed for more. The day before I left, I went to see Dad. We always had to carry our rifle and ammunition with us in case of partisans. Little did they know I was one of them myself. I suggested to Dad we had some target practice to see how good he was.

After firing a few shots, a boy came over from our German neighbour with a message, 'Mr Labot is asking you to stop the shooting at once.'

'Tell your Mr Labot to come here himself if he wants anything,' was my reply. He never came near us. After all, what could he do against a German soldier? I was one of them now.

Next day, I was packed and on my way to see Victor and Irena. When my brother saw me standing at the door, he was speechless.

'Dominik, it is a miracle that you are here. Yesterday, we were warned that I had to get out of here as soon as possible. The gestapo found out about my hiding place. There is no time to lose.' Victor got dressed and we set off with Irena, me in a German uniform carrying a rifle.

After leaving Irena's house we had to walk through some woodlands on our way to Golonog, the new hiding place. Half way through the woods, we spotted a gestapo man with a girl. 'Don't get nervous, Irena, just act natural.' I was prepared for him, should he stop us. As we got closer to them we all called out in unison, 'Heil, Hitler.'

'Heil, Hitler.'

We had made it. Irena was as pale as a ghost and started crying.

'Cheer up, we have made it.' Victor tried to console her. Here was I thinking we would have a nice week together but all I had was three hours with Victor.

I took him to a priest's house in Golonog on the outskirts of a small village close to a church surrounded by woodlands. We cried with relief before we parted and he made his way down the long stretch of steps to the house. As we returned to Irena's we realized how lucky we were.

'What would we have done, Dominik, had he stopped us?'

'Well, it would have been a gentle tap with the rifle butt on his head. I have had good training for that and if the girl had got nasty she would have got the same treatment.'

'You wouldn't.'

'Oh, yes, for our safety I wouldn't have had any choice.'

For the next two days, Irena and I did a lot of travelling to visit all the contacts my brother had so as to give them his new address. It was amazing to think how it had all worked out. Now, I couldn't help but wonder about my mother and her strong belief in prayers. How often she had said, 'I know the good Lord will answer my prayers. We will survive,' and at my signing as a volunteer, 'Sign on, Son, I promise nothing will happen to you. Trust me. I will pray for you.' I couldn't accept that it was all just coincidence. Even my prison sentence, how lightly I had got off. Then getting two weeks' leave from my new CO as a reward, and after three days my mother sending me to see Victor just when he needed me most.

I stayed for another two days. Our time together was happy but also sad because of Victor's move. I could not spend any more time with him in case anyone became suspicious and started asking questions. The risk was too great.

On my last day I managed to slip out and buy a beautiful bunch of red carnations.

'Here, my darling, something to cheer you up and thank you for all that you are doing for Victor; also for being so beautiful, and for all the letters you have written and the money you have sent me while I was in prison.' Irena was thrilled to be given her first bunch of flowers, which she had often dreamed would be from me.

It was suggested we opened one of Father Simon's bottles of wine (Victor's adopted name when ordained) and have a little celebration. We thought it a great idea and that Victor would approve. On reflection, Victor was in a much better place now. His doctor had said it was important for health reasons that he move to a place where he could get some exercise. He must have weighed about 18 stones. Hopefully, he would manage to stay in his new place until the war was over.

'Do you have to go tomorrow, Dominik?'

'Yes, I'd better, Darling. Mother is expecting me. She thinks she may have a large pig for me to kill before I go.'

'I would like to see you doing it.'

'Why don't you come?'

'Victor may need me for messages for the first few days in his new place.'

The next day I was packed and ready for my departure. As usual, I had a lot of money, some gold bars and jewellery to take back home with me. It was a very sad parting. We were certain we would not see each other again until after the war. What concerned us once liberation day came was the effect that Stalin's Russian army would have on us.

I promised that should I survive I would go over to the Americans and I would write as soon as the war was over.

'Just make sure that once the Russians are near, you keep together. There's more safety in numbers,' I said. It was hard to believe how we longed for the day when the war was over and yet how terrified we were of the Russians. What a liberation!

'Look after yourself, Darling. I promise you will hear from me.'

'You sound like your mother.'

'Where would we be without our faith, our hope and dreams? That's one thing they can't take away from us.'

On the journey home my mind was occupied with thoughts of not returning to my unit and of joining the partisans. After telling them at home about Victor having to change his hiding place and about my timely arrival I knew my mother would be offering a silent prayer of, 'Thank you, Lord, for looking after my family.' I only hoped he wouldn't forget me when my time came to go over to our allies.

Dad told me the manager from our wholesaler was wanting to see me before I was due to return. He often used to get meat and other farm products from me. Arriving at his office, I was presented with a case of 12 bottles of wine. Dad later suggested I take them with me as I could give one or two bottles to my new CO who I knew would appreciate the gift.

When I think back to those days now, it was nothing but stupidity on our part, the things we tried to do.

I had spent a whole evening at Eddie's place just so that we could be free to talk about anything. Then, out of the blue, Eddie suggested that I should not go back to my unit. I didn't need much persuasion. A friend of ours, Jaruszuski, a forester, was going to help us with our plan. I was to walk to a certain place in the wood and he was to fire a shot with a revolver through my arm. I would then scratch my face with a piece of bark to make it more realistic and Jaruszuski was to take my rifle. It was supposed to look as if the partisans had attacked. By the time my arm healed we thought the Russians would be in occupation.

The next night I waited for two hours in the wood but Jaruszuski did not appear. I went to his house where he tried to explain to me that even if we had succeeded, the gestapo would have arrested many innocent people and interrogated them. We could not risk this happening and the plan was abandoned. Eddie had another idea. I could break my hand while walking under the influence of drink. That way, other people wouldn't be involved.

We arranged to meet the following night at Clemens's place. After I was well under the influence, which was about ten o'clock, we set off for home. Then in an isolated place I lifted my arm and Eddie lashed out with a stick. After the third time, as I tried to close my hand and open it, we heard a little crack. We thought we had succeeded. I went home on my own but now very sober due to the pain. My hand was swollen and bleeding. Sophie gave me some painkilling tablets. 'Do you think you have succeeded?'

'I don't know but it's terribly sore.'

In the morning, I tried to open and close my hand. It wasn't broken after all. I decided that was enough, no more silly tricks. I was going back. Two days before departure, my mother got a monster of a pig, over four cwt., for me to kill. We even had one of our friendly policemen watching the house to deter anyone from calling at the back door for groceries, which often happened with the farmers working long hours.

We hoped that the pig meat would see us through to the end of the German occupation. I said my goodbyes to all my friends. My sister, Gertrude, by now almost a skeleton, continued her starvation diet to avoid work. We didn't think she would see the end of the war. The poor nuns where Lucy was had their problems, too, due to the Italians declaring war on Germany.

The Italian employing them in his mushroom-drying business disappeared together with the whole family and nobody ever found out what had happened to them. The gestapo were very efficient in dealing with people they didn't like. He had done a lot of good for our people and he was punished for siding with us Poles.

The way things were going at home now, I thought it was just as well that I returned to my unit. I was sure that when the time came I would manage to get over to the Americans. The partisans I had joined had raided the police station to free some of our members who had been arrested. It had been a great success, with no casualties. It worried me that I may be picked up one day by the gestapo. Eddie kept reassuring me though that if anything should happen, all paper, documents, lists, etc., would be destroyed first and foremost.

I had only one more day to go so I went to see my old friend, Lesner, whom I still visited at night with pieces of bread and coffee. Poor old soul, he was quite upset and told me he would continue to pray for me. How could I not survive with so many people praying for me? I only hoped nobody prayed for me to go to heaven; I was too young for that.

It was now time for me to be off and I was rather afraid of that moment. I went on my knees and asked Dad for his blessings. Poor Dad put so much holy water on my head I could feel it trickling onto my back. I thought there must have been a cloud burst above my head. I tried to cheer my mother up by mentioning that with all the holy water I was bound to succeed.

'You will, Son, have trust in God and I'm sure you will,' she agreed.

Sophie, Maria and Eddie came with me to the station. We were still working out how they could write their news from home in such a way that I could get the proper meaning, even if the letters were censored. Eventually the train arrived. We said our goodbyes and I told them not to worry as I would be all right.

It was an hour into the journey before signed-up volunteers started talking to each other. Even then, we were unsure who to talk to as a lot of our ethnic minority travelling with us wouldn't talk Polish. It didn't take long for them to notice that they were not welcome to sit with us and began moving away. In the mood we were in anything could have happened.

Once we were back in our units, it was the other way around. It was we who had to be careful and not get into trouble. In Holland we were scattered all over the place, one or two Poles to ten or fifteen Germans. As for the Cossacks, they were in large groups of their own. They appeared to be more trusted by the Germans, in particular the Cossack officers. But if we did not salute the officers they reported us to our superiors who, most of the time, did not bother doing anything about it. They obviously weren't trusted that much.

After reporting my return to my CO, I gave him two bottles of wine and offered to make supper from my goodies I had brought back with me. He seemed pleased with the idea. He was getting many parcels from home himself. Often when making supper for him from his own supplies, he would tell me to make something for myself as well.

'Will I ask the sergeant to join us?' I asked, and the CO thought it was a good idea. The sergeant was a dentist from Cologne in his early forties, not a bit like a soldier, too much of a gentleman. At the same time, our little unit ran smoothly. We couldn't do enough for one another and for our new commanding officer. We had to march about half a mile to the canteen for our supper. Before the group took off, I approached the sergeant and told him that I was preparing supper from some goodies I had brought from home and the CO would like him to join us. He was delighted.

When he saw me unpacking my second parcel he remarked, 'Is there a war on in your area?' He smiled as I replied, 'Yes, sir, but we have our way of surviving.' What a feast we had, army style, but tasty. We had big chunks of toasted ham, grilled sausages, and chunks of cheese. Out of the blue, the sergeant produced a big bunch of beautiful grapes. Before our CO joined us, the meal was all prepared in his office – except for two bottles of wine which we had drunk whilst preparing the food. There were still eight bottles left. When our CO came in he just stared, then said, 'Dominik, you're making me homesick with your barbecue. It is almost as it was before the war.' We had everything but bread – the sergeant walked across to his room and came back with three slices. That's all the bread we had.

After the feast, there were still a few bottles of wine left. We all felt rather relaxed. Then my CO asked me, 'Grenadier, how long have you been in the German army?'

'Just over a year.'

'What are your parents doing?'

By that time we were all rather under the influence with the amount of wine consumed and I replied honestly, 'Sir, I have one brother who was in the Polish army. He is still in prison in Magdeburg. Another one is a Franciscan missionary who is hiding from the gestapo. My parents are still at home.'

'And you volunteered as a German soldier?'

'I didn't volunteer, I was forced. If I had not signed the form to become a volunteer, my parents as well as my younger brothers and sisters would have ended up in a concentration camp. That's why I am here.'

Before we had a chance to continue our conversation, there was a knock at the door. Who should be there but that fanatic, the one-eyed lieutenant who had court-martialled me in the hope of being rid of me forever. We had control visits most second weeks and a lieutenant from another area would drop in to check for any lack of discipline.

When he saw me in the company of the CO and the sergeant, his first words were, 'How did you enjoy Den Haag Prison?'

'Sir, anything is better than serving under you.'

I could tell that my CO agreed with my comment. The lieutenant's mouth must have been watering seeing all the food we had. He didn't stay very long with us. I know that he was not pleased that my CO hadn't reprimanded me for my comment to him but when the fanatic had left my CO did say, 'Grenadier, I think you went a bit too far with the lieutenant.'

'Sir, I meant it and it was the honest truth.'

After our little party, life went on as before, which included my looking after Max, whom I often felt like drowning. Two weeks later, my CO dropped the bombshell that I was to be transferred. I knew that the lieutenant was connected with the change which confirmed he certainly had it in for me. I was transferred not too far away and my postal address remained the same.

My new place was fine. We lived in spacious bungalows that had been vacated by Dutch families who had gone I know not where. I was given a job from the sergeant after we were asked who loved hunting and I quickly volunteered. Each day, we went off to an area near the sea where there were a lot of rabbits. I was provided with a .22 rifle and would always return with half a dozen rabbits, not that I got any myself.

Yet another bomb dropped on me. As we awaited the 'Stand to attention' order at morning call, I whispered something in Polish to a friend of mine. Much to my astonishment he told me to shut up with my Polish yapping. That remark was too much for me. As the sergeant tried to make a report to a lieutenant nearby I reacted quickly and jumped on the guy, hitting him in front of our CO. Needless to say, I was called to his office and asked the reason for my behaviour.

'Sir, he can't speak proper Polish or German and I am writing letters for that man in Polish to his wife, some of which are very intimate. How dare he say to me, "Shut up with your Polish yapping". I just couldn't control myself,' was my excuse.

From that day on, there was no more rabbit shooting for me. There was always something for me to do. When the rest of the boys went to the town whilst off duty, I was given chores like cleaning the wash room, scrubbing the floor, peeling potatoes and so on. I didn't even have the time to spend the money I was receiving from home.

At the beginning of our training, I was shown how to handle a heavy machine gun. Well, I was now back on to it but it was a heavy contraption from the First World War with a watercooling system. The stand for it was over 70 lbs. in weight. It was murder during any training jumping from one hole to the other with the stand. What worried me more was that should we come into the front line, the machine gun was always the first target to be knocked out and my two partners were Germans. This would make it more difficult for me to seek out the Americans. We would have to stay together as a team. I was determined that soon I would be taken off that duty and go back to ordinary soldiering. There had to be a way out.

CHAPTER 17

It was June 1944 and I was expecting some post from home because of my forthcoming birthday. I did get two letters but it was very bad news from home. My father had been taken by the Germans to dig trenches with other prisoners. I knew it was against the Russian advances into Poland, as many of our German protectors, e.g. the chief of police, Mr Radatz, and the labour exchange manager, Mr Reinke, had left already for fear of being caught by the Russians.

We did not have many people now we could turn to for assistance. What a liberation it was going to be, to be freed by the Russians! If the Russians only knew how we hated them and how afraid we were of Stalin. As far as Poland was concerned, there was little difference between one occupation and the other. A lot of people didn't know what to do: whether to keep running, only this time from the Russians, or to stay put.

How I hated the thought of my dad digging trenches with other prisoners and the German guards/gestapo watching over them. Here was I in the German army and my father, at 64 years of age, digging trenches as a prisoner.

Other news was even more frightening for me in that the gestapo had found one underground bunker with partisans. It was the group I belonged to. Eight of our men were killed along with thirteen Germans during the fighting that had taken place. Two of our men survived. I was now prepared to fight anywhere in order to get the chance to run over to our allies.

I was really afraid now. I couldn't concentrate at all, constantly thinking that if they had found papers with my name on it, punishment would be swift. From Irena's letters, I gathered the end of the war must be near in Poland. We arranged the last time we were together that should the Russians advance nearer she would write me that they may move elsewhere and I would have to wait for their new address. I knew now that this was so. It was possibly the last letter from Irena and Victor also. The money sent with each letter was much more than usual as well. Most likely with the end of the German Reich, nobody wanted to trade in German currency.

With all the money I had, I tried to spend it on myself. I usually went to an excellent restaurant. One night, when I was not on duty, I invited the youngest boy amongst us, who was only eighteen years old, to join me. He had been one of the execution squad sent to deal with the unfortunate Dutch victims in Amsterdam. He was never quite the same after the incident. He was so pleased with my invitation and we became great friends.

One night, while we were having our drink, the facial expressions of the German soldiers suddenly changed - some looked quite frightened. One or two had to hide their smiles. It was repeated news - an attempt on Hitler's life! My young friend looked at me to see my reaction but I still wasn't quite sure of him. Some of the soldiers had tears in their eyes so in pretence I put a sad expression on my face also. I was very good at acting and they did believe me. Should they have succeeded in killing that evil monster, I think I would have cried more than some of the German fanatics, only my tears would have been of joy.

One could see that the Dutch people were not in the least upset, rather quite the opposite. It was really fascinating to watch the various faces and it was so obvious who was pleased. Quite a few left immediately on hearing the news, but the waiters had their busiest night in serving drinks. We all had an excuse, either to drown our sorrows or to rejoice.

At nights, as usual, the men in my bunker were glued to the wireless as I pretended to be asleep but they would tell me nothing. Sometimes, I felt like blackmailing them in order to get a bit of news but I only needed to look at their frightened faces to figure out the way things were.

At the next morning call, we got a little speech about the attempted assassination from our CO. I was surprised that in our little group of twenty, most of us listened without much emotion except for one fanatic about 40 years of age who was almost hysterical with sadness. Because of the attempt on Hitler's life, we were on watch more than ever, patrolling places we had never bothered with before.

I persuaded my new German friend, Meier, to ask our sergeant if we could be put together on night duties to which he agreed. I always had a feeling Meier was not the same as the rest. It was on the night we heard the news of Hitler's attempted assassination that I first noticed it. Now being on duty together, I slowly gained his confidence. The safest place for us to talk was while standing guard beside the sea, with the new type of heavy machine gun. I think it was introduced into the army in 1943 and was called a 0.43.

From where we stood, we could see anyone approaching, any control at night which might come. Then one night, I asked him about his family hoping he would also ask me about mine. I was wanting to see his reaction once I told him all about my home and family. For me it was rather important as he was the third man on the machine gun with me and I hoped to gain his confidence. Escape would be so much easier with two against one, once we were in the front line and the second man chose not to desert. We could deal with him quite easily.

I had it all nicely worked out and it went exactly according to plan.

'What are you doing here then?' said Meier, after I had told him about everyone at home.

'The same as you, I volunteered,' I said.

'You didn't have to.'

'Well, we can shake hands on that. I had to go.'

'Could you have not refused?'

'Surely you know yourself the consequences for refusing to fight for your Führer.'

'Never thought of it,' responded Meier.

'You know the one thing that is rather annoying is the lack of news of what's happening on the American or Russian fronts.'

'Yes, Dominik, that's true.'

'Why are you glued so much to the radio through the night? What news are you getting?' I enquired.

'So you do know we are listening through the night.'

'Of course, I know, more so in the last two weeks, you haven't missed listening any night. You don't need to worry about me, Meier, I am not going to report you. Come on, if there is anyone you can trust it is me.'

Meier hesitated for a while then said, 'Do you know that France which we occupy has been invaded?'

'No, since when?'

'By the Americans and the British on 20 June.'

I was ecstatic. It seemed like I was floating on air but I tried to hide my emotions from Meier.

'Have they succeeded?' I asked.

'It is almost a month since the invasion. So far there is nothing good in the news, Dominik. The way the Americans are progressing they will soon be here.'

'That's not so good, Meier. Most likely we will be moved to the front ourselves.' I was pleased Meier trusted me enough to give me all the news.

I often went with Meier to my favourite restaurant where some of the German officers got quite drunk. On one occasion, our CO was well oiled and the guard refused to let a woman accompanying him through the camp gate. The CO threatened to shoot the guard. There were rumours going round that the CO was going to be court-martialled but nothing came of it.

I was aware of all the extra duties I had to do while other boys were off duty. It was all because of the trouble I had been in with my CO on account of that man I had spoken to in Polish. Often I had to do some cleaning around the CO's house and he would be sitting in the garden with one or two Dutch women drinking. If it was not cleaning, I had to peel potatoes, even though we had some Dutch and French-speaking girls to do the job. Our dislike for one another was mutual. From the encouraging news I was hearing from Meier, I was sure all this was coming to an end very shortly.

Now, I wished they would send us to the front line. I was so sure I would succeed in reaching the Americans. About the middle of August, we had a big army exercise with long marches from early evening to sunrise. It was murder carrying the old-fashioned heavy machine gun stand.

Meier, who was number three gunner, just couldn't cope with carrying the stand because of the weight. After number two carried the gun for a while, I decided to carry it the rest of the time for Meier. When we neared our bunkers the real drill started. The exercise was to recapture our bunkers assuming the enemy was occupying them. What a pity it was only training. I wished it were true that the enemy was occupying our living quarters.

My friend, Meier, was so exhausted, I had to do the jumping with the stand from one hole to another. When we were about 100 yards from our bunkers, our group leader said, 'Grenadier Stoltman, go back and help the boys who are left behind with their heavy machine gun and bring it into position.'

'Corporal, I am not going. You know yourself that it was I who carried the stand most of the night and here I am running from one hole to the other, again only myself as Meier is not fit any more.'

'Grenadier Stoltman, what are you going to do, once we face the enemy? Will you refuse my order when the time comes to fight for your fatherland?' At once, I could feel my temper rising, blood boiling with rage when he said 'fighting for your fatherland'. We were still under cover and there was shooting all around us. I stood up because of his comment. I was so enraged. I started speaking quietly, 'Corporal, I gave you the reason for not going to fetch the other stand and as for fighting for my fatherland, I haven't got a fatherland to fight for. When the time comes for fighting the enemy, I will be thinking of my parents, my brothers and sisters. Had I not signed as a volunteer, it would have meant concentration camp for all of them. That's "my fatherland" and that's the reason I am here.' Before I had a chance to say any more, the rest of the training exercise was called off. We were supposed to be under cover and shooting. The colonel and other officers were observing me through their binoculars not under cover but standing and lecturing. When we returned to our bunkers that morning, the atmosphere was very tense. I was expecting the lieutenant in charge of us to have words with me but nothing happened. Meier was feeling sorry for me.

'Why did you have to say that, Dominik? You know you may get shot for that. You are just impossible, Dominik. You are forever in trouble.'

Midday, we went for our meal and hardly anyone talked to me. About two o'clock the colonel came with another three officers.

'This is it, I told myself but somehow I couldn't have cared less. Stubborn me, I was really hurt though when the corporal had said, 'Your fatherland'. We all stood to attention as our corporal made his report of the room and eight occupants. The colonel asked for Grenadier Stoltman.

'Here, Sir.' As I looked at him, I felt certain no harm would come to me. He was a man in his late sixties and there was something about him that was pleasant.

Then he started speaking, 'Grenadier, what did you mean by saying, "you have no fatherland to fight for"?'

'Sir, I have a brother who is a Franciscan monk in hiding from the gestapo. His only crime is being a Catholic missionary. Another brother was in the Polish army and after release from prison he was taken back to a labour camp in Magdeburg - his crime was being a Polish soldier. My father is 64 years old and he was recently taken to dig trenches with other prisoners at the Russian front. I was asked to sign as a volunteer. Had I not done so it would have meant concentration camp for all my family. It was only because of my mother who begged me, "Son, sign. I will pray for you that nothing will happen. If you won't sign we will all go to a concentration camp." That's what I meant by saying, "I have no fatherland to fight for". I am saving my family by being here.' He could only stare at me. I was really scared now, almost in tears waiting for his decision.

He then turned to his officers and said, 'Well, well, and we are told we have volunteers from West Prussia (the corridor on the Baltic). God help us if we want to win the war with such volunteers.' After he had left with his officers, the boys I stayed with made no comments and Meier became very friendly towards me.

On one occasion, while we were on duty, Meier told me, 'Dominik, the news is very bad. The Americans are on the way to Paris. I'm afraid we are doomed. I will stick with you, Dominik, once we are sent to the front.'

'You have to, Meier, as you are with me on the heavy machine gun so the three of us have to stay together,' I replied.

'You know what I mean.'

'No, I don't Meier,' but I did know what he was trying to say. After a while he said, 'I'm sure there will be many trying to save their skins by running over to the Americans.'

'Oh, I quite believe it, Meier. There may be quite a few who will try to run over to the Americans but you had better watch what you say. You know it could have serious consequences. I promise we will try and stay together. Whatever happens, I am going to survive. You heard what I said to the colonel. My mother constantly prays for me and promises my survival.'

'Do you believe in prayers?' asked Meier.

'Yes, it helps very much. It is high time, Meier, that you started praying.'

'I wouldn't know how, Dominik. I never prayed in my life.'

'That's bad, Meier. You left it very late now. I can see the bullets already dancing around you.'

'Come on, Dominik, be serious.'

'When the time comes, Meier, for fighting at the front against the Americans, we will do something, don't worry. We will make it.'

Poor boy, he was so frightened. As for myself, I couldn't get to the front line quick enough. With Meier now giving me all the news, I had great hopes that the Germans were more or less finished.

A day came when we were taken to a bunker. It was camouflaged so well I never knew it existed. We started cleaning heavy gun shells. There were thousands of them. Well, I thought, it won't be long now when we will be moving to the front line. The very first place I had landed in Holland where I had passed rifle ammunition to the Dutch, they always asked me about ammunition stores and places where the heavy guns were positioned. I had been able to tell them every position exactly as we often had to guard the guns during the night but I had no idea the ammunition stores had been so near. I said a little prayer when we were cleaning the shells that hopefully the Americans would find them before we had a chance to use them ourselves.

After my recent troubles of explaining about 'my fatherland' I thought my superiors would leave me alone but no such luck. Off duty one evening, I was ordered to go to our CO's office. The sergeant there sent me straight to the kitchen to report for duties. I was given a list of all the jobs I had to do. I wondered if it was because I had neither been punished nor court-martialled by the colonel for the comments I had made. They must have all been mad about it. I felt quite smug though.

The sergeant noticed my feelings and he screamed at me, 'You damned West Prussian dog. What are you grinning about?'

'I wasn't grinning, Sir,' I replied and I knew he was annoyed at the way I was staring at him. As for the 'damned dog' that was accepted by every soldier as we were often called that. It was a mild form of miscalling any soldier. What made me mad though was that he had added 'West Prussian'.

Had he said to me, 'You damned German dog,' I would have said, 'I will second that, Sir.'

Then the drill began. Close to the kitchen stood girls and a few of our soldiers peeling potatoes and they watched my performance. I was ordered to do press-ups. After half a dozen, I began to fall on one hand.

'Sir, I have rheumatism in my right hand. I can't do any more.' Who was he to know if I had rheumatism or not? That did it – he told me to go back to the commanding officer.

'Sir, I was ordered to report to you. I couldn't do enough press-ups as I was ordered because of rheumatism in my hand.'

'You have disobeyed orders, Grenadier.'

'It is because of the rheumatism, Sir.'

He screamed at me again, 'You have disobeyed orders as you did at your last training.'

'For that I gave my reason to the colonel, Sir.'

I was told to wait outside. After ten minutes, I was called in again and asked to empty my belt pockets of the ammunition which we always had to carry with us. I became nervous. I was then instructed to go to a place about 500 yards from the CO's office where often we did our training; a kind of assault course with wooden walls to climb over, barbed wires to crawl under etc. I was to wait there. I thought if only I knew some Dutch family I could trust, I would try and get away.

Two corporals arrived and all hell broke loose. They were both screaming different orders at me. I didn't know which one to obey so I decided to obey all orders as long as I was fit enough to. It seemed wise for me to forget about my rheumatism as it could get serious. At one time, about 30 yards away from them, I was tempted to put one clip of five rounds (which I had left in my pocket) into the rifle and put an end to everything. I had never experienced anything like it. It seemed my mother stood beside me say, 'Son, don't do it.' I was now on the point of collapse and I just dragged my feet waiting to fall over. At last, one of the corporals told me to report back to the CO and they went away.

As soon as they had gone, an air-force officer together with a corporal approached me. They had been watching from behind some trees, as it was close to the road. He asked me what the reason was for the drill. I told him that I couldn't do enough press-ups and I was told I had disobeyed an order. He took my address and advised me not to change my tunic and to ask my CO for permission to see the colonel. The air-force officer gave me his address and said, 'Tell your CO that we were watching everything and give my address to the colonel once you see him.'

I felt my energy returning. I was a terrible sight. My tunic was in shreds and I had scratches all over my face and hands from the barbed wire. As I walked past the kitchen, the girls and boys looked at me aghast. As I approached my CO who was standing about twenty yards away talking to a lieutenant, the company sergeant called me over before I had a chance to speak to the CO. 'Grenadier Stoltman, you had better go to the store and change your uniform.'

'Sir, I would like to ask you for permission to speak to my commanding officer.'

'What is it, Grenadier?'

'I want to put a complaint to the colonel about the drill I got. Lieutenant Hoffman and a corporal from the air force were watching while I was getting the drill. He gave me his address and asked me to refer him as a witness. He also advised me not the change my uniform.' I deliberately spoke loudly so my CO could hear me. I was told to wait while he went over to the CO to discuss the matter.

On his return he said, 'Grenadier Stoltman, when I was a soldier I got a drill, it's part of the training. You had better go and change your tunic and put it all behind you.'

'Sir, during my training, I enjoyed every day, including the drill I got. That was not drill I got today from the two corporals. That was physical and mental torture.' My temper and my voice were both rising. I knew the CO could hear me. 'We all know what happened at the party when the commanding officer tried to get a girl into our base. When the guard refused to let them through, the CO threatened him with a revolver. Nothing was done about it. Was it because it involved an officer? Sir, again, I would like to ask the CO for permission to see the colonel.'

Once more, the sergeant went over to speak to the CO. The boys who were at the potato-peeling were giving me the thumbs up sign. I knew the CO was getting rather nervous at my mention of the girl and he knew it could be serious for him as the colonel hated his guts. The sergeant came back and told me to go back to my bunker. I had the rest of the day off and the CO would see me the following morning.

Back at our base, the boys were appalled at the state I was in. I flopped down onto the bunk bed as my mind dwelt on the outcome of my interview with my CO. I was determined to see the colonel, especially with the air-force lieutenant on my side. Unfortunately, sometime during the night everything changed. As I lay on my bunk bed I could hear men on the move shouting orders and engines running. I thought I was imagining things in my exhaustive state but somebody was pulling at my arm. It was Meier, who said, 'Come on, Dominik, we are moving out. I don't know where to but I'm sure we are moving to the front line. We have been loading ammunition most of the night. You seem to be getting special treatment. There is a new tunic for you on the table. I've already packed your rations. Just take anything from your locker you think you will need.' I thanked my young friend.

I was surprised at the energy that was coming back into my body because of the good news. I felt I could have survived another drill session with the two corporals as I was so pleased we were moving to the front. I was ready in no time at all and joined the rest. There was a message from the corporal to put my bike on the lorry as it would save me cycling to the station and he apologized for the drill he had given me.

'You had to give me, Corporal? Well, hmm, just forget it, it is all for our fatherland, Corporal.' I couldn't believe the VIP treatment I was given. Were they frightened that I would try to kill them once we were in the front line? It would have been much easier for the CO to have gotten rid of me there and then.

As all the men from other bases arrived on their bicycles, we were busy loading the train. Most of our equipment was already on board before the men waiting on the platform climbed onto the train. My heart dropped as I was put back on to the SMG heavy machine gun and had to hand my rifle over. Meier was delighted to see me and suggested a few times that once the chance came we would run over to the other side. As for me, I couldn't think what I could do to get away from the machine gun.

We stopped in Belgium, not far from Brussels, away from any railway station. On one side of the track were woodlands and on the other was a monstrous heavy gun standing on the railway track alongside. That was the gun the Germans called 'Big Bertha'. It was most likely out of action, tired of spewing out hatred and death against innocent people. Maybe the Germans had nothing to feed her with now.

Then, out of nowhere, the American planes appeared flying very low. Although they never fired at us, with one quick jump I was off the train followed by Meier and the third man to take cover. When we got back onto the train, the sergeant apprehended me for deserting the heavy machine gun.

'Sergeant, I was following you as my group leader and isn't that what we are supposed to do, according to our training.'

'Why did you leave the train? Don't let it happen again.'

'No, sergeant, I will just follow you. I'll try always to be close to you.' I could tell he didn't take my comment very well from the way he looked at me. He couldn't say that I was threatening him, our feelings towards each other were mutual. How I hated that man. He always tried to get me for something, but now we had to show a little respect for each other. I was hoping the American bombers would pay us a visit after their reconnaissance planes had passed over as we were such an easy target, but nothing happened.

As darkness fell, we got bread rations and a warm meal of thick soup. There was so much meat in it I couldn't find much in the way of potatoes or vegetables. Some Belgian farmers would be missing a few pigs. What a treat after the diet we had in the bunkers. The soup would surely be the only thing I would miss when I left this crowd.

We reached our destination an hour later. It didn't take long before we were on our bikes and I on a tricycle with the heavy gun on it. Will I ever get rid of it, I wondered? It will make it so much harder for me to disappear with the three of us having to stay together as a team to man the gun. Meier was waiting for the chance to go with me but we had to keep an eye on our third man who was a right fanatic, always talking about the Führer and his secret weapon which was going to win them the war. The only way would be to get rid of him and that was too risky. Better to leave him for the Americans to deal with.

At the moment, we had to watch we didn't get run over by the German tanks as they were taking up most of the width of the narrow road as they headed for the front.

The tanks kept rolling past us as, at long last, we stopped for the night at a small farm. I checked the surrounding area. There was a big orchard attached to the farm, stacks of corn still in the fields and about 300 yards from us were sloping woodlands with a thick undergrowth.

Orders came to dig into our position. A soldier came over and told me to report to the sergeant. Meier and I both wondered why. I was soon to learn that I was being taken off machine-gun duty and Meier was to replace me as the first gunner. I was given a rifle and told to dig in somewhere near the garden. It certainly wasn't what I had expected after the drilling I got through him when I promised myself I'd get even with him once we were at the front line. Now I wished him the best of luck - he had made up for everything by taking me off the gun duty. I could only assume that the poor man would not allow himself to trust me to fight for his fatherland.

It seemed in an instant that all hell broke loose. Most likely the German column of tanks had been spotted. One could almost feel the ground vibrating, dark columns of smoke with roaring flames could be seen leaping upwards towards the sky. I was totally bewildered – it was like watching a huge fireworks display. One lone German tank arrived and took position in the orchard. By the time he had manoeuvred into place, every fruit tree was uprooted.

An hour passed, by which time a lorry with one-foot-high sides arrived. The floor of the lorry was covered with wounded men, shouting and screaming. After a few minutes' discussion with our lieutenant, the driver took off again. One could see they were not properly bandaged, yet they were from our column of tanks. When the fighting had started, I had prayed for the guns to continue in order to break the morale between the soldiers but they still believed in victory for the Führer because of his secret weapon. They were still waiting for the promises of Goebels and their beloved Hitler.

I couldn't help but feel sorry for the wounded lying around, but in my mind I always tried to justify what was happening to the Germans. I made myself think about Hitler's speech – 'What do you want, butter or cannons?' and the answer came, 'Cannons, cannons.' To me, the sacrifice was small by comparison to the thousands of innocent men, women and children who had already died in Poland, most of them in the concentration camps. I felt that the harder the Americans pounded at the Germans, the quicker the war would end and those waiting in the concentration camps would perhaps survive. They, too, must have felt as I did.

The sergeant got on to me about my hole not being deep enough but, to my surprise, in a rather concerned manner. With the first morning light came a few planes who machine gunned our position. One could hear the thud of bullets hitting the ground. One Pole jumped out and started running away from the orchard, calling in Polish, 'Lord, you have plenty of targets to hit. That's me here, watch what you are doing.' I couldn't help laughing, hoping nobody understood. There must have been some of our ethnic minority amongst us who spoke Polish. Luckily, nobody was hit.

It was night-time once more. I noticed large objects moving about the sky. I heard the Germans talking rather excitedly and it dawned on me why: those were the flying bombs, the secret weapons called the V1.

Morale went up again. They were winning now . . . or so they thought. I saw some of the soldiers wandering into the farmhouse so I decided to join them as it was almost midday.

Then more planes came over. Our lorry was hit and all the ammunition inside exploded. What fireworks! I continued watching through the farmhouse window wishing more planes could come. The corporal shouted at me to take cover and to lie down but I was confident that I wouldn't get hit. I believed so much in my mother's prayers for my safety. So far, her prayers had been answered. All I had to do was keep running in the right direction and I was good at that.

After we had eaten our delicious soup, rumours went around that we were pulling out. I got busy planning. Would I succeed if I stayed behind and hid? I decided against it as there were no houses to be seen, only open fields.

About 4 p.m., orders came to pull out. It was a good sign, I thought. We were going in the right direction and making room for the Americans. I noticed a sign 'BRUSSELS - 4 MILES' and by 6 p.m. we had reached there. We were lying low in a park full of rhododendrons, and all the time small units could be seen passing through. I got hold of poor Meier who had felt so lost after my transfer.

'Do you think we will make it, Dominik?'

'Meier, just keep your eyes open. One day we will make it.'

During the night, still in the park, I got in touch with a few Poles who were going to come with me. I was aware that they were now afraid to go ahead with our escape plan as, if caught, it would mean a bullet for desertion - but I knew I would succeed. I decided to abandon the plan for that night, though.

I left the park and sat down on a bank to watch the Germans retreating. A German major took a seat beside me - he was somewhat under the weather. He took a bottle of wine from his briefcase, broke the neck of the bottle on the metal arm of the seat we were sitting on and gave it to me to drink.

'Come on, drink with me Soldier,' he said. I was amazed by his actions and I guessed he must have had enough of Hitler's war. I cut my lips drinking from the broken neck. We were enjoying the quiet of the night when, all at once, the peace was broken by orders being screamed from all directions, 'Make room for the SS units.' The streets were vibrating with the speed of the tanks rolling by. Although the major was looking at me he quietly said to himself, 'Yes, yes, make room for the SS.' He then got up, turned to me and said, 'Good luck, Soldier. Look after yourself.'

I thanked him. I was very tempted to disappear into one of the houses nearby but decided against it.

It was now 2 September. With the first light of morning, we were on our way again, cycling along the Marche-les-dames Canal. One of our boys called out, 'I have a puncture.' A message came back from the leader, 'Try to repair it and catch up.' What a wonderful way to get lost, I thought. When we stopped for a short break later, I opened the valve on my bike a little. Fortunately, no one saw me. After cycling for a mile or two, I called out that I had a puncture. As I expected, I was told to repair it and catch up. Some hope of that, I thought. You'll have to wait for me to catch up with you.

I had the bike leaning up against a fence. There was a house close by. It must have been the longest time in my life I had been on my knees supposedly repairing my bike. From 8 a.m. until 4 p.m. I was fiddling about with the valve and keeping an eye on the road. Now there was not a soldier to be seen.

I decided to start moving but still with a flat tyre. Should anyone stop me, I was going to say that I hadn't got the kit to repair it. As I walked along a Russian, a real Mongolian with slanted eyes and squashed nose, dressed in a German uniform, joined me. He suggested himself that we should make a run for it and hide. Great, I have company, I thought.

We reached a place where there were some houses, a sort of biggish cul-de-sac. There was a church on one side and on the other side were rather high rocks. From a small hole in the rocks, a dog jumped out and I knew it meant people in hiding. Above the hole was a small cluster of rocks. I knew that was the place for us. I pointed it out to the Mongolian, 'Come on, we will go there.' I was shocked when he decided against it. I cocked my rifle, pushed it in his belly and at the same time took his rifle and then told him, 'Davai tovarysz,' which meant, 'Come on, friend, get going.'

At the hole, I pushed the rifle in first, then said quietly in German to whoever was in there, 'Please take the rifle and guard that man coming in.' Somebody responded quietly, 'I've got the rifle, quick, quick, come in.' When I crept in, I lifted my hands and said, 'Thank you, Mother, for your prayers. Thank you, Lord, I have made it.' They all looked at me questioningly as they didn't know who I was or what I was up to.

I told them first about the Mongolian and how he had wanted to come with me then decided against it. They threw our bikes into the canal out of the way. What a great place they had for shelter from the bombing and heavy gun fire. The cave was between 18 ft. and 20 ft. long, 6 ft. wide and 7 ft. high. There were three families sheltering inside it, and a young priest who spoke very good German.

I was worried about my Mongolian friend. Should there be any German soldiers passing, one scream from him and we'd be found. That would be the end for us all. I told the priest about the struggle I had to get him inside the cave and how he had changed his mind. While I was explaining it all to the priest, two Belgian men crept in. The priest smiled at me and said, 'They have come for your friend. They watched you struggling with him.' At long last, I was beginning to feel safe.

I carried photographs of all the members of my family and after showing these to the priest and the rest of the company, especially the ones of my brother in his Franciscan robes and my sister, Lucy, in her convent habit, they opened up to me. They must have believed me as they offered me cigarettes, chocolate and some brandy they had. They explained the reason for all the goodies: some SS men on the run had crossed the canal and left their boat nearby and they had helped themselves to what was left in the boat.

One of the girls left us and after half an hour returned with some sandwiches - she was now dressed to kill. The priest must have made some comment about the girl and her dress. Even the others started teasing her, which made her blush.

In the evening, they started leaving the cave for their homes. Two of the Belgian partisans helped me to my hiding place. One watched the road and the other showed me a way to climb up the rocks to my hiding place reassuring me that from the top I had nothing to worry about but to keep an eye on the road. I was going to give them my rifle but I was told to keep it. They then asked if I had enough ammunition and assured me they wouldn't be far away from me.

So that's what it was all about; they were needing my help. I didn't like the idea at all, as I thought the war was over for me. What an awkward space my hiding place was, about 6 ft. in diameter. In the middle was a stone sticking up and I couldn't lie straight or even sit properly. I was coiled like a snake around the boulder. I thought that in a while I would start hissing like one due to the discomfort.

As morning came, I began watching the road wondering how long I would have to stay there or how long they would need my services. I was desperate to get to the Americans. Suddenly, I spotted about 70 yards away a German car coming along the road with four officers in it who kept looking around. I expected the Belgian partisans to shoot them but, no, they let them pass and they were the last Germans to pass by there.

The boys called for me to come down and we were once again inside the cave. Through the Belgian priest as interpreter, they tried to persuade me to stay with them until the war was over. A lot of the persuasion came from a mother and her daughter telling me I could go back to Poland from there once the war finished but my mind was made up. I asked them if the partisans could take me to the Americans as I wanted to join the Polish army to fight along with my countrymen.

The fourth day of my stay was spent on the farm with the lady and her daughter. Then three boys on bicycles came with rifles.

'Are you sure you want to go back, Dominik?'

'Yes, please, I would like to.'

Somebody else came bringing the German Mongolian who just looked at me. We said our goodbyes and the poor lady with her pretty daughter was almost in tears.

We were on our way. One of the Belgian boys, as a friendly gesture, gave me his bike to ride and he walked beside me. Within an hour, we were with the Americans. The day I had envisaged all through my enforced army career and even at home prior to that was here at last. A new chapter in my life was about to begin.

CHAPTER 18

My hopes and dreams had become a reality. It wasn't only me who had the dreams. All the Polish boys who had been forced into the German army used to talk about nothing else when we met up in our home town. All of us had hopes of being taken prisoner by the American or British forces. To us this meant freedom and now here I was. My war was over.

The partisans took us to an American camp where there was a field kitchen. Looking around, I thought it would be great to join them and spend the rest of my war days helping in the kitchen as one of my favourite hobbies was cooking. But the idea of my staying with them and working in the kitchen was soon abandoned. As soon as the Belgian partisans had left, more Americans came to look us over. It seemed rather peculiar to me the way they kept coming over to look at us. I decided that it must be my friend, the Mongolian, who was drawing their attention.

Then two American boys wandered over, one of them still wearing a white apron so I presumed they must be the cooks. One of them took my hand and had a look at my gold ring which I had bought in Bergen to use up the rest of my Dutch money. I was asked by one who knew a little Polish to hand over the gold ring as a souvenir. 'No, I can't give it to you. It is from my girlfriend.' I lied. It made no difference. As one of them took hold of my hand the other one just pulled it off. They took my two fountain pens which were of very little value.

After that, they turned to the Mongolian and went through all his pockets but found nothing. Out of nowhere, one of the men produced a carving knife about fourteen inches long. I wondered what was going to happen next. Then one American got a hold of the Mongolian by his chin and pulled it up. His friend, with the blunt side of the knife, started sawing at his throat. If they only knew what was going through my mind at that time, they would have shot me. I was now feeling a hatred towards the Americans and could have killed them given the chance.

Looking again at the terrified Mongolian's face, the way his enlarged, slanting eyes were following the knife, I couldn't help joining in the laughter with the Americans.

I then remembered being taken to prison before, that time by the Germans, and it was exactly four years ago to the day. What a coincidence. 2 September, 1939, I had landed with my brother, Bruno, in the German front line. Here I was again, four years later, once more a prisoner. The only difference then was that the Germans had decided to execute us on the spot, which we so miraculously escaped, but they didn't bother looking for jewellery. I didn't expect to be greeted by the Americans with a band playing after the partisans had handed us over but I also did not expect to be robbed of jewellery, especially by our allies.

For me, it was a great disappointment. After the Americans had their fun with the two of us, we were taken to a Dutch barn and once again I found myself lying on straw. We were guarded by Belgian soldiers. Through the day, we gathered spent shells from heavy guns and other waste materials. Sometimes unexploded mines were found. I was surprised that there were always volunteers to dismantle them with great success while the rest of us stayed under cover.

The first Sunday after gathering the waste materials, everybody looked forward to a day off. There were about 30 of us, Poles and Germans mixed together, so we had to be careful what we said. I was surprised at the discipline the German prisoners still tried to maintain, as they had in the army, and their continuing belief that some secret weapon would save them.

About ten o'clock that first Sunday, a few Belgian soldiers came to collect us and we were marched a few miles through a village, then into a park which looked more like the private garden of a big house I could see. Here, we had to walk round and round for hours. Then I saw the reason for it - civilians were coming along to look at us. There were civilians of all ages. Some would just look at us whilst others swore and spat in our direction, but the worst were the children who threw stones and tried to hit us with sticks.

As I kept walking, I tried to make excuses for the Belgians' behaviour, wondering what they had experienced during the German occupation. Nonetheless, I felt it was degrading, but more so for the Belgians behaving in that manner. After all, we were prisoners of war and the Belgian army should not have exposed us to an angry mob of civilians. By the time they had had their fun with us and we were back at the barn, it was 3 p.m. and no dinner was issued that Sunday.

The excitement I had felt dreaming of running over to the Americans and then joining the Polish army – encouraged through news we heard at home from Polish Radio London – was waning as the weeks passed.

Then one morning two Belgian soldiers arrived in American jeeps. They needed four men: I was chosen and we were taken to a fairly large estate. I had expected to return that night, but we were given a place to sleep with another two men who already worked there. We slept in a round tower-like building, about 24 feet in diameter and with a little window about 20 feet from the ground. We were given some blankets and good food.

Some of the prisoners worked on the estate. I often helped in the army kitchen for the Belgian partisans, now wearing military uniform. Across the yard from us was the estate house where about fourteen Belgian officers were having their meals in one of the large rooms. Some of the Belgians could speak a little Polish. It was there I got to know a Pole who worked on the estate. His name was Jo and he was in his late forties. One evening he invited me along to the kitchen. The proprietress of the estate and her maid, Monique, joined us. What a pleasant evening we had, talking for hours, drinking wine. When I left, I was given a treat of some chicken wrapped in paper, and some cake. Hopefully, things would start changing for the better.

I was told the Belgian commanding officer wanted to see me. I couldn't think what it could be for. As I entered the hall, he was standing there, rather tall, lean and quite good looking. His German was word perfect as he spoke, 'Dominik, we have decided to give you a job as a waiter in our officers' mess, which may sometimes include working at night if we have a party.'

'Thank you very much, Sir. I would enjoy doing that.'

'You will take orders from me only. Should I leave for a day or two, I will let you know from which officer you will then take orders from. Understood? You can start tomorrow.'

'Thank you, Sir.'

I couldn't sleep that night for the excitement. Although I had no experience as a waiter, it couldn't be that difficult throwing plates about, I thought, as long as they landed in the proper place. The previous waiter had been a Cossack who had fought with the Germans. I suspected that it must have been the lady who had gotten me the job after our long chat the night before.

Serving breakfast was no problem at all but lunch was hard going for the first few days. The food was sent out by the cook who also cooked for the soldiers. The kitchen was about 30 yards from the officers' mess and they would help themselves to the soup. All I had to do was place two or three bowls on the table, depending on how many officers I was serving. The problem was serving meat and potatoes. Whilst holding a big, oval plate with meat in one hand and potatoes in the other, I would move around the table so they could help themselves, but they blethered so much by the time I reached the last officer, I was ready to drop it all in his lap as my arms were so sore.

After a few days' practice, I really began to enjoy it. I also had to wash the dishes after each serving and the women in the kitchen would always have something ready for me; some sandwiches with meat or sausage. Midday, there were usually a few slices of bread with butter and a chunk of beef or a chicken joint.

By now, I felt I was halfway home. I stopped going to the army kitchen for food for myself but the other German and Cossack prisoners asked me to continue. Of course, I went for every meal but handed my share over to them. I was only too glad to help them, thinking of my prison days in Nuremberg. Sometimes I felt rather guilty about the good food I now enjoyed.

When I woke up one morning, I noticed one of the German boys was missing. I knocked at the door to alert the guard, which didn't please the rest of the Germans. In no time at all about 100 men took off to look for him. He must have had help from at least two other prisoners as the only way out was through the little window about twenty feet up. One man would need to stand on top of another. What a fanatic that boy was, how strongly he believed in Hitler's victory and the secret weapon that was going to save them.

The tide was turning fast against them. I felt some pity for that boy as I put myself in his place. What would happen to him, I asked myself, should he succeed in reaching his army again? Most likely he would receive a medal then be sent back to the front line, and maybe an American bullet for his bravery.

From then on, the Belgian guards watched us closely. The door would be open and every hour one of them would come and do a head count. As for myself, I started learning French. Often I had to ask for more cutlery. Although I had a supply in a chest of drawers that stood in the hall, the sergeants' mess was next to the officers' mess and they often helped themselves to my cutlery supply. I didn't bother reporting this to the CO as I didn't want to have any enemies and risk losing my good job.

On Sundays, Madam would take me to church with her maid, Monique, who always pulled out twenty cigarettes from inside her blouse to give to me. Sometimes, during the week, Monique made some excuse to cross the hall where she would call my name quietly then produce a packet of cigarettes. She would blush at times, but this only added to her good looks. I enjoyed her cigarettes more because of the way she gave them to me, with her beautiful, shy smile and the warmth from her body still wrapped round the packet. It was the first time since leaving home I had dreamed of romance. I was coming back to life.

Madam praised me for my efforts in learning French. Anything I needed from the kitchen I could ask for myself now, or so I believed. All the French I did know was complete sentences learned from the two Belgian soldiers. One day my French backfired. As usual, I knocked at the kitchen door and made my request in French. Monique's face went red and Madam looked at me and smiled. I knew something had gone wrong with my French education.

In the evening Madam called me back to the kitchen and Jo, who worked on the farm, was there.

'Dominik, something went wrong with your French. What was it you were asking for?'

'I was asking for chairs.'

'No,' he said as he started laughing and told Madam and Monique what I had wanted earlier. The two women joined Jo in his laughter. Then looking at me, he told me it was a young female I had asked for, not chairs. That was my last French lesson from the Belgian partisans. Madam commented, 'You are on the right track, Dominik, but you have to rephrase your sentences slightly.' Looking at me and Monique, she remarked, 'One day I will see the two of you marching to the church holding hands.' That will be the day, I thought. I didn't intend getting tied up with Monique just because of a few packets of cigarettes.

At night, the deputy commanding officer, who had rather podgy cheeks and a ruddy complexion, would call me over when nobody was in the hall. He would pull out a hip flask of brandy from his pocket and offer me a drink. Life was improving daily but I did have one problem. I couldn't get on with the sergeants who often asked me to serve them, especially when I had only two or three officers to serve. Keeping to the instructions I had been given from my CO, I refused. That backfired badly and my good days were coming to an end.

One evening, the CO called me over and said, 'Dominik, somebody accused you of taking meat from the plate you were serving us from.'

'That's a lie, Sir.'

'You are accusing an officer of lying?'

'No, I'm saying that whoever accused me of doing it is a liar. For the last two weeks, I haven't even touched any food from the army kitchen because of all the food I have been getting from Madam. I'm not very popular with the sergeants who often ask me to serve them because I always refuse as I was told to take orders only from you.'

'Who was it who asked you to serve them?'

'It was the sergeant who always wears sunglasses.'

'I will speak to him.'

'Sir, may I be relieved from my duties and could you possibly hand me back to the Americans?'

'I will see what I can do.'

I felt so hurt when I returned to my sleeping quarters: to be accused of stealing was the last straw for me! I almost cried with anger. I was a stubborn Pole and maybe I expected too much. Perhaps I should have forgotten the whole incident and carried on with my cushy number as a waiter. But I didn't. Had some of the Belgian boys kicked my backside, I would have ignored them - but not in this case. I felt my ego and integrity had been much offended, especially after the way I had been treated with respect and the trust I had been shown by some of the officers, and also the kindness from Madam. Now I had been slandered - but by whom?

The next morning, I decided not to serve the officers. The CO sent a sergeant for me but I refused to go. Before the midday meal, the sergeant came back again, this time with some sweets and again asked me to attend to the officers. To me, it was like giving a little boy an ice cream and asking him to be good.

'I'll do my work again if the person who made the slander against me will admit it.'

'Dominik, if you won't go, you may get shot.'

'Whatever the decision, I'm not serving again until I am cleared.'

I was then sent back to work on the farm, often cleaning toilets and scrubbing floors. On Sunday, I was to go to Mass as usual with Madam and Monique. An hour before, I was asked if I would like to go to confession. Of course, I agreed. I felt so low and thought it would do me good - forgive and forget and make a new start. I was told the priest would come to the farmhouse and one of the bedroom doors upstairs would be left ajar and I was to go whenever I was ready.

I noticed it wasn't the same priest as the one saying Mass in the church. After my confession, I waited what seemed like hours to me. Then in very good German, he asked me if I had taken food from the officers' plate. I could not believe what I was hearing.

'No, I did not.' As I started to get up slowly, I was asked, 'Will you forgive your accuser.' I looked at the priest and suddenly had my doubts as to whether or not he was a priest or someone trying to find out if I was guilty. I looked at him in a determined voice, 'No, I won't forgive that person.'

'Then I can't give you absolution.'

I didn't respond to his comment and did not intend being drawn into any conversation with him. I walked out and closed the door behind me.

That was the end of working with the Belgian army. Within a few days, I was back with the Americans. This time, all in my group, about twenty, were Poles.

Most of the work was cleaning the barracks. How we were treated in each camp depended so much on the person who was in charge of us. As the number of prisoners increased, we were moved every two or three weeks and more Poles kept joining us. In one place, it was near Le Havre, the Americans in charge decided that we could do our cooking so we had our own kitchen. The rations we got were double what we needed.

On one occasion, our chef told a kindly American that we didn't need so much meat. We were told to use it in case our rations were cut too much as he gazed at the stove, almost telling us with his eyes that that was the place for it. What madness! What meat we were burning! In the next camp we were put back on a starvation diet.

There were quarrels between the boys if somebody had a smaller slice of bread. With a little freedom here, the behaviour of individuals was almost unmanageable. There was constant bickering.

We agreed to form groups of twelve men, headed by a leader who would try to cut the bread ration in twelve equal portions. I numbered the men's names in my group from 1 to 12. Number 1 had first choice, and often it would take him one or two minutes to decide which piece he wanted. Next day, he would be at the bottom of the list and Number 2 would have first choice. Peace at last. I always took the last piece and this turned out to be an advantage as most alternate days the men would come back and each would hand me a little piece of their bread which meant I finished up with about one quarter of our daily ration. They did this to make up for my always taking the last share.

It is difficult to put into words how each of us felt about the treatment we were getting from our allies. It certainly wasn't what I had expected for so long.

After a few weeks on this starvation diet, we were moved near to Le

Havre. There must have been about 1,000 of us. It was very well organized despite the large numbers. Some days we would get slabs of meat, especially pork chops that would cover the whole plate. Starvation was at an end – but for how long?

For the first time, we were given a sheet of paper that was especially printed for prisoners of war to write home. It was a great relief for all of us to be able to send the news that we had survived. I could imagine my mother receiving my letter and saying 'Thank you, Lord, for answering my prayers,' thinking of the day she asked me to sign as a volunteer to safeguard the family. How many times she had tried to console and reassure me. 'Son, have faith. I promise you will survive.'

Here I was, safe and sound. Each day, as we searched amongst the prisoners for someone we knew, we would come across someone who had belonged to our ethnic minority. Those same people had been the cause of many deaths and now they were trying to become Poles again. I was glad the way they were being dealt with. Some Poles were ready to deal out punishment to those traitors, but the majority always intervened and stopped it. They were reported to the American in charge of us and were taken away to join the German prisoners of war.

The most heartbreaking scenes involved the Cossacks who were put with the Poles. (These were people who, after German occupation of their country, had joined the German army with the promise of an independent state after the war.) We were on very friendly terms with them. One day, their representative announced in Russian that the war was over for them. It was plain to see that they were terrified of their future. Some of them even cried. One boy, in the bunk next to mine, even took his own life while with us. We could not understand why they didn't want to return to their homeland, but they knew better than we did what Stalin had in store for them. Many of those who transferred to Austrian prison camps eventually ended up in Russia only to be executed for siding with the Germans. The lucky ones were taken to labour camps in Siberia. Their fate is recorded in many books.

The Polish people also had reason to be afraid. We already knew about the massacre of Katyn in the Ukraine area, where at least 2,000 Polish officers had been shot by the Russian military personnel; after the so-called liberation we discovered that many thousands of civilians were killed or had perished in Stalin's Russia. If Russia had had another leader instead of Stalin (perhaps Gorbachev), how many lives might have been spared. After all the prisoners had been divided into their nationalities, including the ethnic minority who had been discovered trying to pass themselves off as Poles, the Cossacks were taken to their dreadful fate. We were once again moved and that took most of the day.

The army trucks took us to Le Havre Station. Our treatment made it seem that it was more like a picnic. Most of the food supply was in tins, except for bread. In the late evening, we arrived at Cherbourg railway station and were ordered to line up four abreast. Twenty of us were chosen to carry the rest of the food for our journey. With all my experience of the prison camps I knew it sometimes paid to be the last in line. I gradually moved backwards in the queue because I had noticed quite a lot of the cases already opened contained tinned meat. It did pay off as I got one of them. After joining the long column we took off.

As it was late evening and rather dark, I asked my mate to start taking the odd tin out of the case I was carrying and drop it in the haversack on my back. By the time we arrived at our new camp, all the tins had been transferred to my haversack. I discarded the empty case. What a blessing I had done it: we were back to a life of hell again.

We were taken into huge tents similar to the ones in Nuremberg. The difference was that in the German camp we had lots of straw to lie on and a blanket; there were taps to give us any amount of water. Here, from our allies, we got three blankets each and no straw. The ground inside the tent was a bog.

We had water and mud but no drinking water and the first night we spent digging little channels to drain the water off. There was no chance at all to lie down. It was the same in all the other tents. We all sat down, crouched back to back to support each other. Some of the older men tried to console us into believing it was just for the one night because of our late arrival. That's what we had been living with right from the beginning of the war - hope and belief for a better tomorrow. We hoped and believed in America after all the promises to those who had been forced into the German army. What a disappointment it was so far.

Some expressed real hatred against the Americans whilst others still tried to blame the Germans. One could justify all that was said by just watching the German prisoners across the fence from us. They got all the food they needed and any amount of water. The conditions we lived in was a case for the International Red Cross to see.

The tins of food I managed to organize *en route* to the camp were exchanged each day for water. For one tin, I could get a one- to two-litre container of water from the German prisoners but there were so many waiting for a mouthful, quarrels began if anyone took one or two gulps too many. As soon as I approached the fence, the boys knew there would be a drop of water and they all followed. Eventually, my tins of meat ran out. There was an open drain running out from the German camp which contained a sort of milky-coloured water. There was nothing else to do but lie down on your belly and take a mouthful then spit it out again.

Within a week I, and some other boys, had contracted some skin disease, with little blisters and itching. We walked like gorillas on two legs having to keep our arms away from our armpits to ease the discomfort. It was very sore to walk.

At long last the American CO who was in charge of us must have decided we had suffered enough. A huge tank of fresh water arrived for our camp. Just to amuse themselves, the Americans put guards beside the tank, daring us to approach. There was no such thing as being afraid. We were all armed with containers. Those that were standing nearest to the tank were pushed forward by the rest of us. When the boy nearest to the tank opened it, the American boys stood aside amused. From then on we got plenty of water. Every day or two a tank full of water arrived.

We went to the doctor, which was some experience. He was a German prisoner of war: whatever we suffered with was treated with a few tablets but the German boys would get the full VIP treatment. On many occasions they were even sent to the hospital. With the plentiful supply of water we were now getting, our skin troubles soon disappeared. A few had to be sent to the hospital eventually.

An American came along one day to ask for volunteers to do some work outside the camp. The work consisted of clearing areas of empty shells and general tidying up. We also had to clean out buildings which had been vacated by the French for future use by the Americans. Needless to say, everybody tried to get the jobs: there was always some extra food and the chance to scrounge something. Again the Americans teased us when midday came and we were given rations. They would be finished with their meal and they'd deliberately leave the back of the truck open exposing half a dozen or so loaves left over. We would be warned not to dare go near until one of them would suddenly say, 'Go on, take it'. The race towards the bread was astonishing. If you managed to grab one or two slices, the bits that were sticking out of your hand were grabbed quickly by someone else.

Some of our men tried to fathom out the reason for the bad treatment given by the Americans, which we had not expected. After all, weren't we supposed to join the Polish army and fight against Germany? Then someone came up with an answer and as we were so eager to find an excuse we believed what he said - the American CO in charge of us must be pro-German, as were some of the people in our country and other occupied countries!

That worked tremendously, lifting our spirits again, how eager we were to believe in something that gave us a little hope for better times. Through the coming weeks, our daily rations of food improved, as did our midday meals. Everyone wondered why.

The rumours went around that quite a few Germans had escaped armed with revolvers and hand grenades and that the camp CO was to be replaced. Whatever happened, our conditions did change for the better - no more starving. Some of the boys who worked were now able to bring food back and always shared it with the rest. Soon it wasn't necessary for anyone to get extra bits of food - it was goodbye to hunger. A lot of boys from Upper Silesia started building miniature coal mines and houses out of clay. They looked like tiny villages. The clay mixture was taken from the ground we were lying on which, by now, had been transformed from mud into dry clay-like material with the heat of our bodies. Some Americans came and took photographs of what the boys were building and encouraged them more by handing over a few packets of cigarettes to those involved.

It was now only a few days before Christmas. I got a job helping in the kitchen and thought there would be a chance for me to organize some extra-special food for us, but no such luck. On certain occasions, when the supervisor was out, I was able to grab whatever was nearest. A few times I would leave with half a pound of sugar in my pocket taken from a box standing on the work bench. When most of the boys were asleep, I would share it among nine or ten of us – what a treat!

At long last the day we had long awaited came. Our midday meal almost doubled and so did our bread rations. We were marched to the harbour in Cherbourg. The ship we embarked on was a huge transporter, most likely used for bringing tanks and army vehicles into France. They were heavy-gauge chains hanging from the sides and chains fixed to the floor. Before boarding, we were issued with generous portions of bread and other treats. In spite of all the extra food and better treatment, the mood amongst us was rather mixed. After the varying treatment from the Americans and the stops at many camps over the last few months, we did not know what to expect.

Sometime during the journey, the huge boat suddenly started swaying up and down and sideways. The noise from the chains hitting the walls was deafening. The mess we were in was a sight to see. The colour of our faces was ghostlike, almost everyone was on all fours like a dog, and we were vomiting our guts out. The Americans came and stood watching us with their tommy guns, most likely thinking that we would panic – but with everyone suffering from seasickness we all wished we were dead. Then, after the long night, the swaying, clattering and deafening sounds began to ease off. Soon after that, we were in Dover.

Almost everyone was back to normal, especially when we learned we were in England, the rich country we had heard so much about – a country of prosperity, a country of milk and honey. That's what we were all led to believe.

CHAPTER 19

It was the beginning of January 1945 and, I hoped, the last year for my country to suffer the German occupation. The Russians had started a big offensive into East Prussia. We were now hearing about events in Poland. More and more information reached us as time went on.

We almost felt sorry for our ethnic minority as they tried to make friends with us again. A lot of them were now suffering from a really bad conscience. Those responsible for shooting innocent people or sending thousands to the concentration camps were disappearing during darkness. Farms which had been taken from Polish families were left unattended. All warnings by the German government, the local authorities and the SS not to leave were ignored.

Some of our friendly policemen – who had been kind, not only to us but to everyone in our community – asked if we could speak up for them to protect them. When Mr Büllert, the friendliest of all the police, called on my family and asked if they could speak for him, reminding my mother how kindly he had treated us all, there was nothing my mother could do. The Polish people were just as afraid of what Stalin may do to them. It must have been a big disappointment for Mr Büllert, but we were not in a position to put a good word in for anyone. It was hard to accept that after more than four years of terror and persecution from the Germans, we would continue to receive the same treatment from our so-called liberators. It was very sad to see those decent people now begging for protection. There were also the people who had taken German nationality at the beginning of the occupation but who had never let on and just kept to themselves, not bothering anyone like the rest of us.

We were able to find out more of what was happening in Poland, including events that had already taken place previously in other areas of our country, by listening to the conversations of our own officers amongst us. We now knew of the murdered Polish officers in Katyn, and the rising of all the Jews and the Warsaw underground movement against Germany at the beginning of August 1944, when Stalin with his army was expected to come to our rescue but instead waited for the Germans to destroy as many as possible of our men.

Eventually, after two months of bitter fighting, Warsaw had to surrender, with most of the city left in ruins. As the Germans retreated the Russians moved in. A new wave of terror started – people, especially the freedom fighters, were now arrested by the Russians. With that kind of experience, it was understandable that the Polish people were frightened of Stalin as our liberator. The Russians were so near to my home town by the Baltic area but still the Germans were sending men, women, children and Jews to Stutthof camp. The heavy guns could be heard blasting away, but that didn't stop them. Jews from camps in Latvia, Lithuania and Estonia were still being sent to Poland to the concentration camp in Stutthof.

From the beginning of October 1944 to nearly the end of January 1945, German troops were still arresting thousands from my part of Poland. From Prussia, where most of the Germans were anti-Hitler, many were still being taken to the camp. Of all nationalities that passed through Stutthof camp, most people were Polish, then there were Russians, the majority of them women, and surprisingly, in third place, were Germans. As mentioned earlier, it was sufficient reason to be arrested if one was accused by two of Hitler's fanatical followers. The minimum sentence was six months in the camp even for just running from a job.

From the beginning of the war, the concentration camp was meant to be for the West- and East-Prussian Poles and Germans. As the war progressed, there were people in there from all the German-occupied countries. The crews that were managing the camp with the German army consisted of some of our own ethnic minority and Latvians, Lithuanians and Estonians, Rumanians and Ukrainians – all pro-German because of their hatred of Russian domination.

The first evacuation from the concentration camp started only at the end of January 1945 because of a disagreement between Albert Foster – the man in charge of our area (West Prussia and Stutthof camp) – and Eric Koch, responsible for East Prussia, who insisted there was no need for evacuation as he still believed in victory.

Soon all hell broke loose. The Russians started progressing quickly into East Prussia. Those evacuated by land, still guarded by soldiers, had the best chance of making it to safety, especially the long columns of people walking through the night. Many of those who were still able managed to escape by hiding with Polish families. Those evacuated on trains had very little chance of escaping their tormentors before arriving in Germany. Again, many perished during the sea voyages to Germany. (Even when boarding the ship by walking up narrow planks, people were so exhausted they fell overboard into the water.) No attempt was ever made to rescue them.

The pro-German East/West Prussian civilians were left to fend for themselves. The more privileged ones who were taken by ship in the hope of reaching Germany safely lost their lives when the ships were torpedoed by Russian U-boats.

News now spread quickly, mostly through the partisans and some of our friendly policemen who were still around. By now, our village was only about 130 kilometres from the panic-stricken area. The man who had been in charge of our labour exchange, SS Reinke, had left a month earlier. It was at the end of 1944. Through the lady in charge of the women's section of the labour exchange, whom my mother had refused to help with an abortion, my sisters were sent again to work on the farm. By the end of March they had returned, as their employers – along with many others – had disappeared through the night, along with their guilty consciences.

At the beginning of the war in 1939, the German guns had started blasting away so unexpectedly that people just ran off into the woodlands hoping for the best. Now people were building little shelters ten miles or more inside the woodlands as everyone believed it was not going to be simply a walkover as it had been for the Germans. All thought the German army would offer more forcible opposition against the Russians.

The shelters had to be prepared secretly. It was then known that the people reported to the German authority for their shelter building were often beaten and taken away to prison camps, accused of siding with the Russians. Our place was now overflowing with Germans preparing for the last battle on occupied land.

Orders came for everyone to evacuate. Even the Polish people now felt sorry for the poor Cossacks who occupied the farms. They had entered our country so triumphantly after our own farming families had been forced into a concentration camp. The poor souls who held up pictures of Hitler and other idols on arrival had no place to go now. Whatever the Russians did to them when they captured them, we do not know, but now, in fear, most of the Cossacks put on their wagons as much as they could take, got the horses and took off westwards into the unknown, away from the approaching Russians.

As we waited in Britain, more news kept filtering through but none of it good to give us hope. It was on my first visit back to Poland in 1959 that I heard how my family had coped during the bitter fighting. During endless talks I heard how my parents, two younger brothers and four sisters had managed to sneak into their hiding place one night. There were other families hiding close to my parents. One thing they didn't know or expect was that German soldiers were searching the woodlands for deserters and partisans. One of the soldiers, finding two women, made advances intending to rape one of them. Her friend, terrified, ran over to where my mother was. Trust my mother . . . in no time she was there, lecturing the soldier. He left the terrified women but gave them a warning that he would make a report to his superior accusing them and my family of waiting in hiding for the Russians. How efficient the German army was, even when everything was falling all around them.

The following day, five soldiers arrived with two officers. All the families were rounded up then questioned in turn as to why they were not obeying orders about the evacuation and following the rest into Germany. One of the officers recognized my mother and said, 'Good morning, Frau Stoltman, what are you doing here?' After talking for a while, the mood changed. My mother was promised that no one would bother them again.

'Good luck to you, Frau Stoltman, and to the rest of your neighbours.'

Again, my mother's previous kindness and generosity had paid off.

That officer, while staying in our village, had often come for cigarettes to the shop. Occasionally my mother would ask him in for a cup of real coffee and sometimes a fried egg and a few rashers of bacon, which was then a luxury for them. The outcome of this incident could have been quite different and resulted in imprisonment if it had not been for my mother.

After five days of living in their wooden shack, they returned home to face our liberators. Very little damage had been done to our village. People were gradually returning to their homes. A few elderly people and some young children did not make it as they had died in one of the camps.

As for my family, my brother Victor who had been in hiding and Jan who had been in Magdeburg Prison came home last. The Russian soldiers were quite a friendly bunch, much better than everyone dared to hope. The last man in our village to arrive home was Leon, a brother of the boy who had escaped and lived with us when he and his parents, along with other farmers, had been taken to the concentration camp at Potulice earlier on in the war.

He told me his experience of liberation on my first return to Poland. Listening to him I didn't know whether to laugh or cry. As the Russians advanced, all able-bodied prisoners were moved further into Germany and forced to dig trenches for the German army. Eventually, one night while the German soldiers were in a rather disorganized retreat, he had managed to hide in a young, thick plantation. As the Russians moved into the area, there were young people and prisoners popping out from every conceivable hole.

What a welcome they got from the Russians. Some of them, after telling their liberators that they had been taken away from their farms, got the surprise of their lives. Leon and others were presented with carts and horses. Others came with clothing. Their wagons were spilling over. Of course, they couldn't refuse their generosity. Some unfortunate German families were deprived of their last possessions. Poor Leon, whose father had died in the concentration camp, was now coming home with two horses pulling a loaded wagon with a spare pair of horses tied to the back. What a good start for him . . . or so he thought. Little did he realize then that as he got nearer home, not only the civilians who had lost most of their possessions, but also the Russian soldiers would be looking for something to take off him for nothing. The generous Russian soldiers believed that if you had plenty you had to share with the less fortunate.

From then on it was Leon's turn to show some generosity and share his gifts with the soldiers – not that he had any choice in the matter. By the time he reached home, he was back to where he had started, bare feet and one scraggy horse. One consolation for all the people who had returned was that they were left to get on with their lives as best they could.

At home, my parents tried their best to make ends meet which was rather difficult now. We were not allowed to carry on with our grocery business. Most of the small businesses became state-controlled. After my mother believing so much in the power of prayers and that we would all survive and be together, the most cruel and unexpected happened. Jan, who had been fighting in the Polish forces and spent most of his time during the German occupation in Magdeburg prison, lost his life.

He often went for long walks in the evenings. On one occasion, he came across a group of children who had found an unexploded device which was used for blowing up tanks. The Germans called it 'Panzerfaust'. He rushed over to take it away from them and whilst walking with it to a safe distance, the object exploded. By the time my mother and Maria reached him, there was nothing they could do to help him and a few minutes later he passed away. It was the hardest thing for my mother to come to terms with, but she consoled herself that Jan had saved the children's lives.

Life went on and improved a little. My mother took a post as a matron in a county hospital. The gold and jewellery from Victor – which we had hidden, thinking it would come in handy some rainy day – had all disappeared, stolen by our new liberators.

Life was full of surprises, some bearable, some harrowing and heart-rending. Unfortunately, there was more of the latter. This was what some called 'liberation'.

CHAPTER 20

As for myself and my companions there were no more prison camps for us any more. We were now with our allies in a strange land we'd only heard about. After a full day's travel we arrived in Forres, Morayshire, in the Scottish Highlands. This was the day we had dreamed of when we had been forced, under threat of imprisonment, to enlist as volunteers. Again and again, we were assured by Radio London that they realized we had been forced into the German army and we were to take the first opportunity to run over, join our comrades and fight the common enemy. Little did we know that the fate of our homeland had been decided already. How much we believed that our dream of freedom was not far away.

Welcome speeches were made on our arrival at the army barracks now handed over for use by the Polish forces. Even here there were still a few members of the ethnic minority who tried to pass themselves off as Poles. They were soon taken away by the Military Police. My experience in Den Haag Prison taught me to feel differently, though, towards those Germans. I remembered only too well the ones I had seen in the death cells.

At our Scottish destination, we were soon put into groups and marched into the kitchen. What a celebration feast we had! The best was that we now knew that the starvation days were behind us. The cooks must have enjoyed watching us, as much as we enjoyed all they had prepared for us. On our way out we still took more bread. Almost everyone had a loaf under his arm, marching away and singing.

Within a few days we were assigned to different units. I volunteered to be trained as a medical orderly to a field hospital. After the treatment we had received in some of the camps from the Americans, my eagerness to fight the common enemy to defeat Hitler was gone. We now feared Stalin just as much, so what was there to fight for?

By the time the training was over, the Polish army had been pulled out of Germany. Our fighting days were over. Most of the boys were disappointed at that news, for we had believed that we would get home after the German surrender if we had been fighting in Germany.

We were then transferred to Inverarity, a very isolated place between Dundee and Forfar. We were installed in a castle and it was like living in a hotel.

Our commanding officer made speeches trying to persuade us not to return to Poland. It was always put in such a way that no offence could be taken by Stalin, but some were more outspoken with their different viewpoints. I could see that they had made up their minds never to return. In spite of all the speeches and warnings some did decide to go back to Poland. Even our CO gave us a farewell speech one day which made us feel rejected and quite low. We were confused and unsure of what to do. Very few letters were arriving from Poland and none said 'Please come home, we are waiting for you.' That was taken as a sign for us to stay where we were. The most heart-breaking thing to see was when the married men saved every penny they got, which was 30 shillings every ten days, and bought presents for their wives and children only for some to receive a letter saying that their wives had married again. Every time it said, 'Darling, I got the news that you were killed in action. It was hard for me to provide for the family. Forgive me. If you return I am willing to come back to you if you want me to.' It was painful for the rest of us to watch a man opening his case, sometimes twice a day, to look at the gifts he had bought for his family, crying his eyes and his heart out.

One of the boys who had returned to Poland had been in charge of all the equipment for our units – from tunics to shoelaces. At one morning call, I was told to report to the CO's office. On my arrival I got the order, 'Stoltman, from today you are in charge of the stores. Here are the keys. You will soon know how a place like that is run. No excuses, this is an order!' Despite my reluctance, I worked hard, checking and rechecking and keeping records. I became an expert, and it turned out to be a little goldmine.

On one visit to the division stores in Dundee for new equipment, I met an old friend of mine from home. What a day it turned out to be.

'Dominik, this calls for a celebration. Can you stay overnight? The treat is on me.' As my friend, Henrik, and I were sitting enjoying our drink there was suddenly great rejoicing all around. People were hugging each other and shaking hands. Soon we were all like one big happy family. Germany had surrendered!

We thought of all that had happened in the last five and a half years. We were happy for those who had survived and the ones who were freed from the camps. But the lights in Poland went out again. While other countries were celebrating, Stalin, the peace-loving man according to our allies, was busy with his feared NKVD (Russian Secret Police) arresting innocent people and sending them to Siberia. For my country the terror had started again. Henrik asked me if I was going to return to Poland but my answer was that I didn't know. I was still waiting for news from home. By now, we had heard that Stalin's men were arresting all freedom fighters who had been in the underground movement, and I had been one of them.

When Henrik suggested a way to make some extra money, I threw caution to the wind and thought, 'Why not?' He was in charge of making up the orders for the different units and offered me any amount of extra boots, underwear, socks, towels, etc. I knew that apart from benefitting myself financially, I would be able to send parcels to Poland. I soon had a little draper's shop.

Once a month all the soldiers' equipment was checked. As I was able to get any amount from Henrik, there was always something missing when I checked as now the boys had a chance to send clothing to Poland. The charge I made for replacements was very low. Our officer in charge was well aware of how the boys were 'losing' things, but as long as it was replaced everybody was happy, including me. I now managed to send even more goods home, which I had to buy of course. Through her medical profession, my mother was able to help a lot of people with the penicillin and other medicines I sent over.

One day, through a letter from my mother, my future was decided. I received the overwhelmingly sad news that my fiancée had been killed. It had happened after the German surrender, when one would have thought all were safe. A bomb from a Russian plane had hit the house she had been visiting and everyone in it had been killed. In the same letter, I also learned that my brother, Jan had been killed. There was no indication in the letter asking me to return home. I knew all mail was censored and we had to draw our own conclusions that it would be wiser to stay and build a future in this free country.

As our unit got smaller we joined up with another one. I was still left with my store for a while until one day my company sergeant accompanied by a corporal ordered me to hand over the keys as there was no need to have the two stores.

'I'm sorry, sergeant, but that is not the way I will hand over my responsibilities. I'll get an agreement typed stating that any shortages would be your responsibility once I am no longer in charge.' He agreed to this, which gave me time to organize myself. For some reason we did not seem to get on very well with each other. Maybe it was because of his small build, slant eyes and fat belly. Perhaps because of what he lacked in some areas, he tried to make up for it by showing off his superiority over us. Even when he spoke to our CO he wore a smirky grin.

When he had to exchange things at my store I sometimes refused, saying that it was still wearable, as the decision was mine. All the time he knew about the big supplies I had received from the division store. He also knew that as my friend, Henrik, had decided to return to Poland, the last load of extra supplies had just arrived. With the help of some of the boys we carried all the surplus stock to our barracks during the night. The boys seemed more pleased with our getting the better of this unpopular sergeant than with the clothes I gave them to send to Poland.

The next morning, the little man and his corporal were waiting for me. I told him that I had informed my CO that I was asked to give up the store and that he now wanted a copy of the agreement. We all signed it. Not long after, I was called to the CO's office where the two men were already waiting. We all got a lecture from our CO 'How come there is always squabbling going on between you men? We have all gone through so much during the war, should we not be more tolerant with one another?' I had heard him saying this before, when someone came with a complaint.

He informed the sergeant that he must try and put any shortages right as, after all, an agreement had been signed. All the boys of my unit were very pleased with the CO's decision. Soon after this, the sergeant returned to Poland.

I was then transferred with some of the other men further north, to army barracks near Alness, a small village in Ross-shire. I now worked with a doctor in the sick bay at the camp where other Poles from surrounding camps would come for treatment or their medicals before being demobbed. My new CO, the doctor, could not have been nicer. He had the rank of a lieutenant and although he was Jewish, he was tall with blond hair and blue eyes. He had received his medical degree in Britain. I was always under the impression that he must have had some sad experiences during the war. Unfortunately, some of the men took advantage of his kindness and after only a short time one noticed the lack of discipline, but he knew how to handle situations when called for and surprised us at times with his firmness.

By now I was missing my extra income and decided to organize a dance, with the doctor's permission. Before the big night arrived, however, a new CO, Captain Zych, also a Jew, was to replace our present doctor. He kept a close eye on me, checking the number of tickets I had sold. He was surprised at how few had paid, although the hall was full of people. He did not believe me when I told him that a lot of the soldiers had climbed in through the windows without paying. It was not a good start to our relationship and I knew the time ahead would not be easy.

I was not the only one who did not like the change. He expected the men to be busy at all times, the corridors polished like mirrors. He always looked as if he was in need of a shave with his dark complexion and small piercing eyes. Heavy black-rimmed spectacles perched on his long, thick nose. He was a chain-smoker and above his thick red lips was a permanent nicotine streak in one corner.

Dr Zych did not like to see us congregating in the kitchen, which had been our favourite gathering point. One day he surprised us by his sudden appearance. We were taken aback when he joined in our conversation then proceeded to tell us a joke which made the Polish peasant seem really stupid. Our cook was quick off the mark and asked the captain to explain, 'Why did the good Lord open the sea for Moses to get to the promised land?' Of course he did not know the answer. 'He was too ashamed of them to let them march through the town.' We thought we would have to pay for this episode, but if anything, things seemed to improve.

There were occasions when we had some hearty laughs working together, when he would take down his glasses and wipe his eyes. The men would come with all sorts of problems to our surgery. On one occasion a young soldier came and said, 'I caught a cold, Captain.'

'Open your mouth and say, "aah".'

'Not there, Captain.'

He looked over his glasses at him and then at me, asking did I know where that cold might be? The soldier got a red face and pointed at his fly. The captain told him very sharply, 'Pull your tail out.' One could see it was a case of advanced syphilis.

'How did this happen, Soldier?'

'I was peeing against the wind.'

We couldn't help laughing. The appropriate treatment was applied.

We were informed that a dentist was coming to work in our unit. He was Captain Friedman, also a Jew, who had escaped from Poland before the Nazi invasion. I decided to try my luck to get a transfer to work for him.

Before his arrival, I cleaned his room and made sure that supper was ready for him. My request to work for him as a dental assistant was granted. We got a dental trailer and worked only from 9 a.m. to 11 a.m. It was like a long holiday for us. Captain Zych asked me to help the rest of the men at their jobs and I said, 'Gladly, Captain, as long as I get permission from my superior, Captain Friedman.' I was never asked again.

We did a lot of travelling in my new job to all the other camps – like Forres, Elgin, Banff and Aberdeen – where we would always stay for about two weeks. This gave me an opportunity to dispose of the rest of the things from my days when I had the store. My extra income was now finished.

One day, while in Aberdeen, I managed to buy some salami sausage from a Pakistani who traded in continental sausages. My Captain Friedman just loved to eat them. When I told him I could make them myself and much cheaper, too, he just said, 'Why don't you?' He did not realize that I could be in trouble if I was found out. But it was enough encouragement for me. With the help of a friend, who was a butcher by trade, we used the outhouse of a nearby farm to work in. I had no difficulty buying the animals, as long as I paid a good price.

I was now very busy on my trips to the camps selling sausages. My best customers in Aberdeen were Polish officers. Everyone enjoyed a taste of Poland and I was pleased to be able to help my family further. I still treasure one of the thank-you letters from my father.

All good things come to an end, and now was the time for me. We had been in Aberdeen a few days when a letter arrived stating that I had to attend the military court for illegal trading. I went straight to my captain and we both agreed the only way out was if I got demobbed. He wrote a letter asking for a postponement of the hearing due to the amount of work over the next couple of weeks and he also wrote off for all the necessary papers for my demobbing. He was not surprised when I told him that Captain Zych was behind this action. He consoled me saying that I did have a good head for business, but that I needed another one for keeping the money I made.

I did not look forward to returning to my base camp in Ross-shire and facing Captain Zych. I was glad he did not get his way after all and I was able to avoid the military court.

I did regret having to say goodbye to Captain Friedman. He was a great man to work with. I remembered the times when officers had come to our dental trailer and talked about the situation Poland had found itself in, about the murdered Polish officers in Katyn and the many soldiers and civilians who had lost their lives in Stalin's Russia. None of the officers believed that the death of our Supreme Commander of the Polish forces, General Sikorski, was an accident.

The final and most dreadful disappointment was the Yalta Agreement, when the Polish Nation was handed over to Stalin by our allies. I recalled all the propaganda we had listened to during the German occupation, calling on us to join the partisan movement (Armia Krajowa). Now while other countries were celebrating victory and freedom, Stalin with his NKVD was arresting thousands of intellects and all those who had fought bravely at the Warsaw Uprising. They were called traitors by Stalin. Where was the justice of it all? For Poland anyway, it did not come true that every life lost, or blood spilled, would not be in vain. For the Polish people, this was not so.

When my papers came through I said my farewells and set off with all my worldly goods tied onto a bike, looking for a job and a better tomorrow. Cycling along through the beauty of the Highlands and approaching a village I saw an old tramp strolling along the side of the road. He had a long, white beard and all his earthly possessions in a bag on his back. I stopped when I got near him, put my hand in my pocket and gave him all the change I had. I noticed his expression of joy. When I was about 50 yards away from him, I looked back and there was the old man happily turning round in circles and looking at the money I had given him. I then realized I must have given about £3, which in those days was a few days' wages.

Smiling to myself, I thought of my mother and how she would have approved of my action. Was she responsible for my putting my hand so deeply into my pocket? Knowing her prayers would still be with me, I cycled on into the future, still with hope and trust inside me. I had survived after all.

POSTSCRIPT

As I settled down to a new life in the Scottish Highlands, initially employed as a farmworker not too far from the camp where I worked in the sick bay, my parents continued to live in the village of Powalki. They no longer had the grocery business as private concerns run for personal profit were not allowed under Russian rule. Anyone found trying to gain from others was punished according to the new laws. My father retired from working and my mother became matron of a local hospital.

As for my brothers and sisters, Victor came out of hiding and took on the role of parish priest in an area which had now been returned to Poland after being part of Germany for 130 years. Gertrude was never to recover her health and sadly died shortly after the war. Sophie was to eventually marry my friend, Eddie, and like Maria, who also married, settled down in the same area. Lucy moved to another convent in Grudziadz, about 50 miles from Powalki.

I was the only member of my family to be permanently separated by the war. I was never to see my brother, Jan, my sister, Gertrude, or my father, who died in 1958, again.

I eventually made a return visit to Poland in 1959. On my next visit, in 1960, I was accompanied by my wife and children, my German-born wife whom I'd met in 1950 when she was in Scotland for an extended stay of one year.

During my visits I was to learn how life was turning out for the people struggling to survive under Stalin's rule of oppression. When the agreement of non-aggression was not honoured, the Polish people felt disillusioned and betrayed, left to the mercy of the ruthless enemy. As Stalin and his dreaded NKWD spread terror throughout the land, there was little animosity left between the ethnic minority and Poles as both were now the oppressed. There was more hatred shown towards the Poles than to the Germans by the Russian dictators.

So often I heard the questions being asked, 'How long is it going to last this time? When we are free again, who will be next to make a non-aggression pact with Poland? Where will it lead us?' Nobody knew the answers then.

It was to be a long time before the winds of change were to sweep through Poland and other East European countries. But freedom is precious and worth waiting for.